# ADAM MICKIEWICZ: POET OF POLAND

*Columbia Slavic Studies*

A SERIES OF THE

DEPARTMENT OF SLAVIC LANGUAGES

COLUMBIA UNIVERSITY

ERNEST J. SIMMONS, GENERAL EDITOR

MONUMENT TO MICKIEWICZ IN PARIS, BY ANTOINE BOURDELLE

# *Adam Mickiewicz*

## POET OF POLAND

A SYMPOSIUM, EDITED BY MANFRED KRIDL

WITH A FOREWORD BY ERNEST J. SIMMONS

GREENWOOD PRESS, PUBLISHERS
NEW YORK

First Greenwood Reprinting 1969

Library of Congress Catalogue Card Number 75-90540

SBN 8371-2783-1

PRINTED IN UNITED STATES OF AMERICA

# FOREWORD

## by Ernest J. Simmons

To an extent which the well-educated person is not always willing to admit, not a little of the common heritage of world culture is imprisoned by the tyranny of foreign languages. The keys to these hidden artistic delights, which so often open up for us new worlds of beauty, of ideas, and of the spirit of alien peoples, are not easy to come by and require much individual effort. In the nineteenth-century graduates of American and Western European universities still held in common some knowledge of the Greek and Latin classics, an achievement which nowadays is rapidly vanishing, and an appreciation of the rich cultures of Italy, France, Germany, and England was considered the hallmark of a truly educated man. But this knowledge did not extend to the cultural contributions of the Slavic countries. Here the language difficulties seemed insurmountable. Only in the second half of the nineteenth century did translations of the famous novels of Turgenev, Tolstoy, and Dostoyevsky begin to stimulate the Western world to take an interest in Slavic culture, and slowly, very slowly, was instruction on the Slavic countries introduced into Western universities. It is an interesting fact that the great Polish poet, Adam Mickiewicz, was one of the pioneers in this effort, for he was called, in 1840, to assume the newly founded chair of Slavic literature in the Collège de France in Paris.

The "internationalism" which is so fashionable in educational circles today is doing much to break down the language barriers in the way of a deeper comprehension of Slavic culture, both of the past and present. To be sure, the Slavic language principally studied in our colleges and universities is Russian, whereas little space is given to the languages and literatures of the Western and Southern Slavs. Though there are understandable reasons for this state of affairs, one may be permitted to regret the lack of comparable concentration on the cultures, let us say, of Czechoslovakia and Poland. Russia's greatest poet Pushkin, for example, is gradually becoming known, in the original and through translation, to a wider circle of American readers. But the same can hardly be said for Poland's foremost poet—Mickiewicz. Yet Mickiewicz's poetry, even more so than Pushkin's, was oriented towards the West, as indeed is Polish culture in general. Western students of Romanticism are not often aware of the fact that Mickiewicz's fine narrative poem, *Konrad Wallenrod,* is superior in literary merit to the verse tales of Byron which provided suggestions for the hero; that his *Forefathers' Eve, Part III* contains some of the best lyric poetry in any language; or that his masterpiece, *Pan Tadeusz,* has been appraised by some discerning judges as the greatest narrative poem of the nineteenth century.

It is no derogation to the honest and sometimes highly competent translations of Mickiewicz's poetry into English to say that the widespread failure to appreciate his true worth and significance is largely because of our inability to read him in the original Polish. In a sense, great verse translations are literary "accidents." Perfect bilingualism in the translator, contrary to a common conception, is not vital and has sometimes been lacking in outstanding achievements in verse translation. Poetic ability of a high order, however, is always essential for the best results, but even more than this, a complete artistic affinity which makes the necessary aim of recreation in the spirit of the original a natural and not a labored effort on the part of the translator. It has never been the good fortune of Mickiewicz to find such a translator in English.

In spite of the obstacle of language, however, the genius of Mickiewicz has won wide recognition beyond the borders of his native land. Among the Slavic countries especially and those of Western Europe and the American continent the fame of his poetry is celebrated and his noble devotion to Poland is deeply admired and respected. In fact, one of the most significant contributions of the present volume in honor of Mickiewicz is its striking illustration of the international reputation of the poet reflected in the varied nationalities of the authors and the several countries represented in its pages.

Romanticism is the keynote of Mickiewicz's poetry and of his whole poetic temperament, and romanticism in a sense has likewise been the ceaseless inspiration of his people despite the harsh realities of their age-old struggle. Consequently, it is little wonder that the Poles find in Mickiewicz, with his lyrical flights of passionate patriotism, his bitter satire on the enemies of his country, and his mystical vision of Poland's glorious future, a great spiritual leader who has captured in bright, deathless verse the full image and ultimate aspirations of his people.

# PREFACE

The aim of the present book is to contribute to the commemoration of the 150th anniversary of Adam Mickiewicz's birth in 1798, which was celebrated in Poland and abroad in 1948–1949.

Since it was our purpose to present to the American public the universal significance of the work of the great Polish poet and leader, his contribution to world culture, and the appreciation of this contribution by foreign writers, we tried to collect opinions and judgments of distinguished contemporaries of Mickiewicz and of present-day scholars in Slavic and Polish literature. We are sorry to say that this task was carried out only in part, because some century-old sources were unavailable and some Slavic scholars to whom we applied were unable to fulfill our request. Nevertheless, it seems to us that we succeeded in collecting enough interesting and valuable material to show the greatness of Mickiewicz, his world-wide significance and influence, his spiritual affinity with the highest minds of his epoch, and the eternal values of his legacy.

The book is divided into two parts according to the character of the material. The first part contains general studies characterizing Mickiewicz as poet and leader and articles devoted to individual works and problems; the second part describes the relationship of Mickiewicz to those countries in which he spent long or short periods of time, or in which he was especially interested. In chronological order, these are Russia, Germany, Bohemia, France, Switzerland, Italy, and the United States. In this part of the book we give general articles about Mickiewicz's relations with the world and evaluation of the man and his work by representatives of various nations.

As to the works of Mickiewicz himself, we did not consider it necessary to give many examples or excerpts from them. The most important are available in English translations by Professor G. R. Noyes and his associates in *Poems by Adam Mickiewicz,* translated by various hands and edited by George R. Noyes (New York, Polish Institute of Arts and Sciences, 1944). We have therefore limited ourselves to less-known excerpts from Mickiewicz's articles published in

*The Pilgrim* and the *Tribune des Peuples;* some of these appear here for the first time in English. Apart from this we have included two ballads of Mickiewicz in an excellent French translation by Paul Cazin.

Our work would have been impossible without the help and collaboration of many people, to whom we express our warm gratitude. We thank in the first place all the contributors in America and abroad who are the real authors of the book. We are grateful to Professor Ernest J. Simmons for his interest and encouragement and for writing the Foreword to this book, to Mr. Joseph Wittlin for his many excellent suggestions and valuable advice, and to Professor George R. Noyes for authorization to quote from his translations. Acknowledgments are also due to the Frederick Ungar Publishing Company for permission to reprint two articles by Mickiewicz ("On the Tendencies of the Peoples of Europe" and "Our Program," published in *For Your Freedom and Ours,* New York, 1943) and to E. P. Dutton and Co. and J. M. Dent and Sons, Ltd., for permission to quote from Voltaire's *History of Charles XII, King of Sweden* and from *Pan Tadeusz,* Everyman's Library.

We also wish to express our appreciation to Professor Wilbur M. Frohock who revised some translations from the French, Mrs. Rulka Langer, Mr. Alden Haupt and Dr. Ludwik Krzyżanowski for their services as translators. Our thanks are also due to Mr. John N. Washburn and Dr. Krzyżanowski for help in editorial work.

M. K.

*New York*
*January, 1951*

# CONTENTS

# ILLUSTRATIONS

# THE MAN AND THE POET

# HISTORICAL AND BIOGRAPHICAL DATA

AT THE END of the eighteenth century the Polish Commonwealth ceased to exist. Extending over vast territories of central and eastern Europe it had been one of the strangest political units in history, a result of the union between the Kingdom of Poland and the Grand Duchy of Lithuania, completed in the sixteenth century. It bore the name of *Respublica;* with a king at its head, it was organized on the basis of distinct estates, but was governed by an omnipotent diet. Its ruling class was the nobility, but a nobility much more numerous than in any other country and ranging from magnates who owned hundreds of thousands of acres to the poor gentry who tilled their land like peasants. Voltaire in his *History of Charles XII*[1] gives a picturesque description of the peculiar institutions of that state:

Whoever saw a King of Poland in the pomp of his majesty would think him the most absolute prince in Europe; yet he is certainly the least so. The Poles really make with him the same contract which is supposed to exist between a sovereign and his subjects. The King of Poland at the moment of his consecration, and when he swears to keep the "pacta conventa," releases his subjects from their oath of allegiance if he should break the laws of the republic.

. . . The nobility, jealous of their liberty, often sell their votes and seldom their affections. They have scarcely elected a king before they fear his ambition and make plots against him. The great men whose fortunes he has made and whom he cannot degrade, often become his enemies instead of remaining his favorites; and those who are attached to the Court become objects of hatred to the rest of the nobility. This makes the existence of two parties the rule among them; a condition which is inevitable, and even a necessity, in countries where they will

1. *History of Charles XII, King of Sweden,* tr. Winifred Todhunter (Everyman's Library, London, J. M. Dent, and New York, E. P. Dutton), pp. 63–64.

have kings and at the same time preserve their liberty. What concerns the nation is regulated by the States-General, which they call Diets. These Diets are by the law of the Kingdom to be held alternately in Poland and Lithuania. The deputies do business there with sword in hand, like the old Sarmatae, from whom they are descended, and sometimes, too, in a state of intoxication, a vice to which the Sarmatae were strangers. Every nobleman deputed to these States-General has the right the Roman tribunes had of vetoing the laws of the Senate. One nobleman, by saying "I protest," can put a stop to the unanimous resolutions of all the rest; and if he leaves the place where the Diet is held they are obliged to separate.

In that big agricultural country the peasants lived the miserable lives of serfs, while the growth of towns was much slower than in neighboring Germany. If the Reformation, which swept through Poland in the sixteenth century, did not take root, it was due mainly to the weakness of the middle class. The gentry, who were not too friendly toward the Roman Catholic clergy and suffered from heavy church taxes, were inclined to accept temporarily some teachings of Luther, Calvin, and Socinus, but after they gained complete control of the state in the sixteenth century and curbed the supremacy of the clergy, they lost interest in Protestantism. Moreover their interests were opposed to a transformation of the social structure which some Protestant doctrines implied. Thus Poland remained Roman Catholic.

Adam Mickiewicz, who was to become the central figure of Polish literature, was born in 1798, three years after the last and final partition of Poland by the Russian, Prussian, and Austrian monarchies. He was born near the town of Nowogródek, on the territory of the former Grand Duchy of Lithuania—that part of the Commonwealth which had found itself under the domination of the Tsarist Russia. His family belonged to the small gentry, and his father was an attorney in Nowogródek. In order to understand what shaped his childhood, one should keep in mind the tragic fate of the country, which from one of the major states of Europe had been reduced to the level of provinces governed by imported officials. The fall of Poland occurred at the moment when the unwieldy organism of the nobility's Respublica started to undergo radical changes. The small gentry and townspeople were in strong opposition to the big magnates. Political literature was flourishing. The new Constitution, passed by the Diet in 1791, though a result of a social compromise, was looked upon with suspicion by the neighboring absolute monarchies and became one of the reasons for foreign intervention. Poland was obviously a center of dangerous radicalism, which came to life not uninfluenced by the ideals of the French encyclopedists. What kind of people led those radical movements is shown by the example of Kościuszko, who, after having taken part in the American Revolutionary War, became the chief of the national insurrection of 1794. Kościuszko's army was beaten, however, through the concerted effort of foreign monarchs.

The partition of Poland did not put an end to these social and national upheavals. The hopes of progressive Poles turned toward France. Almost immediately after the last partition, that is in 1797, there came into existence, under the command of General Henryk Dąbrowski, the Polish Legion in the army of Napoleon, which, until the fall of the Emperor, fought on all the battlefields of and beyond Europe. In 1807 after the victory over Prussia, Napoleon created the so-called Duchy of Warsaw, which included the territories annexed by Prussia in the two last partitions, that is, Western Poland and a part of Central Poland with Warsaw. The army of the Duchy of Warsaw fought with Napoleon in 1809 against Austria, and in 1812 marched to Moscow. Despite Napoleon's defeat, the Congress of Vienna created in 1815 a new Polish State, the so-called Congress Kingdom of Poland. It contained one seventh of the former Polish territory and one fifth of its population and was bound with Russia by a personal union—the Russian Tsar was the King of Poland. Lithuania, however, became simply a part of the Russian empire.

All those events provided a permanent subject of conversation in Mickiewicz's surroundings during his childhood. In 1812 his native town enthusiastically greeted the French and Polish armies. The impression which the year 1812 left upon young Mickiewicz was strong. Many years later, in Paris, he made the entry of Napoleon's army into Lithuania a central point of his great epic poem *Pan Tadeusz*.

In the local school he attended, emphasis was, according to the Polish tradition, on Latin language and literature, but Polish was also taught and the pupils received a considerable amount of knowledge, mostly of history. Polish literature was strongly influenced in that period by French writers of the Enlightenment. Mickiewicz, though reared in a strictly Roman Catholic spirit, loved to read Voltaire, and his first literary attempts were imitations or translations of that writer. Among the poets whom he read, an important place was taken by Polish poets of the Renaissance and the Enlightenment: Kochanowski, akin to Ronsard; ironical and brilliant Krasicki; a magician of Polish verse, Trembecki.

Classical traditions found a counterpart in the world which surrounded him, a world of fairy tales, old songs, and folk legends. The people of that corner of Europe lived a very primitive life. Tales and songs that were the products of centuries still provided an outlet for imagination and belief. Mickiewicz heard them from his nurse, from peasants and fishermen. It should be noted that the peasants of that region spoke Byelorussian but the modern idea of nationality did not yet exist. Mickiewicz, as all his contemporaries born in that land, called himself Lithuanian, in the sense that he came from the Grand Duchy of Lithuania. The word "Lithuanian" was used as an opposite to the "Kingdom Pole," just as "Scotsman" is used in contrast to "Englishman." Only as late as the second half of the nineteenth century, the national differentiation in the modern sense appeared in Lithuania. It went along the lines of class differentiation: the gentry, the middle class, and the town proletariat spoke Polish (in towns a considerable number spoke Yiddish), while peasants used either Byelorussian or Lithuanian. In Mickiewicz's times the "native tongue" of the Byelorussian folk was not used in literature and was considered a dialect.

In 1815 Mickiewicz entered the University of Wilno (founded in 1579), which enjoyed the reputation of being the best among institutions of learning in a land where the school system had a large degree of autonomy. At the university Mickiewicz studied Polish literature, ancient languages, and history. Those studies must have been very thorough, since there are many testimonies of his rare erudition and since he later became a highly successful professor of Latin literature in Switzerland, and of Slavic literature in Paris. The four years of his stay at the university were not exclusively dedicated to studies. Financial difficulties compelled him to seek a position as tutor to younger students. At the same time, he took an active part in student organizations.

Liberal and patriotic tendencies in Poland proved difficult to uproot. After the hope for Napoleon's victory disappeared, these tendencies survived in broad circles of the society and in the universities; the University of Wilno was a leading one in that respect. The circle of Mickiewicz's friends was interested primarily in literary discussion and in writing poems, but their reading was filled with strong political implications. Neither Schiller nor Byron could teach love for the autocratic and foreign monarchy. The teachings of the French encyclopedists and their Polish disciples, as well as the ideas of German and English romantic poets fell upon ground already prepared. Mickiewicz and his friends started to think about methods of action. Choosing a cautious approach, they created an organization, called Philomaths, that was very limited in number. The members infiltrated wider student circles and founded other, broader, organizations, but the existence of the Philomaths was a secret even to the members of the wider groups. The movement had no clear political aims, but undoubtedly it led the young students in patriotic and progressive directions.

While at the university, Mickiewicz began to write poems in the classic style, according to the literary fashion of that time. Their form, however, hardly corresponded with the new thoughts which haunted the minds of the liberal and emotional youth. Mickiewicz and his colleagues began to consider the sophisticated literary conventions as a brake put upon the spontaneity of popular and national feelings. Soon Mickiewicz started to write romantic ballads, using for subjects the folk songs and legends heard in his childhood. The strength and adroitness of his poetic language were such that the date when his first volume of poems appeared—1822—became a turning point in the history of Polish literature, much as, several centuries earlier, the appearance of the first poems in vernacular instead of Latin had marked a new period.

Mickiewicz's poems could be understood even by uncultivated

people, and that is why they were of such great revolutionary and democratic importance. They brought him immediate fame, but also exposed him to the attacks of critics, who angrily denounced the "barbarity" of his provincial idioms.

His first volume, *Ballads and Romances,* was followed the next year by a second which contained *Grażyna,* a tale in verse, and two parts of a romantic drama, *Forefathers' Eve.* Mickiewicz at that time taught in a school in Kowno. As befitted a poet of romanticism, he did not escape a love tragedy. He fell in love with a girl from a well-to-do family. She reciprocated, but after some hesitation, married a rich landowner. Mickiewicz, teacher and scribe, was not considered a serious suitor. For Mickiewicz the affair was much more than a youthful toying with love. His passionate temperament did not permit the loss to be easily forgotten.

This tragedy of love coincided with another serious affair. The Tsarist authorities discovered the youth organization, and Mickiewicz and his friends were imprisoned. After a long investigation, Mickiewicz was sentenced to deportation to Russia. He left Lithuania in 1824, never to return.

In Moscow and in St. Petersburg he found a friendly reception in Russian literary circles. It was the period of a seething revolutionary movement, the time of the Decembrist conspiracy. Mickiewicz maintained friendly relations with the Decembrists and later dedicated one of his best poems to their memory.

Preceded by his fame as the greatest Polish poet, Mickiewicz earned the respect and love of several Russian writers. Close friendship developed between him and Pushkin. He traveled in Russia freely. From his trip to the Crimea he brought back the famous *Crimean Sonnets,* which were published in Moscow in 1826 and immediately translated into Russian. Nevertheless he was constantly watched by the secret Tsarist police, whose agents were often recruited from fashionable ladies who surrounded him. The young and handsome poet had no reason to complain of a lack of love adventures. In 1828 he published a new tale in verse, *Konrad Wallenrod* wherein he presented in disguise the fight of the Polish nation against its oppressors. The censorship did not understand this allusion.

It should be noted that Mickiewicz had some influential protectors among Russian liberals. Their help was instrumental in securing him a passport to go abroad. In 1829 he left Russia and went, via the Baltic sea, to Germany, where he paid a visit to old Goethe in Weimar. He also visited Bohemia and traveled through Switzerland to Rome. In Rome Mickiewicz lived in an international society, a large colony of Polish, Russian, French, and American artists. Suddenly from Warsaw, capital of the Congress Kingdom, came news about the outbreak of the rising on November, 1830. Radically minded young men, enthusiastic readers of Mickiewicz's poems, started the revolution; a provisional revolutionary government was created and the Polish-Russian war began. Mickiewicz left Italy in April, 1831, for the province of Poznań (then under Prussian domination), with the intention of joining his fighting countrymen. His efforts, however, came to nothing, since the frontier was strongly guarded by the Prussians. Moreover, the insurrection was now (August, 1831) already waning. This was the crucial moment in the life of Mickiewicz. He saw the remnants of the beaten Polish army crossing the Prussian border and heard from witnesses about the horrors of war. Tormented by self-reproach for not having taken an active part in the struggle, he went to Dresden. There he wrote the third part of *Forefathers' Eve,* and that long dramatic poem, published in 1832, marked his definite change from a romantic poet into a poet serving the public cause. From Dresden he went to Paris, and Paris up until the end of his life was to be the main terrain of his activity. In 1832 he published a book in prose *The Books of the Polish Nation and of the Polish Pilgrims* in which he assigned to the Polish nation a singular role in the rebirth of Europe through revolution, a role akin to that of the Jews in the Roman Empire. In 1833 Mickiewicz was the editor of the Polish paper *The Pilgrim.* In 1834 his long "novel in verse," *Pan Tadeusz,* appeared, and with that masterpiece Mickiewicz ended his poetic activity. His only later verses are a series of short lyrical poems, the so-called "lyrics of Lausanne," written in Switzerland many years later.

When Mickiewicz was closing his literary career, he was already considered a spiritual leader of the Polish nation and his influence reached far beyond the limits fixed by the Polish language. His position could be compared with that of the Greek tragic poets, because his poems were easy to understand and the passions he expressed in them were something more than subjective and individualistic feelings. His poetry has little in common with French romanticism; its climate is much more rugged and severe.

A poet who, in the most vigorous period of his life, renounces poetry for the sake of action is a rare phenomenon in the history of world literature. It happened with Mickiewicz as a result of his conviction that poetry should have evangelical strength and simplicity; that direct moral and intellectual action is more important than any poetry which does not reach the standard attained by prophets.

An *émigré's* life in Paris was harsh. Mickiewicz, who married Miss Celina Szymanowska in Paris and now had a family to support, was constantly in financial difficulties. The year 1839–40 he spent in Lausanne as a professor of Latin literature at the university. In 1840 he was appointed professor of Slavic literature in the Collège de France and lectured there until 1844. He used his chair as a tribune for promoting, in a fiery way, his ideas. This aroused the suspicion of the French government and deprived him of his professorship. During that period he had fallen into a kind of mysticism under the influence of the Polish mystic, Andrew Towiański, but broke with him in 1847. This event opened a new chapter in his life; the poet ceased to be a teacher and preacher and chose deeds instead. In 1848 he proceeded to Rome to organize a Polish armed force to fight against Austria for the liberation of Italy. After the outbreak of the French revolution, he returned to Paris and founded the republican-socialist newspaper *La Tribune des Peuples.* When *The Tribune* was liquidated in 1849, Mickiewicz received a modest position as librarian in the Library of the Arsenal. In 1855, after the outbreak of the Crimean war, Mickiewicz went to Constantinople to organize a Polish legion with the Turkish army for the fight against Tsarist Russia. There, in Constantinople, on November 26, 1855, the life of this passionate poet and fighter for the freedom of nations ended.

# ADAM MICKIEWICZ

## by MANFRED KRIDL

### THE POET

THE CHARACTER of Mickiewicz's poetical world is determined, as is that of every writer, by two factors: the epoch which furnished the material for his imagination, along with the general literary style prevailing in this epoch; and his poetic personality, which formed and transformed this material. His epoch was that of romanticism, hence his world is basically romantic with a definitely, sometimes exclusively Polish flavor; his poetic (and human) personality was one of the most powerful, hence it expressed itself both in romantic and extraromantic forms in a highly individual manner, uniting national and universal elements.

This world embraced vast and various regions, extended—according to the general romantic spirit and the prologue to *Faust*—"vom Himmel durch die Welt zur Hölle." Heaven and hell were represented both by an absolute faith in the supernatural world and by literary accessories, for instance by employing good and evil spirits, ghosts, witches, mermaids, and so on, as symbols of strong, mysterious forces, not only mingling with the human world, but directly influencing human fate. "Die Welt," therefore, took on a fascinating aspect. It was the real, concrete world, to which many of Mickiewicz's extraromantic works are devoted, and it was, at the same time, a realm of strangeness, mystery, and weirdness, of irrational forces directing human life and passion, of good and evil, beauty and ugliness. Mickiewicz was one of those romanticists who felt, deeply and enthusiastically, the beauty of the outside world, who never turned away from it into the "ivory tower" of his soul, but populated this world with products of a powerful imagination drawn from folklore, from mystic writings, the Catholic doctrine, and other sources, all of them transformed into impressive artistic devices.

Mickiewicz's extensive classical studies in the University of Wilno were probably the reason why his first poetic utterances were expressed in classical form, for instance, the little poem "Winter in Town" (*Zima miejska*), and an excellent translation of some three hundred lines from Voltaire's *La Pucelle d' Orléans*. Then came deeper and more personal experiences connected with student life in Wilno, a life characterized, among other things, by serious work in clandestine organizations. This gave rise to a lot of unpretentious little Anacreontics, songs, and versified jokes never printed in Mickiewicz's lifetime. But it also produced more valuable poems, among which is the "Ode to Youth" (*Oda do młodości*), a powerful lyric poem without parallel in his earlier work. In it he utters novel ideological aspirations, calling on "youth" to "encircle the vast world with chains of harmony" and to push the entire globe into a new path, so that it shall be "freed from moldy bark" and "recalled to its long-lost, verdant day."

Romantic conceptions, already announced in the "Ode," took possession of the poet's imagination after he had become acquainted with English and German romanticists (around 1820). He adapted romantic forms, mainly those of the ballad and the fantastic drama, by means of which he tried to express his *Weltanschauung* and his personal experiences. The demonology of the ballads was used rather as a literary device and adornment without lending them a deeper, more metaphysical meaning. In his first volume (1822), only one poem, entitled "Romanticism" (*Romantyzm*), seems to present a kind of literary and philosophical program, summarized in the lines:

> . . . Feeling and faith to me far more reveal
> Than eyes and spectacles, though learned, do . . .
> Look in your heart, that still may see aright! [1]

This "confession of faith" is generally considered as expressing the underlying philosophy of Mickiewicz both in poetry and in life. As does every formula applied to poetry and life, it simplifies, of course, their character, the antithesis of "feeling and faith" and "eyes and spectacles" (reason, rationalism) being in itself a gross simplification. On the other hand, even "feelings and faiths" are not homog-

1. *Konrad Wallenrod and Other Writings of Adam Mickiewicz,* tr. Jewell Parish, University of California Press, 1925.

enous and indeed were not, either in Mickiewicz's poetical or political activity. Another aspect of romantic "philosophy" is presented in the poem "The Sailor" (*Żeglarz*), that is, individualism in its attitude toward the external world. These verses express in a poetical manner the idea that the individual is not only the sole reality, but represents a world in itself to which nobody, "except God," has access.

The world of folk-fantasy receives different treatment in Mickiewicz's dramatic poem or poetical drama, *The Forefathers' Eve* (*Dziady*). Two parts of this work appeared in 1823, the third in 1832. There is a great difference between them, both in the problems involved and in artistic significance. But there is, nevertheless, a common feature: the use of folklore and the supernatural as symbols of a general moral philosophy and as an expression of individual and national experience. In the first part of the poem (which he entitled the second), Mickiewicz describes a mysterious and fascinating folk rite, still celebrated in his time by the White Ruthenian peasants, which consisted in spreading a feast in honor of the departed spirits of the forefathers; with this he blends some moral conceptions concerning the task of men on earth and the necessity of suffering. Thus in typically romantic fashion he attaches symbolic values to a relatively simple, half-pagan ceremony.

The ghost of a young suicide who appears at the end of this part becomes the hero of the second part (called the fourth) and is again a symbol of a passionate, mad, truly romantic love uttered for the first time in Polish poetry with such force and truth of expression, uniting metaphysical elements with deeply human accents. The impression on contemporary readers was great, not only because of the overwhelming strength of the picture, enhanced by the form of half dream and half vision, but also because of some autobiographical elements involved which the poet expressed frankly yet without altering the purely artistic and fictitious structure of the poem as a whole.

Thus Mickiewicz gave to the eternal love motif an entirely original treatment, interweaving it with the rite of service to the forefathers, combining it with a peculiarly romantic folklore doctrine concerning the ghosts of suicides, and expressing it in the form of a dramatic monologue. Some fragments of the abandoned first part of *The Forefathers' Eve* surpass even the fourth part by their mature and brilliant artistic values, their deep insight into human affairs. This applies especially to the monologue of the "Wizard," an impressive symphonic poem in which motives of sadness, resignation, despondency, and hopelessness follow one another and express the vanity of human efforts.

Love did not always present such a despairing and gloomy aspect in Mickiewicz's works. Three years later (1826) he published his *Sonnets* (*Sonety*), which bear eloquent testimony to a quite different attitude. In them is expressed a joy of life unhampered by "ghosts," a freedom of spirit, a devotion to the life of the senses without any false prudery, as well as without any "metaphysics." Now Mickiewicz expresses quite "normal" feelings and moods connected with love, enthusiasms and disappointments, triumphs and defeats, delights and suffering, with an amazing precision and plasticity.

In his *Crimean Sonnets* (*Sonety krymskie*), published in the same volume, Mickiewicz also turns away from the world of ghosts and pays tribute to the joy of life, here symbolized by the powerful beauty of Crimean nature. Overwhelmed by its splendor and charm and by the mysteries of his own heart the poet becomes aware of his own value and of the treasures of his talent. Nature does not depress him by its power and terror; on the contrary, it enhances his feeling of strength and freedom, the consciousness of an artist encompassing beauty and transforming it into eternal form in works of art.

The religious feelings of Mickiewicz first found expression in his "Hymn on the Annunciation Day" (*Hymn na dzień Zwiastowania N.M.P.*), published in his first volume, in 1822. The poem is somewhat enigmatic through its combination of traditional, classic verse with exaltation, adoration of spiritual power and of the mystery of the Immaculate Conception.

The religious lyric poems written in Rome about 1830—"Evening Discourse" (*Rozmowa wieczorna*), "Reason and Faith" (*Rozum i wiara*), "The Master of Masters" (*Arcymistrz*), and others—are among the priceless pearls of Polish lyric art. They are characterized by a rather unusual attitude toward the Supreme Being. Mickiewicz utters no complaints, reproaches, or grievances, such as are found so frequently in other poets; he expresses merely a feeling of humility, insignificance, and nothingness in the face of God and—what seems to be the very essence of every genuine religion—a feeling of boundless joy and gratitude simply because He is, because He exists, because man can feel His presence within himself, can receive Him in "the little home of his spirit." This attitude is expressed in the purest form in "Evening Discourse." Other religious lyrics contain some elements of abstraction and discussion, for instance the antithesis between reason and faith already present in "Romanticism."

The patriotic elements in Mickiewicz's works also take various forms. Absent in his first two volumes, they explode in *Konrad Wallenrod* written and published (1828) during the poet's stay in Russia. This poem marks a return to romantic gloom, this time of a Byronic type. He depicts tragic, insoluble inner conflicts, moral discords, spiritual storms, remorse, despair, and hopelessness—the psyche of a modern Byron transferred into a Lithuanian of the fourteenth century, who is also endowed with all the conventional external features and grimaces of a Byronic character. But for the poetic world of Mickiewicz, the most important quality in Wallenrod is his frenzied patriotism, which demands absolute self-sacrifice, yet is despairing and hopeless. The lyric portions of this Byronic tale, especially "The Song of the Wajdelota" (*Pieśń Wajdeloty*), express these feelings in a most suggestive way:

> If only I could pour out mine own fire
> Into my hearers' breasts; could I inspire
> A second life in phantoms of old time;
> Could I but pierce with ringing shafts of rhyme
> My brothers' hearts—in that one moment when
> Their fathers' song aroused them, they might know
> The ancient stirring of the heart, the old
> Elation of the soul; one moment then
> Might they be lifted up, as free and bold
> As lived and died their fathers, long ago . . .[2]

2. *Konrad Wallenrod and Other Writings of Adam Mickiewicz.*

Mickiewicz sounds even more pessimistic tones in the poem "To a Polish Mother," which symbolizes the tragedy of a conquered nation and is prophetic of Polish martyrdom after the defeat of the 1830–1831 uprising.

Both patriotic and religious motifs are present in the so-called "third part" of *The Forefathers' Eve* which was written ten years after the other parts, but in the same form, that of a fantastic drama, and which in general character is close to *Konrad Wallenrod* and poles apart from the *Sonnets*. It is a medley of various and contrasting elements; its scenes are sometimes realistic, close to actual history, sometimes fantastic and visionary. A religious and patriotic atmosphere pervades both series of scenes, but under varying aspects. In the realistic scenes it is concerned with the sufferings—naturally somewhat transformed by the poet's imagination—of the students of the University of Wilno who had been imprisoned by Russian authorities for alleged "nonsensical nationalism"; with the doings of the Tsarist satrap Novosiltsov; and with pictures of the corrupt Polish aristocracy, submissive and loyal toward the Russian government. The images are imbued with deep emotion, endowed with power and horror; at times they become grotesque and ironic.

The martyrdom of the nation, its fate and future, become a metaphysical, almost cosmic problem in the visionary scenes of the drama. The Polish problem is brought before the judgment seat of God by Konrad, the Polish Prometheus, who fights for the salvation of his people, challenges the Almighty to combat, and accuses Him of being not the Father of the World, but its tsar. Even if this Promethean outburst, the most powerful in Polish poetry, is condemned and the solution shifted from the rebellious Konrad to the meek Father Peter, this problem itself retains a supernatural character, since the fate of Poland is bound to the expected appearance of a mysterious "Saviour" empowered by God to save, not only Poland, but the whole world under her guidance. Polish Messianism, which had shone dimly through some works of former Polish poets, appears here in a definite and highly impressive artistic form.

The uneven development of the creative work of Mickiewicz, in spurts rather than by a consistent progression, as illustrated by the contrast between the earlier parts of *The Forefathers' Eve* and *Grażyna* (a semiclassical tale in verse), and between the *Sonnets* and *Konrad Wallenrod,* is further exemplified by the conception of *Messire Tadeusz* (*Pan Tadeusz*) almost immediately after the third part of *The Forefathers' Eve.* A greater contrast can hardly be imagined nor a more abrupt about-face than from the summit of romanticism and mysticism to an objective, epic, almost realistic narration. *Pan Tadeusz* has nothing to do with supernaturalism, being entirely concerned with the outside world, that of the Polish nobility at the turn of the eighteenth and beginning of the nineteenth centuries. We shall see later the elements which constitute this modern *epopée* and its artistic values. Now it need only be stressed that Mickiewicz's last great work brought him back from the other world to the real life of his nation; this life is depicted in such a way that *Pan Tadeusz* is rightly considered as immortalizing the basic characteristics of Polish nature.

The works of Mickiewicz include lyric, epic, and dramatic poetry in various combinations—the romantic mixture of literary genres. In general, lyricism dominates his dramatic forms and sometimes penetrates his narrative poetry. It is a natural element in *Konrad Wallenrod,* a Byronic tale in verse; it dominates some of the digressions in *Pan Tadeusz;* but it is almost completely absent in *Grażyna.* The third and fourth parts of *The Forefathers' Eve* are much more lyrical than the second. In this way the traditional classic genres, when applied to the poetry of Mickiewicz, must be interpreted very loosely.

A typical work of purest lyricism is "Evening Discourse." Its components are religious feelings devoid of any material elements and of any intellectual conceptions. Even what seems to be an "idea" (for instance, "Thou art my King, and yet my subject too") is only a direct transposition of an emotional state in which the personal relationship to the Creator takes the form of an almost physical unity. An equally emotional and symbolical aspect is presented by a few words taken from the external world, as midnight, storm, tears.

The *Crimean Sonnets* may serve as examples of descriptive lyrics;

lyricism permeates, more or less, the descriptions and images of the majestic Crimean nature which constitute the first part of every sonnet. They are, as it were, transpositions of states of mind into nature and not objective statements about its phenomena. Moreover, they are drawn in very general although expressive strokes which also distinguish them from detailed epic descriptions.

Some of the *Crimean Sonnets* are composed in the form of dialogues with a more or less dramatic coloring. In the "View of the Mountains from the Steppes of Kozlov" (*Widok gór ze stepów Kozłowa*) the powerful beauty of Chatyr Dagh is expressed in two different ways by the Pilgrim and Mirza; the latter's statement is a kind of sober answer to the questions of the former, conceived in a metaphoric style. In "The Road along the Precipice at Chufut Kale" (*Droga nad przepaścią w Czufut-Kale*), it is the Mirza who describes the horrors of the abyss, while the Pilgrim limits himself to a short but even more expressive utterance emphasizing the impressive greatness of this phenomenon of nature:

> I have beheld it, Mirza—seen the vast
> Abyss, and what I saw my dying breath
> Shall tell. For it there is no living speech.

There is even a little action involved, although not described, since both have to leap the precipice on horseback.

Another sonnet, "Baydary" (*Bajdary*), is composed almost entirely of mobile elements, the rapid movement of a rider galloping past "valleys, woods, and cliffs" and finally "leaping into the sea." These elements, although not bound together into a definite action, are, nevertheless, basic ingredients of any dramatization. Some of the erotic sonnets contain analogous dramatic motives ("I Speak unto Myself," "Good Morning" [*Mówię z sobą, Dzień dobry*]).

A definite action in the dramatic sense is found in "Romanticism." We have here three actors (the Maiden, the Poet, and the Old Man), an invisible ghost, and a "curious crowd"; we have dialogues among them, even an argument between the Poet and the Old Man (a scholar); finally, we have a sort of development of events: the appearance of the Maiden, her behavior and utterances concerning a love drama, the activity of the Poet trying to console her, the sympathetic attitude of the crowd, and at the end the dissonant voice of the scholar.

As an example of oratorical lyric we can quote the "Ode to Youth." Addressed to "youth," the word being employed both in an abstract sense and to denote young men, it is a sort of poetical oration, composed in a semiclassical, elevated, and rhythmically uneven form. It unites, in an organic whole, abstract watchwords with concrete poetic images, both containing explosive ideological and emotional material. It expresses in a sublime manner the liberal and idealistic tendencies of the epoch opposed to the world of old forms.

The *Ballads* (*Ballady*) are basically epic; they are narrative poems with some romantic tinges, characters, and events of the supernatural world are used as literary accessories. This combination of an apparently objective narration with fantastic subject matter is the main structural device of the ballads, connecting them in this respect with fairy tales. Folklore motives are used for the purpose of enlivening the imaginative element, and of constructing out of them symbolic truths. A third element consists of poetic images drawn from nature, one of the most artistically valuable parts of the ballads.

The tale in verse is also basically epic, affected, to be sure, by the romantic reaction against classicism and its freedom in treating established literary forms. The conception of *Grażyna* follows the romantic predilection for historical matters and local color (the plot turns around the deeds of a Lithuanian princess; the scene of action is Mickiewicz's native town, Nowogródek). Its structure is based on a highly dramatic action full of suspense, tension, and mystery (a tribute to romantico-Byronic poems). Classical traditions, however, compel the poet to explain in an epilogue everything that may not be clear. The same traditions influence the language and verse of the poem.

Much more Byronic and romantic is the structure of *Konrad Wallenrod*. Its constituent epic element is the history of the tragic patriot, but the development of the plot does not follow traditional epic patterns either in chronology or in motivation. Moreover, it is interrupted by lyrical parts, only partly connected with the real plot, and by timely allusions and digressions. This overflowing sentimentality contributes to the looseness of construction, but at the same time forms a kind of binding element. The hero is a symbol of the poet's own inner struggles rather than an historical character. In order to solve the difficult problem of motivating the course of action that he followed in accomplishing his superhuman task of self-sacrificing patriotism, Mickiewicz used symbolical devices comprehensible to Polish readers of that epoch.

Epic in the genuine and noblest sense of the word is *Pan Tadeusz.* Planned at first as a modest idyll in the style of *Hermann and Dorothea,* the poem grew constantly during the process of writing and emerged in final form as a great work composed of twelve "books" and containing about ten thousand verses. This growth was undoubtedly an asset. Started as a descriptive poem with a simple plot, it finished as a true *epopée,* according to some critics the only modern *epopée* in world literature. It did not follow all the classic rules of that genre, but certainly bore its general character; that is, it presented a universal picture of a whole nation at a turning point in its history. This universality became the structural principle of the whole poem; the epic detail and moment, so disdained by average romanticists and so important in any epic work, were here rehabilitated, so to speak, and made important devices of poetic technique. Another epic feature is the multiform plot, composed of parallel subplots connected more or less with each other, plus a number of episodes and "delaying moments" (the German *retardierende Momente*). In the first half of the poem all these constituent elements are concentrated around the affair of Messire Tadeusz and the quarrel about the castle; in the second, the main plot is shifted to another theme, dominated by the powerful personality of Father Robak. The result is a certain derangement of the structural balance.

Mickiewicz's dramatic poems show a variety of structural devices. The second part of *The Forefathers' Eve* is chronologically and atmospherically close to the ballads and consists virtually of three dramatized ballads (about children in purgatory, the wicked lord, and the inaccessible shepherdess). The poet tried to bind these ballads together by the conception of the necessity of suffering on earth and not by a definite action. Hence the action is poor, or nonexistent. The whole is, of course, not a drama in the proper sense of the word (and was probably not intended to be), but rather a kind of ballad-opera spectacle. There is, without doubt, an atmosphere of gravity and mystery in the presentation of the rite; there are skillful contrasts in the introduction of characters and a certain dramatic suspense caused by the appearance of the young suicide's ghost, but it is at this moment that the performance ends.

The fragments of the first part are, unfortunately, only *disiecta membra* of a whole, contemplated but never finished. Some of the fragments probably belong together, but it is impossible to guess their sequence and place in the scheme.

The fourth part is more uniform, thanks to the domination of the scene by virtually one person, the unfortunate ghost. We have here, then, a typical dramatized monologue which replaces every other dramatic element: dialogue, action, conflict, and so on. The figure of the priest, in whose home the ghost of Gustaw appears, is a passive auditor of his heartbreaking confession, merely interrupting it from time to time by questions and words of consolation. The whole drama is transferred into the soul of the suicide and is expressed through his chaotic narration, visions, and outbursts of passion and madness. This monologue gives glimpses of events, incidents, inner conflicts, and struggles; it is impressive by the very chaos of its changing images, reasoning, and even discussions with imaginary persons. It is, finally, full of romantic love-metaphysics, accompanied by no less romantic accessories, mysterious signs, voices, phenomena of supernatural forces.

The third part is structurally much more complicated. The two series of scenes already mentioned are not only ideologically, but also structurally different. The whole structure is based on this presentation of two distinct worlds, treated, however, by the poet as equally real, and on a continual passage from one to the other. Though Mickiewicz had faith in the integral unity of his conceptions, from the literary point of view the elements of which the whole work is composed are heterogeneous. The six visionary scenes shape the general character of the poem, its background of religious, national and Messianic ideology. The three realistic scenes are in a totally different mood, so that their connection with the general ideology of the poem is rather loose. They do not sufficiently characterize either the epoch or the influence of the supernatural world on the fate of the characters, although they contain more truly dramatic elements. The outbursts of patriotic suffering in the "Improvisation" of Konrad and the far-reaching Messianic vision of Father Peter are not (in the artistic sense) sufficiently prepared for by scenes depicting the imprisonment of the student, the attitude of high Warsaw circles, and the persecutions of Novosilcov. There are also other artistically irreconcilable elements; for instance, the introduction in the scene of exorcisms (immediately after the Improvisation) of a very primitive and vulgar kind of devil, who allegedly was in possession of Konrad's soul.

All in all, these diverse elements in the third part of *The Forefathers' Eve* are fused not by definite, realistic, motivated compositional ties (which is more than natural in a work of this kind), not even by the person of the hero, but rather by the unprecedented heat of lyricism which permeates the whole work and manifests itself in an extremely rich range of emotions and moods. In this way a "higher," or at any rate an emotional, unity is achieved in the work.

The language of the early poems of Mickiewicz (both printed and unprinted), especially his "occasional" writings and his ballads, contains numerous dialect words and expressions used by the Poles living in the former Grand Duchy of Lithuania; these are often influenced by White Ruthenian (the language of the rural population of the Wilno district) and much less frequently by Lithuanian. Some of these expressions can be found even in his later works, endowing them with a pleasant local flavor. But in general, Mickiewicz early overcame his provincialism and developed a language versatile in its adaptation to different types of subject matter and yet preserving a fundamental individuality of its own.

Mickiewicz drew his linguistic material both from the literary language of his own epoch (enriched by his study of writers of the sixteenth and eighteenth centuries) and from the vivid speech of the social class in which he was brought up, the middle-class country gentry, a class whose way of life differed little from that of the peasants. It is an evidence of the strength of Polish culture that the writer who was probably the greatest master of the Polish language came from a region where the Poles were a linguistic minority.

The language of Mickiewicz is marked by simplicity raised to the highest level of poetic art. He relies mainly on elementary words, those already in existence for centuries, homely words that every Pole can understand. He avoids neologisms and even artificiality in his language; he does not devise new and difficult and amazing combinations; he shows none of the linguistic virtuosity characteristic of Słowacki, Norwid, and Malczewski. Yet out of this simple, colloquial material he builds a style not only incomparably clear, clean, and precise; not only infallible in its designation of both material objects and psychological processes; but full of amazing force, light, color, epic exactness, and emotional dynamics. This he does by his unerring choice of words, by their application and localization—their apt association with other words and adjustment to them—by their rhythmic accent and cadence.

These basic properties are in all the masterpieces of Mickiewicz: in the dreams and visions of *The Forefathers' Eve* the epic descriptions and characterizations of *Pan Tadeusz,* and the purely emotional utterances of the lyric poems. Even his most abstract images, his boldest flights far above the earth into the unknown, he expresses in a concrete, solid, and precise style. Even his most romantic passions and conceptions are free from any romantic verbosity, vagueness, obscurity, or carelessness.

This basically concrete and real linguistic material he of course organizes and artistically transforms in different ways according to the subject matter and poetic aims. Let us take, for example, two passages from the third part of *The Forefathers' Eve* the narration of Sobolewski and the dream vision of Eva. The first depicts the deportation of the Polish youth to Siberia from Wilno, and is accordingly an image of concrete reality, although, naturally, "poetized." It presents authentic incidents and even quotes authentic names. It is an epic narrative full of concrete, realistic episodes and details, although certainly with a lyric undercurrent.

Eva's dream is that of a pure, innocent girl. Its main theme is flowers, but spiritualized, symbolic, mystic flowers, their colors, fragrance, and the shapes of garlands formed in the skies. Eva's state of mind is mainly one of delight, ecstasy, trance, an intoxication with unearthly happiness. The language is, therefore, devoid of any real, earthy element; it employs pure emotions, abstracts, symbols, colors.

Further instances of this "dematerialized" style are found in some of Mickiewicz's lyrics. At the opposite extreme is his purely epic style, applied throughout *Pan Tadeusz,* except in some lyric invocations and digressions. This is rich in objective values. Because of them, everything depicted in this poem possesses the undeniable and overwhelming quality of truth (in the artistic sense of the word) and fidelity to reality. Mickiewicz treats with the same Homeric carefulness and love of detail both great and small subjects, even very common things, mean and base phenomena of life, such as food and drink. Nature and the life of animals occupy an important place in the whole picture because men live in nature and nature in them. Every detail is, so to speak, autonomous and as if treated apart, and yet deeply involved in the whole picture. People live in themselves, and they live in other things, through them and for them. This penetrating insight of the poet, his all-embracing poetic attitude, his understanding of nature and human beings, enabled him to create a work that is both highly individual, original, specifically Polish, and at the same time universal, close to every human soul, independent of nationality.

Polish versification attained in Mickiewicz's works one of the highest degrees of perfection. Its general aspect is analogous to that of the language; that is, there are no amazing novelties in his meter, rhythm, and rhyme, no "discoveries" or revolutionary trends against tradition. On the contrary, many of the metrical forms used by him had been known in earlier Polish poetry. And yet his verse is really new and highly original because it is endowed with new force and light, new rhythmical movement, disposition of main and secondary accents, stressing the value of significant words by rhymes, and so on.

In this respect his was a mastery hitherto unknown in Polish poetry. One would be inclined to speak, in connection with him, of an absolute mastery of verse in all its aspects. He could be, and really was, sometimes, unsuccessful in structure, could compose his works of heterogeneous elements, could introduce into them components motivated by extraliterary reasons, but his mastery of versification was indeed marked by an unprecedented certainty and infallibility—it does not know hesitation, mistake, or stumbling. It is impossible to enter here into details of such a vast problem. We must, therefore, limit ourselves to general remarks. Mickiewicz's verse is the traditional Polish syllabic. In this general framework there is a great variety of metrical and rhythmical forms, depending not only on the number of syllables, but on the differentiation of accents, the use of caesura, and of *enjambements*. Let us take, for instance, *Pan Tadeusz*. The whole poem, with a few artistically justified exceptions, is composed entirely in a thirteen-syllable verse, called the "Polish hexameter." Every line consists of thirteen syllables and is divided into two parts, the first of which numbers seven, and the second six syllables; the caesura always follows the seventh syllable, the scheme, therefore, is 7 || 6. The principal accents are almost always, as in the *Sonnets*, equally distributed. What introduces variety and movement into the verse is the secondary accent, irregular, extremely vivid, and mobile. The result is that along with the fundamental uniformity of the rhythmic tempo it is never monotonous, always variegated according to the poetic function of every word and its aim within the given structure of particular elements.

Mickiewicz's rhymes are relatively simple and easy; at any rate, they do not distinguish themselves by any special refinement or virtuosity (we even meet many of the so-called "grammatical" rhymes). Yet they achieve in a perfect way their natural task, which is the unification of verses in a structural and sonorous whole, the stressing of significant and important words—or rather investing the words with significance and importance by virtue of rhymes—the emphasizing of accents, collaboration with rhythm in creating "sounding" pauses and borders and in rhythmical repetition. These qualities are, *mutatis, mutandis,* shown in all his mature works.

### THE LEADER

Mickiewicz belonged to the type of romanticist who did not retire from the world but made attempts to transform it in accord with his own ideas. This attitude was sometimes called in Poland, "introducing poetry into life," or "realizing poetry in life." From his student days in Wilno until the end of his life he was interested in public affairs and engaged in public activities. The terrain of these activities changed during different epochs in his stormy life, and their methods were suited to different conditions, but in every epoch and under every condition he showed the same devotion to the cause of Poland and the world, the same ardent enthusiasm, the same unshakable faith in the great destination of mankind. In Wilno he plunged wholeheartedly into the organization of a clandestine students' association, the Philomaths. Established primarily as a study club, it evolved quickly into a large organization embracing various groups and broader goals. These goals were given general names, such as "fatherland," "learning," and "virtue," but the practical aim of the young men was to organize all the society about them and to collaborate with patriotic groups in the Congress Kingdom. Mickiewicz was one of the most outstanding and active leaders of the Philomaths. He played an important role in establishing the character and the statutes of the organization, showing an amazing talent for organization, energy, knowledge of conspiratorial methods, and leadership. Together with some intimate friends, he was responsible for the extremely clever organizational principle adopted by the Philomaths; that is, to keep the society strictly clandestine and limited to a small number of absolutely certain and worthy members, and to found a series of other student societies, legal or half legal, directed in a firm though invisible manner by this central organization. In this way the Philomaths could influence and "shape" their colleagues ideologically, preserving their organizational nucleus intact in case of political persecutions. When, after a few years, the Russian authorities stumbled upon their trail, they arrested many students, including several Philomaths, but they never discovered the center of this organization, which was entirely revealed only by the publication of the Archives of the Philomaths a century later.

Mickiewicz found himself in completely different circumstances when he settled in Paris after the defeat of the 1830 Polish uprising. In Wilno, on his native soil, he had had to do with young men living and acting under relatively normal conditions, and could then apply relatively normal, sober, realistic methods of organization. The Polish *émigrés* in France were exiles, virtually outcasts, and the Polish cause was lost. What was needed, therefore, first of all—in the opinion of the poet—was not so much a political organization similar to that in Poland before 1830, but to save the souls exposed to pessimism and despair, to preserve their faith in the future, to keep them on a high moral level. Considering the emigration as the "soul of the Polish nation," Mickiewicz directed all his efforts toward these idealistic and moral aims. They were expressed in a very simple and popular but noble, elevated, and sometimes beautiful form in *The Books of the Polish Nation and the Polish Pilgrims* (*Księgi narodu polskiego i pielgrzymsta polskiego*) published in 1832. The first part contained a synthesis of Polish history which stressed, for pedagogical reasons, all the high lights of the Polish past, omitting almost entirely all its shadows. Exaggeration, inexactness, even mistakes are here too evident to be enumerated and rebuked. The Messianic ideas which in *The Forefathers* were presented as a poetic vision, here took the form of a program and have to be judged by nonliterary criteria.

The second part stands intellectually and artistically on a higher level. This "catechism" for the pilgrims contains some sound and true advice in regard to the preservation of national traditions, patriotism, and high morality. It is permeated by a deep Christian spirit, by love of humanity, and by devotion to the cause of the common people. On this point Mickiewicz agreed with the democratic party among the Polish exiles, although he differed from it in many other basic problems. In general, he advocated, not a political, but a moral program. It was not very popular with those to whom it was addressed, but had awakened an immense enthusiasm in progressive French Catholic circles (those of Lamennais, Montalembert, and others) and visibly influenced Lamennais's analogous work, the famous *Paroles d'un croyant.*

Mickiewicz wrote his political articles of this period, published in the *Polish Pilgrim* (*Pielgrzym polski*), in the same spirit as the *Books,* preaching the same general ideas, and applying them to contemporary national and international problems and events. He sees and presents the cause of Poland and of humanity in too simple a fashion, but it must be noted that at that time such was the attitude of the most progressive and democratic forces in Europe. They regarded the world as divided into two opposite camps: the "peoples" (by which Mickiewicz meant "nations," not common people, peasants and workers) and their "governments," all forms of which they thought morally dead. Poland's liberation was strictly connected with that of the "peoples"; her place, therefore, was in their ranks, fighting arm in arm against tyranny, oppression, and slavery. Mickiewicz always (then and later, even when entirely dominated by the Messianic idea) united the Polish cause with that of the whole of humanity and never lowered his ideals to the level of narrow nationalism. For him, "liberation" meant independence, together with what we now call civil rights; social problems did not interest him so much as they did some of the political leaders of his time, although social thought and theory were still in their infancy. He was close to contemporary democrats in believing that the masses and not individuals are the creators and bearers of truth, that the criterion of certitude has to be placed in common reason and sentiment, that, finally, in the hands of the masses lies the future of humanity. On the other hand, he differed fundamentally from the democratic movement by condemning all rationalism, all theoretical deliberations about detailed political and social programs, about future constitutions and polities. For him all such things depended on intuition, on feelings, faith, and enthusiasm, and would be accomplished at once, without preparation, by the *élan* of the victorious peoples.

A strange paradox: this poetic and romantic political leader apparently believed more in the right, pure, and "sacred" instincts of the masses than did their sober and experienced representatives. Mickiewicz also differed from the leaders of democracy by laying emphasis on the religious element in every political and moral action (one and the same thing for him) and by his mystical leanings, which he had shown already in some of his poems and which finally led him into a long-lasting, integral mysticism. His former mystic implications now come to the fore and grew into a whole doctrine which, as any philosophy in the traditional sense of the word, was to solve all the problems of existence. His former belief in the masses was replaced by an absolute faith in the individual, who became the only source of truth and certitude provided he won the right to be so by the force of his moral elevation and strength. Romantic individualism here becomes combined with moral greatness. He rejected all intellectualism, every method of logical thinking and reasoning. By such methods, he maintained, man can discover only what he had called "dead truths" in "Romanticism," that is, intellectual, scientific laws, but no "vital truths," a term that now means ethical norms. Moreover, truth is attainable, not by thinking, but by action. Mickiewicz does not reject all his former belief in tradition, in feeling, in the "voice of the people," the "national spirit," nor, of course, in the revelation through which man receives truth. But all this is not given beforehand or found, but perceived, defined, felt, and materialized by the "purified" and elevated individual. Such an individual has the right and the mission to be a leader of the people. So the cult of heroes leading humanity to its destination enters Mickiewicz's doctrine as a natural conclusion of his emotional-mystic premises. The masses have no significance by themselves. Their historical mission is fulfilled by the all-embracing Man. Nor does this lead to despotism, for despotism is not the rule of one man, but reigning without love, and such a reign can be exerted equally by one man, many men, or an assembly. The notion of progress receives, consequently, a purely spiritual meaning; it depends upon the development of our "interior being," upon its drawing nearer to God. The word "people" does not mean necessarily peasants or workers. "You may wear the rags of a Slavic peasant or the blouse of a French workman and not belong to the people; and you may glitter with gold and be of the people. To the people belong all the suffering and longing men, men of a free spirit, not encased in any formulas or systems." It is the same with such notions as liberty, education, even material misery. Even the idea of the motherland changes. While formerly Mickiewicz condemned any deliberations about Poland's future constitution and polity, the main goal being its free existence, now he declares: "We do not want a Poland unless she materializes God's will," and, "It would be useless to destroy the whole world (and without this Poland will not arise) if, as a result, one small nation, similar to other nations, were restored."

These are only a few of the statements by Mickiewicz characteristic of his new attitude. He developed his theories mainly in his lectures at the Collège de France. These were later published in French. (The first year of his professorship, however, he had devoted entirely to Slavic literature, which he presented against a large comparative background, depicting in synthetic, plastic outlines the spirit of Slavic culture, especially that of Poland and Russia. His knowledge of the subject was on the level of contemporary Slavic philology.) His practical activity was limited to moral and spiritual "exercises" and "practices" in a small circle of adherents aiming at the preparation of future leaders. But he could not endure for more than a few years the atmosphere reigning in this circle, and in 1847 he wrote to Towiański, the nominal founder of the sect, sharply criticizing this form of organization. This criticism applies to all kinds of similar activity, which necessarily degenerates into what he called spiritual terrorism, moral exhibitionism, torturing of the souls of the "brethren," imposing on them by force feelings and thoughts of the "master," scolding them for any doubts or deviations from orthodox doctrine, and inventing refined "penances" for nonconformists.

An opportunity for more concrete activity presented itself with the outbreak of the 1848 revolution. According to his own attitude, expressed both in *The Books* and in *The Pilgrim,* and in accordance with some Polish traditions, Mickiewicz believed that wherever there was a struggle for liberty, the Poles must take part in it, a kind of token fight for the liberation of Poland. This very idealistic and romantic conviction, which led the Poles into every battlefield of Europe during the nineteenth century, plunged Mickiewicz into hectic activity during this time of renewed hopes and dreams. He was against the idea of organizing an uprising in Poland, an idea represented by the majority of the Polish emigration. He wanted to unite the Polish cause with that of another people or of other peoples fighting for liberty. In this way it would be easier to establish a Polish army, which could in an appropriate moment be sent to Poland. One must agree that this was a more sober and practical project than an uprising inside the country. At the news, then, of the outbreak of the Italian revolution, Mickiewicz proceeded to Rome to organize a Polish legion within the Italian army. The history of this legion and of Mickiewicz as its organizer is really, without exaggeration, a lofty example of the romantic "translation of poetry into life." Mickiewicz published a manifesto, called the "Political Symbol," which contains the ideological program of the legion and an outline of Poland's future polity. It is a characteristic amalgam of religious, Messianic ideas with a radical program of social reforms. Along with a regenerated Catholicism that should lead the "peoples" toward liberation, Mickiewicz presented a new Poland as first among the nations, a fortress of liberty, equality, social justice, living in brotherhood with all nations. One point of the social reform was the establishing of a common property of land, an echo of the contemporary socialist thought.

In Rome, Mickiewicz gathered together a group of young men, mostly students of art academies, and proceeded with them to Milan. It was really a triumphal procession and a unique sight. Wherever the Poles stopped, they were received with enthusiasm by the Italian population and greeted as heroes. Italian papers of that time are full of descriptions of these celebrations and of the Polish group and its leader, who made inspired speeches to the gathered crowds and impressed them by his striking appearance, his voice, his faith and enthusiasm. A real brotherhood was celebrated and sealed between the Italian and the Polish people.

This was not merely the acting out of a fantastic poem. After arriving in Milan, the legion organized by Mickiewicz was considerably enlarged by new volunteers coming from Poland and by Poles from the Austrian army. Thus the Polish legion was organized, and, under the professional direction of Polish officers, took part in the brief

Austro-Italian War. The issue of that war destroyed the hopes of a liberation of Poland, but the participation of Poles in the campaign had its moral value.

Meantime, the revolutionary movement had begun in France. Mickiewicz went to Paris to continue his work for the cause of the revolution and of Poland. His activity now centered around a newspaper, *La Tribune des Peuples,* which he founded in company with a group of fellow editors chosen from various nationalities. It was literally an international paper, with Mickiewicz as the head of its editorial committee (a proof of the confidence and authority that he enjoyed in republican circles). His articles published in the *Tribune,* more than one hundred in number, deal with a variety of timely subjects inspired by defense of the gains of the Revolution and of the Republic. His attitude was radically revolutionary and republican, to a degree hardly surpassed by the most radical contemporary democrats and socialists. Yet he differed from them by preaching ideas incompatible with any democracy and socialism, as, for instance, the "Napoleonic idea," which was nothing less than Messianism applied, under another name, to current events and based on the faith in a great man (Napoleon and his legacy). The election of Louis Napoleon to the presidency of the Republic, was regarded by Mickiewicz as proof of the vitality of the Napoleonic idea, while the attitude of the majority of democratic leaders toward this fact was hostile, or at least very skeptical. We see, then, how deeply the mystic and Messianic inclination was rooted in Mickiewicz's soul and how strongly it colored his political activity of this epoch.

The revolutions of 1848 did not fulfill the hopes and dreams of the "peoples," not to speak of those of Mickiewicz. The *Tribune* was liquidated when reaction set in in France, and the bearer of Mickiewicz's Napoleonic idea proclaimed himself Emperor of France. The poet was compelled to retire from the political arena, but he did not lose his faith, his enthusiasm, or the inner necessity for activity. Nor could he long remain at rest. His work in Turkey after the outbreak of the Crimean War (1855) in organizing a Polish legion with the Turkish army to fight against Russia was again in line with "incorporating poetry into deed," but this time under conditions much more difficult and painful than had existed in Italy. This last heroic flight was again doomed to failure. The Polish military formation which came into existence in Turkey could not, in the face of the outcome of the war, attain Mickiewicz's aim of transporting the scene of battle to Poland. However, his other aim was at least partially fulfilled: the demonstration to the world of the unwavering determination of the Poles to fight for the liberation of their homeland at every opportunity.

The importance of Adam Mickiewicz in the history of Polish poetry cannot be overestimated. He was the first Polish poet of true genius, surpassing all former poets of his nation, including Jan Kochanowski, the great Polish poet of the Renaissance, by the range and wealth of his talent, by the scope and extent of his creative work, by his significance in Slavic and Western European literature, and by the influence which he gained. Romanticism sometimes limited his poetry to forms of expression that reflected only temporary trends. On the other hand, his frequent treatment of specifically Polish problems, close to the heart of every Pole, is apt to limit the appeal of his work to foreigners. But the greatness and universality of Mickiewicz lie in the fact that he created, beyond the limits of romanticism, works of permanent and general value, and that in some of his works he endowed Polish problems and Polish life with a universal meaning. Owing to his works, Polish literature gained a high place among Slavic literatures and entered the orbit of world literature.

Mickiewicz's influence in Poland has continued to this very day. In the realm of poetry this is apparent, both in the adoration with which he is regarded by almost every succeeding generation of Polish poets, and in the influence which he exerts upon their creative work. The Polish people consider him, however, not only as a great poet-artist, but also as the nation's great educator, who in the trying period of its history sustained the spirit of the nation, healed its suffering, and instilled into it a faith in a better future. In fact, he is the main spiritual source of modern Polish patriotism, this "religion of the homeland" which frequently seems to foreign observers too romantic, idealistic, fantastic. In the moral and political spheres, in the realm of certain established feelings and attitudes, his spirit also continues to hold sway over the nation. There is, of course, no question of accepting all his teaching in this field. It contains universal, permanent values, but it also contains ideas that have passed away with the epoch to which they applied. What remains is the spirit that created them, the psychic type, the interior rhythm of his life, his attitude toward the world. Mickiewicz will always remain amazing through his inexhaustible store of spiritual energy and through the wide horizons of his beliefs and emotions, which were not confined to the affairs of Poland but embraced all humanity, rejecting all manner of separation and egoism in relations among nations. This noble and lofty idealism, sealed by an entire lifetime, makes the Polish poet an unfaltering herald of a united world such as has always been the dream of the greatest spirits of mankind.

# POET OF TRANSFORMATION

by Wacław Borowy

I

All of Mickiewicz's major works deal with people who become transformed. Grażyna,[1] whom we meet as a young maiden who though apt at "wielding hard arms" does so only in sport, becomes later a woman-knight who leads an army into combat and falls on the battlefield. Alf-Walter,[2] a youth imbued with friendliness, love, piety, and patriotic ardor, highly sensitive to the idyllic beauty of nature and to the masterpieces of civilization, turns into Wallenrod, who settles down among his foes and dedicates his life to a gigantic scheme of betrayal, preparing with gloomy coldness the doom of those who put their trust in him. Gustaw under our very eyes *obit,* and under our very eyes Konrad *nascitur* of him [3]—the lover blinded by personal misfortune is reborn as the bard who wrestles with God over the fate of his nation. Jacek Soplica,[4] that irrepressible rogue, turns into the gray and humble monk Robak, who devotes his life to penance and to anonymous work in the service of his country.

And alongside these great transformed ones we see others who, thanks to them, also undergo a complete change. In the poem about Grażyna not only she but, because of her, Litawor, too, is transformed. The proud princeling of unbridled ambition turns into a hero: he falls upon the enemy with whom only recently he was ready to ally himself, wins a crushing victory, and to atone for the sin of his intended (though never committed) defection seeks suicidal death on the pyre. In *Konrad Wallenrod* not only Alf-Walter is transformed but Aldona as well: from an emotional young woman who loves forget-me-nots and dreams of flying like a lark she turns

1. The heroine of the tale in verse *Grażyna.* [Ed.]
2. The hero of another tale in verse, *Konrad Wallenrod.* [Ed.]
3. In the romantic drama *Forfathers' Eve.* [Ed.]
4. An outstanding character in the epic poem, *Pan Tadeusz.* [Ed.]

into a resigned recluse who deliberately locks herself up in a murky tower and scorns the thought of leaving it even at a time when she could do so. In *Pan Tadeusz,* under the influence of Robak, quite a few of the various members of the Soplicowo and Dobrzyń set become transformed. Many of these inveterate talkers and brawlers whose concerns never extended beyond local animosities and petty ambitions become soldiers and appear in the last book of the poem not merely dressed in uniforms but already distinguished in combat. And, in the Third Part of *Forefathers' Eve,* too, in the background of the transformation of Gustaw into Konrad still another change becomes manifest: the hero of Father Peter's vision turns from a child into an "awesome man" endowed with the attributes of prophets and magi, and "raised above nations and kings."

And so, even amidst the loftiest flights of poetic fantasy, there is ever the same theme: transformation.

2

Are these concepts Mickiewicz's own or do they in some measure belong to the literary tradition of his time?

The eighteenth century—the epoch on whose works Mickiewicz was brought up both intellectually and as a writer—was fond of depicting how life in general, and upbringing in particular, mold the character of man. It produced numerous works of fiction for which the classifiers later coined the name of educational novels. In this category one might place *Robinson Crusoe,* Fielding's *Tom Jones,* Jane Austen's *Pride and Prejudice,* and many other famous works of English writers. Here, to an even more marked degree, belongs a book which is hardly a novel but very much educational: *Emile* by Rousseau. Here, too, to a large extent falls *Wilhelm Meister* by Goethe. In Polish literature, typical of the "educational novel" was *Doświadczyński* by Krasicki. The eighteenth century was likewise familiar with versified "educational tales," such as, for instance, *Education d'un prince* by Voltaire, in which Mickiewicz, in the days of his youth, took a particular delight and which he even adapted into Polish, changing its title to *Mieszko.* The hero of this tale, whose improper upbringing has made him indolent and helpless,

PORTRAIT, 1823, BY WALENTY WANKOWICZ

thanks to circumstances and to the help of a courageous girl with whom he falls in love, becomes a brave, intrepid man, and from the captivity into which he has fallen breaks through to freedom. The Polish Doświadczynski similarly profits from the painful lessons of experience and, once a naive youth concerned solely with revels and clothing turns in due time into a solid citizen.

But these changes which take place slowly and gradually have little in common with the transformation of Mickiewicz's heroes. Mickiewicz's transformations are not evolutionary; nor are they, for the most part, due to the influence or prodding of another person. In the majority of cases (if we disregard those which are derivative in character, such as the case of the petty nobility of Dobrzyń and Soplicowo), they are acts of will, self-imposed and deliberate decisions, always connected with a moment when a man tells himself: "I will be different." This moment can be anticipated, sensed; it can be to a certain extent prepared; it can be at times "stretched"; nevertheless, it always remains a definite moment. In the *Forefathers' Eve* that moment is even precisely fixed by a calendar date. In *Grażyna* there are two such moments: the first—the dismissal of the envoys—still leaves several ways open, the second, when Grażyna takes over command, marks the final decision. In *Konrad Wallenrod* the hero for a long time contemplates a step which will utterly alter his life, he prepares his wife for it by allusions; at last comes the moment when the transformation becomes a reality, in which, as it were, Alf-Walter dies and Konrad Wallenrod is born. The same is true of the transformation of Jacek Soplica: he, himself, links it with one single moment which he describes as a moment of revelation (Book X, l. 821). So none of these transformations is the result of evolution, of gradual ripening, of progress, of outside pressure; in general these changes are not in the nature of development but of crisis.

Significantly, all these transformations manifest themselves sharply even on the outside. The transformed Grażyna appears before our eyes in the armor of Litawor; the transformed Litawor, in the armor of an unknown knight. The sensitive, tender Alf is well-nigh unrecognizable in the guise of the grim ironic Master of Teutonic Knights, known under a completely different name. And

Gustaw, too, once he becomes transformed changes his name. And the proud reckless squire Jacek—how unlike his old self under an assumed name and in a monk's frock!

A disguised figure, a man living under a false name—that was the traditional effect of the old adventure play and novel. At the beginning of the nineteenth century Walter Scott had brought it back to life. So, after him, did Byron and a countless throng of their imitators. But as far as Mickiewicz is concerned this is not just an effect, not merely a technical device to facilitate the task of the narrator and to hold the attention of the less discriminating reader. That outward change is for Mickiewicz a symbol: the visible mark of a deep and final inner transformation.

3

Naturally, the question arises, if not in the eighteenth century where else, then, are we to look for the kin of Mickiewicz's transformed heroes?

In the European culture of our era, and from its very dawn, the idea of a spiritual crisis was propagated by Christianity. One might say that the first model and the archetype of all later crucial transformations was the conversion of St. Paul, that change in the direction of activity and in the nature of belief so complete and sudden that, as St. Paul says himself in the Apostolic Acts, "all that heard him were astonished" (Acts 9:21). A modern theologian writing about St. Paul says that the most striking trait of the spiritual history of this great propagator of Christianity is the degree to which his thought before conversion and after it lacks continuity. In the subsequent Christian writings—and that on all levels—such matters as conversion, the renunciation of worldly goods for the love of God, the rise from fall to sainthood, were among the favorite subjects. To mention but one typical example in the popular literature of the Middle Ages we have *The Lives of Barlaam and Josephat.* This tale, which circulated all over Europe from the tenth century onward, was the story of a king's son who after coming in contact with suffering and death becomes a Christian and later renounces the throne to become a hermit. The main plot of this edifying book originated, as it turns out, in Buddhism; nevertheless, it expressed one of the ideals of medieval Christianity. We find the same ideal in every collection of Lives of the Saints. The protagonists often went to God from the heights of wealth and power, sometimes they went sullied by sin or even crime, but their love was so great that it atoned for their guilt.

The Renaissance era reveals a duality in its approach to man. On one hand, following the example of antiquity, it seems to believe in the supremacy of the mind over the entire structure of human character; on the other, it shows the consistency and durability of that structure even under the impact of greatest passion. The Renaissance is full of all sorts of formulas: a formula for the ideal ruler, the ideal senator, the ideal courtier. Yet there is no lack of skeptics, too, who refer to such formulas with an ironic smile. And the poets place a particularly strong emphasis on the continuity of the inner life of the individual. That is, for instance, what Shakespeare, the greatest poet of the Renaissance, does. Both his criminal Richard III and his hysterical Richard II up to the very end remain essentially the same. Granted that Henry V does change when, after ascending the throne, he sends Falstaff and his band packing. This step, however, looks like one dictated by external circumstances and not like a change in character. The distintegration of Anthony comes about slowly and gradually. What is more—and the point is a significant one—it does not destroy the positive elements of Anthony's character. Macbeth, a man endowed with a superior mind and a poetic imagination, turns into a murderer. Yes, but the drama about him does not show only that. It also shows that Macbeth, though guilty of many crimes, has not lost his spiritual attributes; toward the very end of the play he is still worthy to utter lines that are perhaps the most sublime of all of Shakespeare's poetry. The case of Othello is not simply that of a brave, wise and tactful knight who, driven by jealousy, turns into a raving maniac; throughout most of the play he is both the former and the latter.

The Shakespearean hero who wishes he might change is Hamlet. When his father's ghost imposes upon him the task of avenging his death Hamlet decides:

Yea, from the table of my memory
I'll wipe away all trivial fond records,
All saws of books, all forms, all pressures past
That youth and observation copied there.

And yet, for all such impassioned resolutions, for all his efforts, Hamlet is unable to turn into a cold, calculating avenger. It is not courage that he lacks, he is not burdened with excessive scruples, nor is he obviously a neurotic (as many of the nineteenth century commentators would have him), and yet he procrastinates. Why? Because in spite of all promises, in spite of moral self-flagellation he still remains his old self: the refined, ironic, sensitive Hamlet, unable to exist without philosophical reflections. When angered he is capable of the most violent deeds, but to perform in cold blood the task of vengeance—and this, under the circumstances is the only possible form of justice (and indeed, is so accepted by him)—is contrary to his nature. Hamlet, otherwise so gifted, lacks the gift of transformation.

In the seventeenth century the theme of spiritual transformation reappears again, and with all its former vigor, in the literature of the triumphant Catholicism of Spain. There it finds its most monumental embodiment in Calderon's drama *La vida es sueño* (Life Is a Dream, 1636). The hero of this drama, the royal prince Sigismund, by nature wild, violent, and tyrannical, has been brought up by his father as a prisoner in shackles. Set free, he reveals all the depth of his egoism and of his bestial instincts. But when once more he awakens in shackles, and, still under the influence of a narcotic, finds himself unable to distinguish between reality and dream, he alters completely and becomes judicious, restrained, and humane. All his actions are henceforth tempered by the thought—the fruit of his experience—that perhaps in life all is but "illusion, a shadow, a spectre, and the greatest happiness is petty indeed if all of life is merely a dream, and even dreams are nought but a dream" (the close of the Second Day):

Qué es la vida?—Una ilusion,
Una sombra, una ficcion,

Y el mayor bien es pequeño:
Que toda la vida es sueño,
Y los sueños sueño son.

Once more set free and called to perform the duties of a warrior and a statesman, Sigismund no longer lets himself be blinded by power and success. Whenever his violent nature threatens to get out of hand he curbs it by reflecting that perhaps he is only dreaming and will have to wake up. At the root of this transformation there is doubt and practical consideration in equal parts: whether life is reality or a dream—"to act right is all that matters; if it be reality, for its own sake; if not, then to win friends for the time of awakening" (Third Day, Scene 4):

. . . sea verdad ó sueño,
Obrar bien es lo que importa: si fuera verdad, per serlo;
Si no, por gagnar amigos para quando despertemos.

Thus the will, the choice, are here the direct outcome of a certain reasoned judgment; indeed, they are practically identical with it, much as in the Moralities of the medieval theater. As a matter of fact, Calderon's drama is spiritually closely related to that theater, though it differs from it in a dazzling wealth of dramatic inventions and a magnificent profusion of poetic language.

We shall not find transformed people in the great French tragedies of the seventeenth century: the heroes of Corneille are too indomitable, the heroes of Racine too dominated by passion.

The literature of the eighteenth century predominantly concerns itself with characters that are either unalterable, or, as mentioned before, undergo a gradual change as a result of experience or education. Mademoiselle d'Aisnon, the heroine of the moving tale *About Madame de la Pommeraye and the Marquis d'Arcis,* which forms a part of Diderot's novel *Jacques le fataliste* (1773–1796), is an exception to this rule. This unfortunate creature, good at heart but weak, by passively submitting to persuasion, threats, intimidation, and main force, lets herself be drawn into vice and even crime; yet a moment comes when in the face of a wrong in which she has been instrumental she first falls into despair, then finds strength to confess her past, to resolve to mend her ways, and to act in a way which brings her moral rebirth. As Benedetto Croce, who wrote a beautiful essay on this little tale, put it: that which, at first, was in her no more than a trait of temperament became henceforth the ethical factor of her character.

At the threshold of the Romantic period we meet with a larger number of people climactically transformed. Foremost among them is Goethe's Faust. (Part One of *Faust* appeared in 1808.) Faust represents an entirely new departure in the category of the transformed. Why does he sign a compact with the devil and start life afresh? Simply to satisfy his craving for knowledge. He has spent years in intellectual speculation, now he wants to plunge into the pleasures of the flesh. He was a recluse; now, he wants to share the joys and sorrows of his fellow men. As a matter of fact, he knows in advance that this new life will not give him full satisfaction even as the previous one had not. Hence the paradoxical style in which he expresses his plans:

> Dem Taumel weih' ich mich, dem schmerzlichsten Genuss,
> Verliebten Hass, erquickenden Verdruss.

Thus in this new life, too, Faust will remain what he has been in the former one, the embodiment of eternal search.

We find a host of transformed people in the writings of Byron (among them the heroes of the two poems *Giaour* and *Dream* which Mickiewicz translated into Polish). All of these Byronic characters are very much like one another, but quite unlike their literary predecessors. The turning point of their lives invariably marks a downward trend. Once, in their youth, they were full of joy and friendliness, they trusted life; later, they met with misfortune and the preposterousness of this wrong fills them with loathing for the world and society. They turn into proud recluses, if not into demoniac enemies of men, all of whom they lump together in their hatred.

Balzac's Vautrin is another offspring of the same literary family. There is a difference, however. Unlike Byron's protagonist, Vautrin never goes through a period of friendly feelings toward his fellow men; from the very beginning he is their enemy. Whereas Byron's heroes are rebellious angels, Vautrin is a born fiend, which is typical of Balzac's realism. A semblance of transformation, analogous to those described above, occurs at a later stage of Vautrin's life when he, by now a hardened criminal, suddenly develops paternal feelings. But even this quaver of human affection does not actually break the continuity of Vautrin's inner story: he becomes attached to Lucien de Rubempre because he hopes to find in him the spiritual heir to whom he might leave the accrued capital of his hatred. An artist in evil, he wants his ward to become his masterpiece. "Je suis l'auteur," he tells him, "tu sera le drame."

Nevertheless, Vautrin belongs to a somewhat later period; the *Splendeurs et misères des courtisanes* from which the quotation is taken was published between 1843 and 1846. Much earlier there began to appear in literature new transformations of evil characters into good ones. In Manzoni's much discussed *I Promessi Sposi* (The Betrothed), a novel more or less contemporary with the early parts of *Forefathers' Eve* (1825), we find a rascally potentate—"the Nameless" (*Innominato*)—who admits of no power superior to himself and jeers at all authority and whose personal whim is the only valid motive and force, the only means. This man is converted at the sight of one of his victims, an innocent girl whom he had ordered abducted for one of his followers. This conversion, on purely moral grounds at first, is soon followed by a religious one, when to the influence of oppressed innocence is added that of the magnanimous charity of a representative of the Church. The transformation of the "Nameless" is reminiscent of the medieval conversions, except that Manzoni presented it against a psychological background for which he drew colors from Rousseau's optimistic belief in the inherent goodness of human nature. Indeed, even before the "Nameless" repents we are told that he is becoming bored, even oppressed, by his own rascalities, and that his thoughts turn more and more often to the memories of his happy and innocent childhood.

In the literature of the Romantic period such transformations are fairly numerous, and in some cases fairly extreme. For instance, in one of Merimée's comedies, "The Spaniards in Denmark" (*Les Espagnoles en Danemark*), which forms part of the cycle *Le Théâtre de Clara Gazul* (1825), a woman spy overcome by love abandons her ignoble profession and turns to virtue. ("O Don Juan! l'amour que je sens pour vous . . . m'a rendue toute autre . . . je commence à voir ce que c'est la vertue . . . c'est . . . c'est l'envie de vous plair.") The condensation of the situation lends to this conversion, as it does to the entire play, a tinge of the grotesque.

Frankly grotesque is another playlet included in the same cycle under the title "A Woman Is a Devil" (*Une femme est un diable*). Here we meet with an inquisitor whose entire faith, fervor, and steadfastness of purpose go to pieces under the impact of a single temptation: for the sake of a woman's embraces he not only breaks within a short hour every vow he has taken but commits murder, to boot. Situations typical of the literature of the Romantic movement are handled here with the ironic wit of the preceding century.

But even when represented in all earnestness, the transformations described by some of the romantic poets seem like caricatures. For instance, in Victor Hugo's *Hernani* (1830) the Spanish king Don Carlos is throughout the first three acts a brutal, cunning rascal; in the fourth, where he becomes the Emperor Charles V, he is transformed into a magnanimous, wise monarch.

And yet, even such works did not discredit the theme of transformation. The family of the transformed in the literature of the nineteenth century was destined to be a large one. It includes such diverse members as Scrooge in Dickens's *A Christmas Carol,* whose conscience is shaken by a sudden vision of the results of his selfishness; as Jean Valjean in Victor Hugo's *Les Misérables,* who turns honest because he has met with big-hearted Christian kindness; as the hero of Leo Tolstoy's tale, *The Master and the Man,* who undergoes a moral rebirth in the face of inevitable death.

Such examples could be multiplied almost indefinitely (among the writings of Leo Tolstoy alone we could have chosen several others, such as *The Resurrection, The Death of Ivan Ilyich,* or *Father Serge*). But even those already mentioned suffice to demonstrate that distinguished works of literature show various types of people who either strive to change spiritually, or actually undergo a transformation. There are among them those who wish to become different and are unable to do so, like Hamlet, and, let us add, his numerous literary progeny. Others are transformed: through the fire of religious revelation, like the saints and the heroes of medieval legends; through philosophical reasoning combined with self-seeking prudence, like Sigismund of Calderon's drama; through an unquenchable lust for life which cannot be satisfied with a single form of existence, like Faust; through the majesty of the office to which they have been called, like Don Carlos in *Hernani;* through moral shock produced by the sight of the consequences of their own evil deeds, like Mademoiselle d'Aisnon, the *Nameless,* Scrooge, and the hero of Tolstoy's *Resurrection;* through the kindness and forgiveness with which they have met, like Jean Valjean; because of the wrongs and misfortunes which have befallen them, like Byron's heroes; or because they are close to death, like Tolstoy's "master."

4

None of these motives prompts the transformations depicted in the major works of Mickiewicz. The motive behind them is different, though in every case the same—the love of the Fatherland. It is this love which moves Grażyna to dismiss the envoys of the Teutonic Order, to don armor, and to go to her death on the battlefield. It is this love which causes Alf-Walter to undertake his gigantic scheme of striking the Teutonic Order from within. It is this love which turns Gustaw into Konrad. Jacek's penance, it is true, is prompted by two motives: the expiation of murder and the atonement for collaborating with the enemy. To expiate his sin of murder Jacek becomes a monk, but it is the expiation of his sin against his country which comes chronologically first. What is more, Jacek, even as a monk, is primarily a political emissary, obviously more concerned with his patriotic than his monastic duties.

Thus Mickiewicz introduces into the poetry of character transformation a completely new element. He shows people for whom the country is the highest moral tribunal, people for whom patriotic duty is the source of highest inspiration and of greatest strength. It is because of this inspiration and through this strength that they become transformed. Admittedly, Jacek may strike some as bearing a close resemblance to the "Nameless," but what this likeness actually amounts to is the similarity in just one detail: in both cases the transformation takes place after the perpetration of a crime. Beyond that, however, the difference in the nature and the circumstances of the crime is tremendous. As for any resemblance between Mickiewicz's heroes and Byron's self-centered, hatred-consumed protagonists, those who speak of this clearly show that while reading they see nothing beyond gestures, incidentals and . . . stage props. The heroes of Mickiewicz and Faust belong to two altogether different worlds. Nor have they anything in common with the half-metaphysical half-prudent morality of Calderon's Sigismund. Even if we did not know, as we do, how harshly the poet spoke of *Life Is a Dream* we could easily guess how alien to his nature he would have found it. From the heroes of medieval legends and of hagiographical tales Mickiewicz's protagonists differ in the degree of psychological realism and in the very concept of Fatherland.

Of all the poets of modern times the one spiritually closest, perhaps, to Mickiewicz is Corneille, a poet with whom Mickiewicz was so little familiar and whom, thanks to the prejudices of his times, he so unfairly condemned. There are no transformations in Corneille's tragedies, but all his heroes are men of strong will capable of sacrificing their lives and all that they hold dear for the sake of a principle which, reason or conscience tells them, is more important than their personal happiness or the happiness of those they love. No matter what their motive, whether honor as in *Cid,* reason of state as in *Otto,* or religion as in *Polyeuct,* the capacity for sacrifice is there. Similarly, Mickiewicz's heroes sacrifice, or are ready to sacrifice, everything for love of country.

There is, however, a vast difference in the way in which Mickiewicz and Corneille present these supreme decisions. In Corneille's tragedies all the "for" and "against" of every decision, all the details of spiritual wrestlings, all future possibilities, all prospects of conflict are fully and meticulously set forth in long monologues and dialogues, which, though they contain all of Corneille's most sublime poetry, at times degenerate into pure rhetoric (or, as a malicious critic put it, "those tears in Alexandrines"). In the works of Mickiewicz both the motives and the consequences of decisions are presented indirectly, sometimes simply by inference. Grażyna is almost wordless. Alf-Walter talks over his great scheme with his wife and father-in-law in broken sentences which leave much unsaid, and when the narrator takes over he uses only a metaphor (IV, ll. 492 ff.):

Thus waxed the flame of vengeance long nourished in secret and silence.
Fed by the sight of disasters and sufferings, till in consuming
Blaze it flashed forth and enveloped his heart, and destroyed every feeling
Even the feeling of love. . . .[5]

The metaphor is completed not by a return to straight narrative but by a simile, the famous comparison to a Bialowieża oak, "which consumed by a fire kindled in its core loses not only its leaves and branches but its crown of mistletoe as well." What lends the parting scene between Alf and Aldona its peculiar poignancy is precisely the fact that it is fraught with so much unexpressed feeling. The transformation of Gustaw into Konrad is forecast merely by a few words of the Prologue in which the hero-prisoner expresses his fears lest the enemy should take the shackles off his hands and feet "only to press them upon his soul." As for the transformation of Jacek, we learn about it only from his deathbed confession made in short, broken sentences, which exhaustion, pain, and humility prevent him from amplifying and sometimes even from completing. With the sole exception of Konrad, for whom, as a poet, words are the natural medium of expression, we know Mickiewicz's heroes first of all by their deeds. Personal disclosures and poetic revelations about them do not come until later and are always short and concise.

## 5

And yet, in spite of all these traits they share in common, the range of dramatic situations which confront Mickiewicz's protagonists is wide indeed. With what novel and rich poetic dissertations would their ordeals provide a Corneille! Here is Grażyna—the tragedy of a woman who can save her country from civil strife and the man

5. *Konrad Wallenrod and Other Writings of Adam Mickiewicz,* tr. Jewell Parish, University of California Press, 1925.

she loves from disgrace, but only at the risk of disaster and by facing almost certain death. Grażyna experiences hours of supreme heroism. The problem confronting Alf-Walter requires not hours but years of self-denial. He knows that the threat looming over his nation means not merely defeat but complete extinction. Here the sacrifice of personal happiness or even of life will serve no purpose. Indeed, no honest means is of any avail. So Alf, although his ethical nature shrinks from it, makes up his mind to use a measure which he looks upon as criminal. He sacrifices his conscience, he sacrifices his peace of mind. He sacrifices the happiness of the human being closest to his heart. He is not even deterred by the thought of eternal punishment, of which, as a Christian, he is fully aware; when he mentions the hereafter it is only to say that he foresees nothing but hell for himself. The drama confronting Gustaw-Konrad is that of a poet of genius who dedicates himself to the service of his hapless country and nearly shatters the whole edifice of his faith and convictions in his search for effective means of action. Jacek's life—that is still a different story, the story of an average though high-spirited and passionate man. Wounded love and outraged pride have driven him to crime. Aroused to do penance, he realizes from the very start that the atonement must take the form of action, of constructive activity pursued for the sake of honor and country.

Nor do these supreme acts of will come any easier to Mickiewicz's heroes than to Corneille's protagonists. The inner transformation is by no means simple. The old self does not die to be replaced by a new one; it is only curbed, and to keep it in check requires constant effort. Grażyna goes to her death with determination, but her body trembles, and even her customary presence of mind deserts her. Konrad Wallenrod cannot lose himself completely in the pursuit of his grandiose (and monstrous) scheme. His conscience torments him, his thoughts escape him to fly back to memories of the past: at crucial moments he complains and weakens. He does accomplish his task in the end, but even then only with reluctance. Regardless of the loftiness of its purpose, regardless of the magnitude of all that he has sacrificed for its sake, it fills him with loathing. He meets with an unexpected stumbling block in the form of love, which suddenly revives in his weary heart, and, at a time "when the fate of nations hangs in the balance," obscures reality by idyllic dreams. Gustaw-Konrad even in his Great Improvisation, even while wrestling with the loftiest metaphysical and moral problems, complains that God has "torn away his personal happiness." Jacek Soplica notes that in the face of approaching death he should not talk so much of matters and feelings pertaining to his youth and begs his listeners' indulgence.

Thus the theme of transformation appears in the writings of Mickiewicz not only in a form that is specifically his own, but also in a highly varied orchestration.

6

Obviously, to demonstrate that the major works of a poet are variations (no matter how abundant) on one and the same theme still falls far short of giving a full picture of his poetry. Besides the poet of transformation there is also in Mickiewicz the poet of love and the poet of friendship, there is the poet of loneliness and the poet of humble prayer, the poet of Promethean courage and the poet of lofty flights of fancy, and the poet of joy derived from the simple realities of life, and still other poets as well. Or, to put it differently, the poetry of Mickiewicz flows in many streams. Here we are concerned with only one of these streams, but a main one, nonetheless.

For we must bear in mind that aside from being the main subject of his major works, transformations (though of a different kind and prompted by other reasons) appear also elsewhere in Mickiewicz's poetry. We may pass over his youthful Ballads ("The Fish"; "Świteź"; "Tukaj"; "Świtezianka"; "I like that"), in which such transformations bear the mark of Ovid-like pure fantasy, and are not always meant to be taken seriously. But the collection of love sonnets closes with a far deeper change: the singer of light love shall henceforth turn into a bard who "with spirits from high above grasps the lyre of Alcaeus." A kindred theme, the breaking away from a certain mode of life and the forecast of a different flight, appears also in the parallel series of Love Elegies ("Musings on the Eve of Departure").

Of the many heroes of the November Insurrection, 1830, Mickiewicz paid in his poetry a special tribute to Emilia Plater, the woman transformed into a soldier ("The Death of the Colonel"). In the poem "The Road to Russia," in which he muses on what the future shall bring to that country and its people, Mickiewicz sees it as one of two possible transformations.

> But when the sun of liberty shall rise
> What kind of insect then will greet the light?
> Will a bright butterfly soar from the earth,
> Or a dark moth, of dark, uncleanly birth? [6]

The poem "To My Russian Friends" is essentially a poetic meditation on various transformations; some of them tragic and sublime, others—profitable and ignoble. Even the future of his own nation appears to Mickiewicz as a transformation. That is how Konrad speaks of it in the Improvisation ("I would turn my people into a living song"). In the vision of Father Peter, Poland appears not only risen from the dead, but (as critics have noted long ago) transformed in the image of our Lord's Transfiguration.

And again we find the same motif running through Mickiewicz's religious lyrics. "The Evening Discourse" is indeed nothing but a meditation on the subject of God the King who becomes God the Subject, and of Man the Servant transformed into the master of his Lord. "Reason and Faith" reaches its poetic climax in the stanza which describes how human estates "vast and turbid" when seen through the eyes of reason are transformed into "small and clear" ones when viewed through the eyes of faith. Even in his earliest religious poem, the youthful "Hymn for the Day of Annunciation," Mickiewicz waxes ecstatic over the transformation in the Madonna, representing the Annunciation as though it were the Transfiguration.

Likewise in his most intimate personal lyrics the theme of transformation crops up time and again. There is Eva in the poem "I Dreamed of Winter"—the woman-bird "as beautiful as Our Lord's

6. *Forefathers' Eve,* Part III, "The Road to Russia," tr. Marjorie Beatrice Peacock, *Slavonic Review,* Vol. XIII, 1935.

Transfiguration." And there is, again, that strange "Vision" which is actually the vision of a great mystical transformation of man's entire nature:

> A ringing roused me, and my body there
> Like down that wraps some flower of the field
> Burst open, by an angel's breath unsealed,
> And laid the kernel of my spirit bare.
> And, so it seemed, I wakened suddenly
> From the dread dream that had so wearied me.
> And as one newly wakened wipes the sweat
> From off his forehead, so I wiped away
> My unshed past—as in a fresh array
> Of greening herbs the old husks linger yet.[7]

And the poem dedicated to Bohdan Zaleski which was Mickiewicz's farewell to poetry, what else is it if not one more development of the theme of change—a change in the sense of rising higher and growing stronger?

> My nightingale, thy wings will fail
> The eagle's thou must wear. . . .[8]

Thus Mickiewicz wanted even the poet-nightingale transformed into a poet-eagle; he ordered even his lyrical ego to change. He looked for transformations in the lives of his great contemporaries; he conferred upon the inspired protagonists of his great drama the visionary gift of seeing his nation transformed; in religion he worshiped above all else the mystery of Transfiguration. Transfiguration, Transformation—here is indeed one of the most frequent and the most significant themes of his poetic vision. And in most cases this theme appears as a mark and token of spiritual value. For Mickiewicz's poetry shows principally transformations for the better, transformations that lift up, ennoble, render more perfect, that prove the strengthening of the inner self, or, even when they involve a tragic burden, reveal a passionate transport of the soul.

7. "A Vision," tr. Dorothea Prall Radin, *Slavonic Review,* Vol. XVII, 1938.
8. "To Bohdan Zaleski," tr. Dorothea Prall Radin, *Slavonic Review,* Vol. XVII, 1938.

We repeat: this favorite theme of Mickiewicz's poetry has nothing in common with the motif of continual changeability which we find, for instance, in the poetry of Shelley ("Nought may endure but Mutability"). Mickiewicz's transformations do not result from a continuous flow of changes; on the contrary, they break the continuity of life.

Yet, at the same time, the very magnitude of these changes lends special glory to everything that is not affected by them. How strong is the friendship which binds Alf and Wajdelota is best shown by the fact that, started in the first period of Alf's life, it continues, unchanged, in the second, in spite of the gigantic transformation which divides the two. The same is true of Alf's love for Aldona, and, again, of the feelings which the beauty of nature never fails to stir in his heart. Similarly highlighted in the *Forefathers' Eve* are the friendships of Gustaw-Konrad, and in *Pan Tadeusz* the love of Jacek-Robak for Eva, whom even on his deathbed he cannot forget. And what is one to say of the power of feelings which bind all these people to their nation and their Fatherland, feelings that are, indeed, the cause of their transformation!

But Mickiewicz's poetry contains other instances, too: instances in which the permanence of certain psychological factors is brought out by means of negation, by showing that no change can affect them:

> Begone from my memory! No! That one command
> Neither mine nor your memory shall obey.

Here is an example chosen at random from one of Mickiewicz's minor masterpieces. From an analogous source springs the poignant eloquence of the opening line in the poem "To X" ("In the Alps at Splügen"):

> So never, never with thee can I part!

7

The important place which the theme of transformation holds in the content of Mickiewicz's poetry has its counterpart in a certain trait which manifests itself in the development of his artistic devices.

Anyone studying his writings must undoubtedly be struck by the great diversity of his poetic media. Whether in matters of structure, or versification, or of style, this wealth is remarkable, indeed. Yet it is not that wealth alone which is characteristic of Mickiewicz; characteristic, too, is the fact that after using a given form—and using it in masterly fashion—he never goes back to it.

The volcanic outbursts of mixed verses in which Gustaw pours out his feelings in the Fourth Part of *Forefathers' Eve* is never to appear again in the subsequent writings of the poet. True that *Farys,* the great Improvisation, and the visions in the Third Part of *Forefathers' Eve* are likewise cast in the pattern of mixed verses, but these patterns—and partly too, their elements—are quite different, as Łoś demonstrated long ago in his book on Polish verses. *Grażyna* may at first glance seem in its outward form not unlike *Konrad Wallenrod*. Actually, however, the structure of these two poems is completely different, even their versification is dissimilar. In *Grażyna* the regular flow of an eleven-syllable meter only in the epilogue yields place to a different type of verse, and, incidentally, one that is equally regular. In *Konrad Wallenrod* there is a profusion of inserts dissimilar in rhythm; even in the course of the main narrative the flow of isometric verses passes several times into the form of mixed verses (though the principal *metrum* never ceases to be the unifying element). And, most important of all, a large part of the poem, several hundred lines in fact, is written in an altogether different meter: a hexameter which constitutes one of the miracles of the Polish language. This hexameter was, as everyone knows, Mickiewicz's own invention, perhaps his greatest feat in the field of versification, and one which was to prove extremely fruitful in the subsequent development of Polish poetry. Yet, Mickiewicz himself, after casting his *Wajdelota's Tale* in it never used it again. Nor did he ever return to the form of sonnet after attaining such artistic heights in that form in the two collections written in 1826. Then, after all these brilliant achievements came the Third Part of *Forefathers' Eve,* with all its dazzling new contributions to the art of versification, its realistic conversations alternating with songs, "singing scenes," visions, monologues, and satyrical rhapsodies. And once more, Mickiewicz did not continue along this path. After overwhelming his readers with the rich inventiveness of *Forefathers' Eve* he chose as his poetic medium in *Pan Tadeusz* the traditional, common, "easy" thirteen-syllable meter. We know what a magic tool this form becomes in his hands, how much enchanting serenity and tragic storm it can express in its easy moving flow, with what force and what subtlety it speaks to the reader's ear.

Even apart from Mickiewicz's major compositions one may point out a number of "unique" instances of his prosodic art, to mention but such gems as "Tears" or "By a water broad and clear."

And what a wide diversity of style and mood does his poetry display! The dreamy, sometimes jocular, sometimes mocking fantasy of the ballads; the stylized, somber primitif of "The Lilies"; the volcanic fire of the Fourth Part of *Forefathers' Eve,* the gallant, and at the same time feminine drama of Grażyna, the elegance and airiness of poems inscribed in albums or composed for special occasions; the sensitiveness veiled by irony of the "Love Elegies"; the monumental grandeur of the *Crimean Sonnets;* the tragic loftiness of *Konrad Wallenrod;* the tender intimacy of religious lyrics; the corrosive grief of the poem, "To a Polish Mother"; the heroic dash of "Ordon's Redoubt," the manifold power of the Third Part of *Forefathers' Eve;* the devout abdication from his own style in *The Books of the Polish Nation and of the Polish Pilgrims;* the succinctness and vigor of the fables; that incredible combination of epic power, vividness, humor, pathos and tenderness which is *Pan Tadeusz;* the whimsical subtlety of "Princess Lala"; the chamber-music lyricism of personal poems written in the Lausanne period, the singing lilt of "My Nightingale"—what a vast scale!

So also in matters of form, the same spiritual forces which shape the climaxes of Mickiewicz's major works seem to be at work. The force which urges a change, and the force which brings it about. Of course, in the artistic sphere things do not happen as they do on a religious and moral plane. In matters of religion and ethics one great climax decides the course of a man's future life. In art, transformation may follow transformation. Nevertheless, the nature of the process, itself, seems to be similar. One has almost the impression that as soon as the poet has triumphed in a given medium his "artistic conscience" forces him to change it. And change it he does.

But, in this sphere, too, aside from elements subject to transformation there exist others which remain constant and unaltered. Mickiewicz, who disposes of such wealth of artistic media and changes his forms so often, in moments most important from the structural point of view almost always uses the simplest words, and it is that simplicity which wins the reader's heart: "Joy did not dwell in his house, when his fatherland knew naught but sorrow." What can be more simple?

Lately there have been attempts to explain the moving eloquence of such verses by a peculiar theory, namely that "from a number of possible definitions of certain facts by various words and sentences the poet *did not choose* any particular word, but, as it were, *extracted the essence of all these possibilities,*" and that "back of Mickiewicz's word there quivers, still vividly perceptible, a swarm of other possible verbal substitutes." This theory, rather obscure in its semantic meaning, has perhaps been transplanted into the realm of poetry from the realm of certain post-impressionistic schools of painting (by substituting "words" for "dabs of color"), but, frankly, it does not apply to Mickiewicz's poetry.

What we find in that poetry is rather a great "clarity of lines" in the sense of clarity of meaning. The words he uses mean precisely what they purport to mean, no more and no less. It is that clarity which lends such force and poignance to his language.

And simple and stirring Mickiewicz's poetry remains through all its transformations.

## 8

There came a time when the poet of transformation who had so often transformed himself artistically was to transform himself in still another sense: he renounced poetry and stopped writing. The history of literature knows many similar instances of a poet falling silent at the height of his creative powers. In much the same way Racine had once, at the age of thirty-seven, given up writing for the stage, and at about the same time as Mickiewicz the Polish playwright Fredro withdrew into stubborn silence for a period of twenty years. But Fredro refused to write because the literary atmosphere of the times was hostile to him. Racine had grown weary of theatrical intrigues and jealousies, and perhaps, too, of the puritanical sternness of his critics. Mickiewicz stood at the crest of fame and popularity. The clamor of his opponents from the classicist camp had abated long since, and besides, no one listened to them any more. It is true that Mickiewicz, like anyone else, had his adversaries but mainly as a man of action and the exponent of certain beliefs; as a poet he was surrounded with almost universal veneration on the part of his countrymen, and highly esteemed by foreigners.

There is no point in speculating whether or not his was the case of genius prematurely "running dry." The history of literature is familiar with such cases, and knows that poets who have "run dry" often continue to write for a long time if they have the will to do so. Mickiewicz stopped writing because he did not want to write. He said once that it would be ridiculous if he, in his old age, still continued "to make verses." Whether this was a loss to literature or not, we do not know. One thing is certain, however: the great theme of his poetry became manifestly the theme of his life. The sudden silence of any great poet is a striking phenomenon. But the silence of such a poet as he, and after such poetry as he wrote, is particularly arresting. For here, the poet of self-willed transformation wrought a transformation in himself: he transformed himself into a non-poet. Indeed, literature presents perhaps no other case in which it is as difficult to draw a dividing line between a man's poetry and his personal life.

*Translated by* RULKA LANGER

# MICKIEWICZ AND MODERN POETRY

by Czesław Miłosz

It is a more or less accepted truth that the last hundred years of European poetry have been marked by a process of radical change in the structure of the poetic phrase. The logical or "understandable" sequence of words has proved to be less and less in favor with the poets, and a new aesthetics based upon the purely emotional appeal of words has emerged. That process reached its peak in Dada and surrealist movements, and seems to be parallel with the antirationalist trends in philosophy.

To pronounce such a judgment does not mean dismissing modern poetry as modest in its achievements or deprived of meaning. Nevertheless, living in a changing world, we are compelled to evaluate the present developments in the name of the future, or of what we imagine the future of poetry will be. We can assume that the serious setback suffered lately by surrealism and kindred literary schools in Europe signifies the poets' desire to trim the overgrown garden of words. There is undoubtedly a tendency once more to revise the past, and to accept the usefulness of some older techniques scorned by the followers of Father Brémond's *poésie pure.* One can find in literary magazines of different countries many statements by poets who see in intellectual vigor the only hope for the survival of poetry. However great a love a poet may have for free images that suggest a meaning by creating a "special atmosphere" in a poem, he would be unwise to deny the dangers that threaten poetry as soon as it becomes too addicted to emotional refinement. It seems to be futile to look for inspiration among poets who continue the Victorian tradition. There is no way back in art, and one can fight what is modern only by applying modern methods. We have not yet severed the umbilical cord tying us to Victorian art and, therefore, we should rather try to enrich our technique through the examination of epochs separated from our own by a greater distance of time and by a completely different discipline of feelings. We must wait some time before we can form a just estimate of Robert Browning, but we can already approach Pope without prejudices.

The modern poets of various nations are striving to establish new connections with tradition. Attention is being focused on those poets of the past who would enlarge the possibilities of the modern poets without making them mere imitators. A poet of any language who feels that he should add something enduring to the resources of his native tongue, and not merely be in revolt against his predecessors, usually invokes the literary figures of the day before yesterday, searching their works for the elements which, in the light of his own experience, will prove to be new and unexplored. So far as Polish poetry is concerned, Adam Mickiewicz is such a figure.

Mickiewicz has been more than often described as the chief representative of the Polish romantic school. His manifestoes, his tumultuous life, his political activities, and his role as national prophet were in complete accord with the ideas of the romantic poet. At the beginning of his literary career he revolted against the French classicism then dominating the Polish literary scene and published a volume, *Ballads and Romances* which was labeled by the Polish admirers of Delille as "monstrous and barbarous." In defiance of the classical unities still accepted by Polish dramatists, he wrote his great poetic drama, *The Forefathers' Eve,* which, when staged by Wyspiański, a pioneer among directors of the twentieth century, showed his infallible instinct for effective theatrical detail.

Nevertheless, Mickiewicz does not quite belong to European romanticism. The importance of classifying should not be overestimated, but the word "romantic" has some definite connotations. The great political upheaval and struggle for national independence, which so influenced the romantic writings in Europe, still preserve their dignity and shape the history of European nations. The same cannot be said of the romantic technique, which is in direct conflict with the present renewed enthusiasm for a dry and somewhat rigid rhythm. By saying that Mickiewicz cannot be classified as entirely romantic in his technique, I wish to stress the elements in his poetry that make him dear to the new poets writing in Polish. Unfortunately, that quality of his is inaccessible to readers who can judge of him only by English translations. English translations of his poems, so far as I can pronounce an opinion, have a very definite late romantic or Victorian touch.

The work of Mickiewicz has its roots in the literature of the eighteenth century and in the philosophy of the Enlightenment. In 1815–1819, the years of his intellectual apprenticeship at the University of Wilno, the rules of French classicism were strictly observed, and a group of able professors taught in that spirit. Mickiewicz acquired a knowledge of Latin and Greek that was then regarded as the necessary equipment for a man of letters. Let us remember that many years later he became a professor of Latin literature at the University of Lausanne in Switzerland. Among his first literary works were a translation of a brief excerpt from Voltaire's satiric epic *La Pucelle* and a poem of his own entitled *The Potato*—"a poem with a subject," in this case the discovery of America by Columbus and the blessing of introducing the potato to European agriculture. The poem expresses the author's sympathy for the American Revolution and, in somewhat veiled allusions, prophesies the victory of the ideals of freedom. These first poems were constructed in a "rationalistic" and "artificial" manner.

The young Mickiewicz admired Krasicki and Trembecki, the two masters of Polish eighteenth century neoclassical verse. He read attentively Jan Kochanowski, the great Polish poet of the Renaissance, who was kindred in spirit to the French *Pléiade* and who had no sympathy with the wilder and more impetuous elements in Renaissance literature. He worshiped Voltaire and was rather well read in Latin and Greek authors. In short, he was the perfect image of an eighteenth century young gentleman of good taste. His acquaintance with German authors, especially Schiller, and English authors, especially Scott and Byron, came later. The same is true of Russian poets, first of all Pushkin, whom he met during his stay in Russia.

To the historians of Polish literature, Mickiewicz has been a sort of prophet who opened a new era by breaking the rules of the dry, slavish classicism which had repressed Polish national feeling. He introduced folk beliefs, folk customs, and legends into his poems. He became *the* national poet, not afraid of expressing contemporary emotions and more widely read than any of the "classicists" who used allegories taken from antiquity and incomprehensible to unschooled readers. The nineteenth century, owing to the strength of the Polish romantic school and the part it played in the national struggle for independence, made the words "Polish" and "romantic" almost identical in meaning. In school, for example, I was taught to appreciate in Mickiewicz everything that was considered pathetic, moving, and sincere; my teachers obviously underestimated the poet's craft, which was based upon the solid precepts of his predecessors.

It is needless to describe in detail the quarrels between the Polish classic and romantic schools. But it is important to remember that the one word "romantic" does not cover all the elements in the poetry of Mickiewicz.

The style of Mickiewicz is manly and simple. He knew how to use conventional phrasing and, without straying beyond its limits, how to transform it into something completely new. That is not easy. Many poets maintain their standards only at the price of being unconventional, and drop into dullness as soon as they venture to use traditional methods. Through a slight retouching of words, a genuine poet is able to invest a commonplace sentence with charm. But genuine poets are rare, and there are periods of history when such an operation is impossible, because the use of a "common style" is then beyond the reach of even the great poets.

Mickiewicz attains his effects by fusing a classical ("dry") control with a free flow of images; his style is natural, not because he does not care about the method of expressing what he wants to say, but because his effort is hidden. He does not appear learned nor does he give the impression of being a master. His teachers' verse was learned and somewhat overburdened with literary allusions, while his romantic rival, Juliusz Słowacki, though he was a great poet, indulged in "melody" and in "mastership." Słowacki (1809–1849), although he was born only eleven years later than Mickiewicz, was subject to the same vice as Swinburne: he worshiped the word, which became an end in itself, not a tool.

The equilibrium attained by Mickiewicz suggests the thesis that the richest periods in art are the transitional periods, the periods when a certain way of feeling and thinking is broken but still exists as a basis for a new effort. Such a thesis would be risky, but it may be accepted in a modified form: that stability does not exist in art; that from the youth of a certain trend to its old age is only one step; that the mature years are no more than an imperceptible moment.

Mickiewicz's work is not homogeneous. It is full of pulsations, of different tendencies, succeeding each other. The first phase was purely classicist. The second—that of *Ballads and Romances*—was a revolt. What is often overlooked is that the ballads are not so sincere and naive as they have seemed to be. Mickiewicz's approach to folk superstitions and legends is sympathetic and half serious, but his simplicity is a device. He made use, however indirectly, of popular songs (as a matter of fact I have heard, in my childhood spent in the remote and wooded country of what was historically the Grand Duchy of Lithuania, some original versions of folk songs used by Mickiewicz). Mickiewicz transformed those popular songs into poems which derive their simple charm from a contrast between the conscious aim of the artist and the apparently primitive quatrain: he knew how to suspend his belief or disbelief, while his imitators (he started a wave of ballads in Poland) tried to be as naive as their subject matter. Of course, he believed in nymphs and miraculous metamorphoses no more than Ovid did. His preoccupation with such subjects was for him a way to show his conviction that through the "wisdom of the heart" of humble people we are nearer to the mystery of the world. But he was not a folk artist: his obvious enjoyment in imitating a folk credulity creates a world *als ob,* a country of fairy tale. What is puzzling is his tone, rather deep, solemn, and religious: he betrays his detachment from the subject through the general character of his structure. We later find the same puzzle in his novel in verse, *Pan Tadeusz.* Some critics have accused the heroes of that poem of being petty, egotistic, and interested only in hunting, drinking, and quarreling. Mickiewicz never tells the reader that he judges them severely; ergo, he approves their way of life. Of course, such an accusation can only recoil on the critic. Mickiewicz does not judge his characters, because he enjoys them as they are: they are not great figures or examples for mankind, but they are very human, average people, noisy and goodhearted, and a little stupid, seen from a remote time and place. The year 1812 in a quiet Polish province was mythological indeed, for a poet who was writing in Paris in 1832–1834.

Before Mickiewicz attained a quiet tone in his epic, he went through divergent modes of expression. Some parts of *The Forefathers' Eve* and *Farys* are marked by a turbulent tone far removed from that of either his earlier or his later writings. Other parts of *The Forefathers' Eve* such as scenes of political depravity and a long digression descriptive of Tsarist Russia that ends the drama, rank among the scanty examples of poetry that combines strength with political insight. We live in an era of concentration camps, and many a representative of the nineteenth century seems a little childish today, but not Mickiewicz. No poet of France or England is so politically terrifying. He has suffered and he has seen his people suffer—that is the explanation. Characteristically, in his most poignant poems he presents or paints rather than makes a direct appeal.

The concreteness of Mickiewicz's language contributes to the ambivalence of the poem *Grażyna*. It would be a well-known type of romantic story in verse were it not for the steadiness of its lines, which have a metallic ring. I want to spare quotations, which are effective in Polish only, but I cannot refrain from giving a sample of the quality of the poem:

Jakowiś ludzie biegą tu po błoniach
*A gałąź cieniu za każdym się czerni,*
A biegą prędko—muszą być na koniach,
A świecą mocno—muszą być pancerni.[1]

That "branch of shadow" following the riders on a plain, under the light of the moon, is a proof that Mickiewicz did not embellish his lines; it is not poetical—it is an observation, or, which in art is

1. Men of some sort are running over the meadows and behind each of them a branch of shadow shows black; and they are running swiftly—they must be on steeds; and they glitter brilliantly—they must be clad in mail.

the same, a discovery. *Grażyna* presents influences of the Homeric style and influences of Torquato Tasso (known to the poet in Piotr Kochanowski's seventeenth century translation).

I am not attempting to write a commentary on the works of Mickiewicz, so I refrain from mentioning some of his poems that are perhaps the most interesting from the point of view of technique. But I must emphasize the fact that his striving for precision never weakened. *Pan Tadeusz* was the return of a prodigal son to Homer and Vergil, but the prodigal returned rich in experience. "Mickiewicz," writes Professor George R. Noyes in the Introduction to the American edition of the poems of Mickiewicz, "was a man of many sides. From lyrical outbursts of passionate patriotism, from mordant satire on the enemies of his country, from mystical interpretations of history and visions of the future, his mind turned back to the scenes of his childhood." And further: "Had *The Forefathers,* Part III, and *Pan Tadeusz* been printed anonymously it would be hard to believe that they were the work of the same poet, written within the space of two years." The secret of continuity may be found in the poet's latent yearning for order, and "order" was considered the first literary principle by his literary educators. Neither his nostalgia for the land of his childhood nor his enjoyment of Walter Scott's affectionate descriptions of the scenery and the men and women of Scotland—a country that in many respects reminded him of his own Lithuania—nor his delight in Goethe's classic treatment of the commonplace in *Hermann und Dorothea* would have given him the idea had it not been latent in him for years. His idea of that type of writing showed itself occasionally in many fragments of his earlier poems. Now came the time of realization, and he wrote the best literary work ever written in Polish.

That is a paradox: Poland has never had a great novel which could be compared with Stendhal's *The Charterhouse of Parma,* Tolstoy's *War and Peace,* or Fielding's *Tom Jones.* To be quite honest, Poland has produced very few good novels at all, but her masterpiece is a poem having, in addition, all the features of a good novel. I say "in addition" as if such a quality could be deducted from a poem. Since it cannot be done, we have to define *Pan Tadeusz* as an epic poem with characters who survive no less than do Sancho Panza or Gargantua.

*Pan Tadeusz* is virtually unknown to non-Slavic nations—and no wonder, for translated into prose it loses its balance. Once the atmosphere given by the meter is destroyed, the actors move either too quickly or too slowly—the effect is that of an opera recited without music. The joy which a Polish reader derives from the poem is similar to that which one has from watching a perfect theatrical performance. What matters is not that reality has been more or less successfully imitated or parodied, but the mere movement of actors who pretended to be somebody else; or, to be more exact, it is the joy of watching a ballet: the apparent freedom of dancers is limited by the regular pace of Mickiewicz's verse.

Another paradox is that Poland's most popular poem is humorous, realistic, and merry, despite the fact that it was written in one of the several black moments of Poland's history, after the unsuccessful uprising of 1831. Such moments are not especially propitious for calm and objective literature, which we are inclined to associate with a golden age or with periods of buoyant growth. Mickiewicz wrote *Pan Tadeusz* in a spirit of contradiction, at more or less the same time that he wrote *The Books of the Polish Nation and of the Polish Pilgrims,* a prophetic, passionate prose tract by a political *émigré.* He did it, I suppose, because he always had before his eyes the dream of a golden age—that of antiquity, or the Polish golden age of the sixteenth century. In *Pan Tadeusz* he is one of the few really "civilized" poets. Let us hope that the adjective has not yet lost its meaning.

Mickiewicz was so rich a personality that commentators on each literary period emphasize a different side of his nature and his interests. He is either a devout Roman Catholic, or a mystic, or a revolutionary—and each time with good reason. The interest which Polish poets of the nineteen-forties take in his craft is perhaps narrow, when compared with the interest of those who enter into polemics about the causes for which Mickiewicz crusaded. Through his craft, however, we discover that he was first of all a good European, faithful to the heritage of humanism. Every aspect of his activity serves as a confirmation of that truth.

I should mention here that a book which might have been a fundamental study of Mickiewicz's indebtedness to the European tradition remains unfinished. During the Second World War one of the ablest critics of the younger Polish generation, Ludwik Fryde, was at work on a volume to be entitled *The Classicism of Mickiewicz*. In 1942 he laid aside his task, since the Nazis decided that he had to die, for a reason quite unconnected with humanism, simply because he was a Jew.

Fryde placed the poetry of Mickiewicz between the two general modes of writing verse typical for the history of Polish poetry, as well as for the history of European poetry in general: midway between the logical-rhetorical structure of the Renaissance, of the Baroque, and of the Enlightenment on one hand, and the emotional-expressive structure which was initiated by romanticism on the other. If both of them, combined, are exemplified in Mickiewicz, the first one is strong enough to show that its possibilities have not been exhausted by poets.

Since we observe today in the poetry of many nations the emergence of a new sort of logical-rhetorical structure, let us hope that future studies of Mickiewicz will contribute to a better understanding of the periods of transition.

# *PAN TADEUSZ*

by Józef Wittlin

I

To the world at large Polish literature is known as an unknown literature. True, a few outstanding works of the nineteenth and twentieth centuries appeared and were read in translation. One can hardly say, however, that they achieved any degree of popular success. The only exception, perhaps, was *Quo Vadis?*, and—who knows?—maybe it was that very novel which deterred foreign readers from pursuing further the works of Polish authors. "The world" preferred to be carried away by the writings of other contemporaries of Sienkiewicz: Zola, Tolstoy, Ibsen, Hamsun, Kipling, Maeterlinck.

What is the reason for such coldness toward Polish literature, particularly on the part of the so-called "Western World"? Various explanations were advanced. Some put the blame on the long years of the country's political subjection, others on the economic destitution of the nation, on its wretched geographical position, or even on hostile propaganda. That the devotees of Russian, Swedish, Norwegian, and Danish literature should shun the literature of Poland some tried to attribute to the exotic character of the latter's subject matter, the quaintness of its folklore, its national mysticism intelligible only to the initiated. Even in the best of Polish books they detected a stamp of purely local sentiment and fancy which makes it difficult for the foreign reader to submit freely to the charm of any work. And so there developed among Poles deeply concerned about the prestige of their national culture a sort of complex based on bitter resentment against "the world." "They accuse us of mysticism," they say, aggrieved, "and so they ignore us. Yet, look how they wallow in the mystical depths of Russian or Spanish writers. They are thrown off by our folklore, our magic, our superstitions and rites, but see how readily they go all overboard for the far weirder antics of really exotic people." And so those whose national pride has been hurt are apt to fall into one of two extremes: they either accuse their native literature of being trivial, purely local in character, and therefore unworthy of wider renown, or else they consider it so great and lofty that none but the well-trained natives can scale its cloud-topped peaks. But a dispassionate observer will soon discern the true crux of the matter in the fact that those soaring peaks of Polish literature rise out of its poetry, not its prose. And even the best translations of poetry often lack what in the psychological jargon of Ehrenfels is called "Gestaltqualität." Or, to put it in less abstract terms: translated poetry is like denicotinized tobacco.

Yet translatable or untranslatable poetry will be born. In the case of Poland not only did the Muses decree that our language produce a rich lyrical poetry as far back as the sixteenth century, in the days of the Renaissance, but, Slavic Muses that they were, they made the nineteenth century Romantics (who, incidentally, were rather closely related to Lord Byron) write even historical novels in verse. Herein lies the secret of the unpopularity of Polish writings abroad. Polish literature has produced no *Don Quixote,* or *Wuthering Heights,* nothing comparable to *The Human Comedy, Madame Bovary* or *Brothers Karamazov.* Instead, however, Poles do possess *Grażyna, Konrad Wallenrod, Forefathers' Eve,* and, of course, *Pan Tadeusz,* to mention the works of Mickiewicz alone.

And why go further? Mickiewicz is enough. For had no one else ever written a word of poetry in Polish, there still would have been enough to nourish amply the aesthetic sensibilities of the Poles. True, when Mickiewicz was alive his compatriots—as frequently happens in exile—often made life miserable for him. Nevertheless, even then he was acclaimed as the greatest Polish poet. He made his mark from the start, from his poetic debut.

To a people overwhelmed by captivity and misfortune he became an authority even in matters which actually have little in common with poetry. He became a "bard," a spiritual leader, like the Celtic bards or Hebrew prophets. Even though, born in Lithuania, he knew Poland proper hardly at all (he spent only a few weeks in the district of Posen), even though he never set foot in Warsaw or

Cracow and spent most of his rather short life abroad, he has expressed almost to perfection Poland's nature and man, and all that the Polish heart holds dear. From Paris, where he lived, his personality radiated upon all who read in Polish and felt like Poles. And today to the educated Pole excerpts from Mickiewicz's works are like verses from the Holy Scripture. Or, to make a less lofty comparison, Polish sensibility is so saturated with his poetry that its lines have become like arias of famous and even a trifle hackneyed operas: in joy or sorrow they rise unbidden to our lips. The figure of Mickiewicz as it appears on countless monuments has passed into eternal glory and the halo which surrounds it is so great that all attempts to bring the poet closer to us, by revealing his human traits, even his weaknesses, have been decried by the general public as nothing short of sacrilege. Aside from their admiration and respect Mickiewicz has also won the love of posterity. Long after his death (and still within my own not so remote memories) it was customary in drinking circles among the so-called "intelligentsia" to sing a song-toast ending with the words:

> To the health of Mickiewicz let us drink
> He brings us moments so sweet.
> All cares dissolve in that nectar divine,
> The singing of his lute.

I have never heard of revelers in the United States toasting in similar fashion Edgar Allan Poe. Yet, Poe was not only a great poet but, alas, a great alcoholic as well.

Of all of Mickiewicz's writings none in Poland is better known nor more beloved than *Pan Tadeusz; or, The Last Foray in Lithuania, a Story of Life among Polish Gentlefolk in the Years 1811 and 1812, in Twelve Books in Verse.* To the Poles this is truly a Holy Book, even though its contents are rather secular. It is so sacred, indeed, that many of its devotees refuse to notice its often satirical tinge. For the poet, though not without an indulgent and forgiving smile, has dealt here with some of the national faults, and in particular with the defects of the class which in his days constituted the sole and colorful façade of the nation—the landed gentry. Actually, *Pan Tadeusz* is not so much a Polish Bible as a sort of Koran full of earthly charms and of promise of delights in the life to come. It is a nostalgic work, and that is how it was born—under the painful pressure of nostalgia. It was written by an exile for other exiles, in Paris, between 1832 and 1834, and so under the still fresh impact of the disaster which befell Poland in the so-called "November Insurrection," the Uprising of 1830 and 1831. The nostalgic character of the work explains many of its peculiarities. The numerous and magnificent descriptions not only of banquets but also of culinary preparations of Lithuanian dishes might lead us to suspect that the author had not always had enough to eat. Or that he wanted thus to brighten the lot of his hungry fellow exiles. Anyhow, the entire book is so profusely larded with every ingredient of earthly bliss that at times it gives the impression of being the glorious hallucination of a soul driven out of Paradise. Professor Manfred Kridl in his beautiful essay on Mickiewicz in the book *Great Men and Women of Poland* [1] has justly called *Pan Tadeusz* "an epic idyll." For it provides an instance, rare if not unique in all of the world's literature, of an idyll combined with an epic fairly brimming with violence and bloodshed. Mickiewicz himself admitted that at first he intended to write something light in the vein of Goethe's *Hermann und Dorothea.* But, as happens so often, the subject led the author, and not the other way around. Mickiewicz fell under the spell of a world of which the background only was idyllic. And so, perhaps against the author's will, was born a monumental epic poem which has no equal in nineteenth century literature. As a matter of fact the nineteenth century had abandoned this form of versified narrative; and only a few of its attempts, such as the works of Frederic Mistral and of Karl Spitteler, may be termed successful. On the whole, and that is true of Goethe's poems, too, there wafts from these long-winded versified yarns a breath of solemn boredom.

Anything else can be said about *Pan Tadeusz,* but never that it is a bore. There is a charm and a harmony about it that hold the reader spellbound throughout all of its twelve admirably balanced and skillfully contrived books. Humor—and a truly Olympian humor it is—steps in whenever the scene threatens to become too glum, while

1. New York, Macmillan, 1941, p. 201.

lyrical invocations and incomparable descriptions of nature temper the bitterness of satire. *Pan Tadeusz* has been likened to the epics of Homer. This, to my mind, is not a fortunate comparison. The Polish epic not only lacks a mythical background but its whole subject matter is modern, and, as we shall see a little later, is not unlike the subject matter of a well-constructed novel. Homer's descriptions of nature tend to be conventional and recur again and again like a liturgical refrain. In *Pan Tadeusz* each of the many sunsets and sunrises has its own hue, almost a countenance of its own. The great epics of Homer ended more or less sadly: the *Iliad* with the burial of Hector; the *Odyssey* with the massacre of suitors, both innocent and guilty. There is no optimism in Homer—only man's fatalistic submission to the gods and to the will of that Moyra who guides the gods in their course. *Pan Tadeusz* ends not only with the Christian penance of a great sinner but, likewise, with a love match between the descendants of two feuding families. And more: it ends on a mighty chord of patriotic hope, the hope felt by all of Polish nobility in Lithuania, of liberation from the Tsarist yoke. Delirious joy fills the last pages of the book all aglitter with Napoleonic standards and eagles which, side by side with Polish standards and Polish eagles, are setting out on their way to Moscow.

For the benefit of foreign readers unfamiliar with *Pan Tadeusz* let us also point out the importance of the role which crime plays in this idyll. One might almost venture to define it as a sort of "Crime and Punishment" set against the background of a delightful Arcadia. An Arcadia over which ramble innumerable good-natured eccentrics, movingly anachronistic Don Quixotes who live no less on the memories of past glories than on the delicious specialties of Lithuanian cooking. This Arcadia, to be sure, also swarms with hotheads ever prone to bloodshed. But the crime and punishment here transcend the limits of a purely private affair. Mickiewicz managed to weave with admirable skill the tempestuous passions of his protagonist, Jacek Soplica, the future Father Robak, into the broad loom of authentic history. For the locale of the story lies right in the path of Napoleon's armies marching on Moscow, and the action takes place from the fall of 1811 to the spring of 1812. And in the personal tragedy of Jacek Soplica, conceived somewhat in the manner of Walter Scott, the fate of the individual is closely linked to the fate of the nation—it becomes purified through heroic deeds and acquires patriotic overtones. Jacek Soplica's crime, though it smacks of national treason, is presented without any morbidity. On the contrary, Mickiewicz treats it with a serenity so complete that one might be tempted to call it "Latin" if such a race-conscious definition had any sense whatsoever. So let no foreign reader who wishes to get acquainted with this epic imagine that he is about to enter a world in any way similar to the dark and fathomless worlds of Dostoievski. If we insist on looking for some analogies with Russian literature we might perhaps say that the Russian Captain Rykov who appears in *Pan Tadeusz,* and who, incidentally, is friendly to the Poles, might be a distant kin of the characters of Gogol, and that the Count, at times, reminds one of Gogol's hero, Khlestakov.

It is difficult to give a true idea of *Pan Tadeusz* to people not brought up in the Polish tradition, of which the cult of Mickiewicz is so much a part. It is like trying to explain the contents and meaning of the Holy Mass to someone who had never heard of the New Testament. To what extent *Pan Tadeusz* became, in time, an object of veneration among the Poles is perhaps best illustrated by the following incident. Not long ago the Polish schools staged a mock jury trial. By means of popular vote the students were to decide the innocence or guilt of the hero of one of Sienkiewicz's best-known short stories: "The Lighthouse Keeper." This lighthouse keeper, on duty somewhere on the Panama coast, is an ex-soldier, an old Polish immigrant. He lives in his lighthouse, completely isolated from the rest of the world, and for years faithfully attends to his duties. Then, one day, the mail brings him from New York a package of books, among them—*Pan Tadeusz.* And that is his undoing. Immersed in his reading, he is assailed by hallucinations and forgets to light the beacon. This, as might be expected, brings on a shipwreck. Only the fact that no lives are lost saves him from prosecution. The story ends with the arrival of a port officer who is to take the old Pole to the consulate where his future fate is to be decided. Guilty or not guilty? The young Poles brought up on *Pan Tadeusz* turned in the verdict of "not guilty." To them, the reading of *Pan Tadeusz* justified the lighthouse keeper's lapse.

I decided to look at *Pan Tadeusz* with fresh eyes, to break away from the magic circle in which, like every Pole, I've lived since my childhood days. So I reread it in English, in the brilliant translation, in prose of Professor G. R. Noyes.[2]

The translator, though an American, also fell under the spell of the poem and has fully grasped what it means to the Poles. In the introduction to his translation he says:

> Perhaps no poem of any European nation is so truly national and in the best sense of the word popular. Almost every Pole who has read anything more than the newspaper is familiar with the contents of *Pan Tadeusz.* No play of Shakespeare, no long poem of Milton or Wordsworth or Tennyson is so well known or so well beloved by the English people as is *Pan Tadeusz* by the Poles. To find a work equally well known one might turn to Defoe's prosaic tale of adventure *Robinson Crusoe;* to find a work so beloved would be hardly possible.

But to an American who, unlike Professor Noyes, is unfamiliar with the Polish lore, *Pan Tadeusz* might easily appear as not unlike a highly poetic and romantic "Western story." It is full of violence, high-handed justice and anarchy that is quite incomprehensible to a law-abiding mind. Even Mickiewicz was aware of this since he deemed it necessary to supply a commentary even for the sake of his Polish readers. He gave it in an introductory note in which he writes:

> In the time of the Polish Commonwealth the carrying out of judicial decree was very difficult, in a country where the executive authorities had almost no police at their disposal, and where powerful citizens maintained household regiments, some of them—for example the Princes Radziwiłł—even armies of several thousand. So the plaintiff who had obtained a verdict in his favour had to apply for its execution to the knightly order, that is to the gentry, with whom rested also the executive power. Armed kinsmen, friends, and neighbours set out, verdict in hand, in company with the apparitor, and gained possession, often not without bloodshed, of the goods adjudged to the plaintiff which the apparitor legally made over

2. Adam Mickiewicz, *Pan Tadeusz,* tr. George Rapall Noyes, New York, E. P. Dutton, 1930, Everyman's Library.

or gave into his possession. Such an armed execution of a verdict was called a "zajazd" (foray).

The story takes place in Soplicowo, the country estate of Judge Soplica. Soplicowo lies in a charming nook of Lithuania. Lithuania had, since 1386, been joined with Poland by union, but had passed, after the third partition of Poland, under the rule of the Russian Tsar. Still—Poland was not far away. Right beyond the river Niemen lay the very small but independent Duchy of Warsaw, created by Napoleon. It was there that in the years preceding Napoleon's war on Russia the patriotically minded Lithuanians flocked to join Polish colors and serve under Polish generals. As we said before, Soplicowo lay on the trail which was to lead Napoleon to Moscow, and so on the trail of great hopes. While waiting for their political liberation, the inhabitants of the Soplicowo manor led a very pleasant life though under the shadow of crime. The crime, an old one, for it dates back to the days of Thaddeus Kościuszko, was committed by the brother of Soplicowo's present owner, one Jacek Soplica. We meet him in the poem, shortly before his death in the fall of 1811, under the assumed name of Father Robak (Robak means "worm") and in the garb of a Bernardine monk.

It is an ungrateful task to retell in one's own words the contents of a masterpiece. Still, if we must, we must. So, to begin it, back in the days of his youth Father Robak happened to fall in love with the daughter of his neighbor, the proud aristocrat, Pantler Horeszko. The Pantler showered him with marks of confidence and friendship, and entertained him often in his magnificent castle. But give him his daughter in marriage he would not. Incensed at the rebuff, for he knew that the beautiful Eva returned his love, her suitor shot the magnate. And he did so, as it happened, right after an unsuccessful attack of Russian troops against the Pantler's castle. For all this was taking place in the days of Kościuszko, shortly after the Constitution of May 3, 1791, had been proclaimed. The fairly numerous opponents of this Constitution had sought the support of Russian bayonets. Pantler Horeszko was an ardent partisan of the Constitution; he was forced, therefore, more than once to repel, arms in hand, Russian attacks upon his castle. Owing to an unfortunate coincidence, Jacek Soplica, his pride severely wounded, had set out to settle his personal accounts with the Pantler at the precise moment when defeated Russian troops were retreating from the Horeszko castle. The triumphant Pantler steps out on the terrace to watch the Russian flight. Just then Jacek shoots and kills him. Though it was pure chance that he should appear in the vicinity of the castle at that particular time, he is branded as traitor. No one believes his protestations that his act of vengeance was carried out on his own responsibility, and not in connivance with the Russians. He, the gallant young noble once so popular among men, the handsome Lithuanian Don Juan whom all women worshiped, must henceforth hide to escape general contempt. Out of despair he begins to drink and marries a woman for whom he does not care. His unloved wife soon dies, leaving him a son, and the wretched Jacek goes into exile. In hard, soldierly life he seeks to redeem his past. He fights for freedom wherever he has a chance. Time and again he has to pay the price of his heroism; imprisoned by the Austrians he even spends some time in the notorious fort of Spielberg. At last, battle-worn and sick of wandering, he takes the frock of a Bernardine monk, and out of humility assumes the name of Father Robak, implying that he is as lowly as a worm. As for his son, the child born of his loveless marriage, he is none other than the hero of the poem —Pan Tadeusz. Of course, the young man is never to learn the true identity of the sullen and mysterious mendicant monk who seems always to hover close by Soplicowo.

Meantime, Eva Horeszko, following her father's wishes rather than the inclination of her heart, had married a wealthy aristocrat, only to die in exile when both she and her husband are deported to Siberia. Fortunately, however, her daughter Zosia, has remained in Lithuania. As might be expected, it is the penitent Jacek who takes the orphan under his wing, entrusting her upbringing to his brother, Judge Soplica, master of Soplicowo. And it is in Soplicowo that (in the first book of the poem) Pan Tadeusz and young Zosia meet. What follows is easy to guess: after many innocent intrigues the two young people fall in love and decide to marry.

The main plot of the story, however, is not this happy love affair; it is, instead, centered in the wretched feud between the Horeszko and the Soplica clans. In the foray from which the poem takes its subtitle, this feud reaches its climax. Several hundred Horeszko partisans raid Soplicowo. And again, as ill-luck would have it, Russians become involved in the private squabble of two Polish families. While the victorious Horeszko party, after freely imbibing from the Judge's well-stocked wine cellar, lies deep in slumber, there appears on the scene a whole battalion of the Tsar's infantry, a battalion of "dei ex machina," as it were. It is introduced so that the two embattled Polish factions may become reconciled and join forces against the common enemy of their country! Let us not forget that all this happens only a few months before Napoleon's armies are to march into the country, and takes place in an atmosphere already filled with thunder. This atmosphere is largely due to the work of the chief agent of the Polish "underground" in Lithuania, that mysterious monk, Father Robak. It has been his task to prepare the uprising in Lithuania in advance of the entry of Polish troops into that country.

The bloody incident with the Russian battalion ends as befits an idyllic epic. The Russian Captain Rykow whom we had occasion to mention before, and who is friendly to the Poles, offers them some sound advice. As a result, the commanding officer of the battalion, Major Plut, vanishes without a trace. The Poles, however, and particularly the younger ones among them, must immediately flee across the Niemen. They return a few months later dressed in resplendent uniforms, a part of Napoleon's army. Among them, it goes without saying, is young Tadeusz Soplica. The poem ends at just the right moment: with Polish troops under Generals Dąbrowski and Kniaziewicz making a stop at Soplicowo.

We must admire Mickiewicz's restraint in stopping where he did. He spared us the sight of Napoleon's defeated army fleeing from the ruins of burnt Moscow. Nor do we ever learn what became of the young officer, Tadeusz Soplica. Did he perish somewhere in the snows? Did he fall at Wiazma, Krasnoye, or Beresina? Or did he come back safe and sound to his beloved Zosia, to pursue by her side the life of a country squire? From what we know of his character and temperament we can only be sure that he was among those gallant Polish cavalrymen whom Napoleon's aid, Count de Ségur, mentions with such admiration in his famous book, *La Campagne de Russie*. Mickiewicz breaks off his narrative at a time of general rejoicing, a moment—so rarely experienced by Poles—when all hearts unite in elation and hope. Let us not forget that he wrote the poem in Paris, in the years 1832–1834, amidst the atmosphere of dejection prevalent then among Polish exiles. How differently do those years of the Moscow campaign appear when viewed through the eyes of Tolstoy in *War and Peace!*

The romance of Tadeusz and Zosia woven into the bloody history of Eastern Europe may be considered as a sort of *Romeo and Juliet* with a happy ending. But the comparison is fruitless. No drawing of analogy, no summary, no matter how detailed, can render the true content of *Pan Tadeusz*. For this content is the very substance of life, as well as the very substance of poetry.

To be sure, to the casual reader, life as depicted in *Pan Tadeusz* may seem somewhat extraordinary. Take, for instance, the daily routine of the Soplicowo manor: breakfast, hunting, mushroom-picking, lunch, flirting, and, from time to time, murder. A sort of never-ending party, a continual social season interrupted now and then by a more or less bloody brawl. Anything serves as an excuse for a round of banquets, sports, and hunting—even the court session which is to settle the long-standing litigation over the ownership of the ruins of the Pantler's castle, which stands on grounds that belong to the Soplicas. The chamberlain who arrives in state to preside over the court brings with him not a retinue of clerks, but his wife, and the daughters for whom, incidentally, he hopes to find good matches. The count who represents the opposite side, and who is the legal claimant of the castle, continually and without the slightest compunction takes part in all the banquets and hunting parties given by his greatest enemy, Judge Soplica. Nor does this prevent him, when the moment arrives, from yielding to the persuasions of the inexorable warden of the castle, and using force against his genial host. Peculiar, indeed, is this Lithuanian "Western."

Peculiar, too, the whole company of likable, titled idlers! Who, actually, works in Soplicowo that so many people may continually play? As far as that goes, in none of the romantic fictions of the age do the heroes lower themselves by toil. Nor, for that matter, did heroes of earlier periods. We do not know what was the source of Tristram's income, or what Lohengrin lived on, or how Don Juan earned the money required for his exuberant mode of life. Someone, somewhere, must have worked for them. And so, someone worked for the heroes of *Pan Tadeusz*. Invisible in the poem, they lived in Soplicowo, tilling the Judge's fields. They were the Lithuanian peasants, having no part in history as yet because they lived in serfdom.

The social status of peasant serfs does not have to be explained to Americans, familiar with the background of their own Civil War. The skin of Soplicowo serfs, however, was the same color as that of the Soplicas and of the Horeszkos. In the hour of general rejoicing, when Polish troops enter Soplicowo, and the engagement of Romeo-Tadeusz to Juliet-Zosia is being celebrated, Tadeusz, in a transport of joy and happiness, liberates his peasants and distributes land among them. Not without reason does the last book of the poem bear the title "Let us love one another," strange as it sounds to our modern ears. As we see, Mickiewicz, the future editor of *La Tribune des Peuples,* did not altogether omit introducing social touches in a spirit which in his days was quite revolutionary.

2

As is the case with all objects of general worship, one can at times grow tired even of *Pan Tadeusz*. The most beautiful prayer will grow trite through daily repetition so that in the end its original deep meaning is lost to the ear. What ruined *Pan Tadeusz* for us was school. When I say "school" I mean the old schools of former Galicia.[3] For six months in every Fourth Form, school robbed the poem of all its charm, squeezed it dry of every bit of aroma. Any masterpiece read under compulsion can in retrospect become a nightmare. What subtle sadism, to poison young souls by means of poetry! There

3. The part of Poland under Austrian rule.

ought to be a law, protecting the masterpiece of literature; they should be preserved untouched in a sort of National Park of Poetry. My resentment toward school is not based solely on the memories of an ex-student. I also was a teacher, and it so happened that for three consecutive years I had to "work" on *Pan Tadeusz* with my class. That was quite long ago. Nevertheless, I afterwards avoided the poem, as one avoids the witness of a rather shabby deal. It was not until 1929 that, quite unexpectedly, I took it out of moth balls. As it happened, and the fact is not without significance to me, I did so in Paris where *Pan Tadeusz* first saw the light of day. Dazzled by its beauty, intoxicated by its fragrant greenness I felt as though I had found a buried treasure. Forgive me these personal digressions but without them my conscience with regard to *Pan Tadeusz* would not be clear. Strange as it may seem, it was Proust who led me, the prodigal son, back home to the Lithuanian epic. While reading *Du côté de chez Swann* I found myself transported through some secret channel of sensibility right in the midst of Soplicowo. There can be no question, of course, of any similarity of subject, and still less of technique. Yet there is something about these two so dissimilar works which somehow makes them kindred. It is as though the two poets wrote them—one in verse, the other, in prose—under identical pressures and suffering from identical venoms of the soul.

What, to the modern reader, is most striking in *Pan Tadeusz* is that spiritualized realism which makes all of Mickiewicz's poetry recognizable at a glance. This dominant trait of his art appears as markedly in the Third Part of *Forefathers' Eve*. Here, too, we find an acuteness of observation that many a nineteenth century novelist might have envied the Polish poet. I believe that no one in Poland before Mickiewicz was able to transfer the reader so easily and painlessly into unfamiliar surroundings or draw him so completely into fictitious events and make him take part in someone else's life. I also believe that in all of Polish literature Mickiewicz alone knew how to stir, and by use of the simplest means, the whole sensibility of his reader. These means are not confined to metaphors and associations of ideas alone. *Pan Tadeusz* assails us through all our senses at once so that we not only see it, but hear, feel, taste, and almost touch everything it describes. We feel now warm, now cold; we smell the fragrance wafted from the woods and orchards; we are swallowed up by the primeval silence of the forests. We lose ourselves completely in its world of images and sounds. The reading of this fairly long book takes no effort on the part of either mind or imagination. It is an adventure. Nor does it disturb the serenity of the soul. We come out of the adventure without any sense of guilt.

The contemporaries of Mickiewicz reacted to *Pan Tadeusz* somewhat differently. They did not understand poetic realism; the passion for depicting everyday life in its most minute details was quite beyond their grasp. They were shocked by the language in which the very real people of the poem talk of very ordinary matters. And, amazingly, the poet himself shared the opinion of his Paris colleagues. That *they* felt as they did was hardly surprising. To them Mickiewicz was an inspired prophet and a spiritual leader: they could not grasp this sudden leap from *The Books of the Polish Nation and of the Polish Pilgrims* to a versified novel about ordinary people and human frailties. *The Books,* world famous in those days, had been published in 1832, and were thus the last of Mickiewicz's writings to appear before *Pan Tadeusz.* Written in a solemn, biblical style they had set their author somewhat apart from the world of simple mortals. Translated into many foreign languages they had lifted Mickiewicz in the eyes of his fellow exiles to the rank of a Polish Moses. With the appearance of *The Books* there almost sprouted upon the brow of the author the golden horns with which God had once adorned the brow of Israel's lawgiver. And here—after Mount Sinai, after the flaming Bush—an ordinary country place, Soplicowo, with its cattle, its fowl, and its people engrossed in their prosaic pursuits! No wonder that even the author himself made light of the work which was to make him immortal, just as the father of modern fiction, Giovanni Boccaccio, thought little of *The Decameron,* setting far less store by these "light" tales than by the didactic works which he wrote in Latin.

Let me quote here part of an apocryphal but quite probable conversation which clearly brings out this point. Mickiewicz, having just finished *Pan Tadeusz,* was reading it to a group of his Paris friends. One of them, Bohdan Zaleski, a gifted lyrical poet whom Mickiewicz once called "the Ukrainian nightingale," remarked that some of the sayings of the poem's characters, and particularly the squabbles of the petty nobility, lowered the tone of a serious epic. To which Mickiewicz replied: "My dear man, I know exactly what you mean. Not only in the places you point out, but all through the poem the tone ought to be raised by half a note. This cannot be done offhand. I will do better, God willing, in another *novel* [italics are mine]—in 'The Son of Pan Tadeusz,' and, most likely, in the subsequent parts of *Forefathers' Eve*."

*Pan Tadeusz* was a sudden burst of lucidity amidst an atmosphere loaded with mysticism. Its realism and its serene—one is almost tempted to say Apolline—optimism were bound to confuse not only the bard's followers in Paris but also his whole Polish public, somewhat used by then to his Byronism. A prophet is expected to live at all times in a state of wide-eyed ecstasy, in constant contact with the supernatural. Now a prophet, who, up to that time, had conformed in a fairly orthodox fashion to the tenets of Romanticism, peopling his poems with spirits and ghosts, had suddenly turned into a lucid narrator and had written a novel about people who were real and very much alive. A novel, despite the fact that he bound the chapters together with the strong bonds of verse—a thirteen-syllable meter that shimmers with all the hues of the rainbow. Herein, in the disparity between subject and form, lay the opening for criticism, which even the author himself apparently accepted, since he agreed with Zaleski's objections. Versification implied loftiness. And of loftiness, in the eyes of the Romantics, *Pan Tadeusz* had not enough.

It is difficult to understand today the obstinacy with which all Polish Romanticists, except young Zygmunt Krasiński, shunned unversified fiction. Perhaps this, too, was a matter of orthodox Byronism. In verse, and only in verse, they wrote numerous novels; dramas, too, though they could not even hope to see the latter produced on stage. They were writing them for a stage *in partibus infidelium*. As for the novels, perhaps they were deterred from the use of prose by its demand for verisimilitude. Prose does make this demand: even the tales of E. T. A. Hoffmann and E. A. Poe, so remote from reality in the ordinary sense of the word, use a technique akin to realism. These narratives are, for the most part, free of grandiloquence; no matter how weird the situations, the prevalent atmosphere is still that of everyday life; the most irrational happenings are subject to the laws of reality. Not so in versified novels. Here rhythm and rhyme put the reader, just as music does, in an exalted mood regardless of the contents of the story. Had Mickiewicz written his historical novel in prose, probably no one would have accused him of lowering its tone, nor would he have felt constrained to apologize for it and to promise to do better in the future.

The fact that he wrote *Pan Tadeusz* in verse cannot be ascribed to the trend of the era or to Mickiewicz's subservience to fashion. He wrote it in verse, rather, in spite of the prevalent fashion. At that time, all over Europe, and particularly in France, novels were being written in prose. Indeed, to judge this epoch by what has survived of it to our days, this was the golden age of the French novel. Let us not forget that in that very year, 1834, Balzac's *Père Goriot* was published. And *Le Rouge et le noir* by Stendhal had appeared in 1830. It does not seem likely that Mickiewicz, who was living in Paris and very much part of its literary atmosphere, should have been unacquainted with these two novels. The decision to write *Pan Tadeusz* in verse must have been, therefore, influenced by old habits and by Mickiewicz's awareness of his mastery in this medium.

Prior to Mickiewicz, Polish letters included a number of fairly good novels. On the whole, however, the genre was considered as light entertainment, unless it happened to be didactic. None of these novels in prose, purporting to "depict life," contained that fullness of life which characterizes *Pan Tadeusz*. None gave such a true picture of an epoch and its customs. Even if here and there we find among the earlier writings, works of fiction or memoirs which mirror faithfully the surface, the outer layer of life, they still lack that most important truth, which transcends mere reporting—the truth of poetry. Without it no novel survives its own times. The visions of reality of the early Polish novelists were either so pale and blurred or else so quaint and personal that today they no longer have the power to draw the reader within their own magic circles. Poetry was precisely what they lacked.

The poetic vision of *Pan Tadeusz* is based on honest and unbiased observation of a real world, a world firmly planted in space and time. This is the hardest sort of poetic vision, and the most binding as far as means of expressing it are concerned. The somnambulistic visionary, dreamer of nebulous visions, is far more free as an author. He escapes all control, nobody can hold him responsible for the world he depicts. Visions such as Shelley's or those of the Polish poet Słowacki altogether defy comparison with objective truth. But Tolstoy's vision of Russia in *War and Peace* and Mickiewicz's vision of the Lithuanian countryside in the same years of 1811–1812, are pictures of a real time and of definite places; no matter how much fictional element they contain, they can be checked against our own ideas of reality. And, as it turns out, they suffer nothing from such comparison. The people of Soplicowo are so real to us that we do not care where Mickiewicz took them from. What does it matter whether they were all products of his imagination, or whether they had been copied from living models by his memory? Either way, these people belong to real life and their creator belongs among the great visionaries of reality.

The illusion of realism in *Pan Tadeusz* is so powerful, even today, that a modern Polish critic accused Mickiewicz of glorifying in his epic the worst traits of the nobility. In my opinion the critic was mistaken: an epic poet does not glorify anything. His job is to reproduce as clearly as he can the vision he sees. That is why a true epic genius is essentially amoral. The epic poet treats good and evil with equal sympathy. That is what Homer did, and he, too, might be accused of glorifying crime in both the *Iliad* and the *Odyssey*. As a matter of fact, on another occasion I tried myself to prove that Ulysses was a highly immoral character and that his author did not set him up as a model for anyone. Mickiewicz in *Pan Tadeusz* is an epic poet, though a less inexorable one than Homer was. And a less unbiased one. Here and there a satirical or lyrical tone betrays where the sympathies or antipathies of the author lie. It is hard to tell who was closer to Homer's heart: Hector or Achilles. He compels one's compassion for human sufferings no matter whether they occur on the right or the left bank of the Scamander river.

Mickiewicz neither condemns nor absolves Soplicowo. One thing is certain, however: he is homesick for it. If he glorifies anything, he glorifies life itself—the very existence of man, of mushrooms, of frogs. Under the circumstances, the heroes of the poem must differ somewhat from the typically romantic characters of Byron and Walter Scott. They differ, too, from the protagonists of Mickiewicz's previous poems where the "tone" was "half-a-note higher." Father Robak, alone, might possibly pass as one of the heroes in the earlier Mickiewicz's style. He is also, morally, the most interesting character of the story, and probably closest to the author himself. There is no denying that the shifts from *Konrad Wallenrod,* and from Konrad and Gustaw of the *Forefathers' Eve,* to the flirting golden youth, to young and old maids, to the Assessor and the Notary—a shift, that is, from supermen to very ordinary people—came about with the swiftness of lightning. Mickiewicz's earlier heroes might well have served as models for simple mortals. This model-like quality of Grażyna, and of Gustaw-Konrad, let alone Konrad Wallenrod, finds expression in their artificial manners, in their theatrical gestures and speech. If the characters of *Pan Tadeusz* were equally grandiloquent they could never have endured the normal life of Soplicowo and would have been doomed to die under some unusual circumstances. Or they would have turned into slightly grotesque figures like the Count, in whose person the author wanted to ridicule certain aspects of early Romanticism. The most solemn figure of the poem is that of Father Robak. His is the pathos of death. But even so, one is bound to admit that his deathbed confession does not quite fit the harmonious framework of the epic. Its style is too reminiscent of the emphatic monologues of the earlier Mickiewicz's heroes. The latter were, by and large, extraordinary men endowed with superhuman qualities of character and mind. Imagine describing at length a meal of that noble madman, Gustaw, of the Fourth Part of the *Forefathers' Eve!* Or enumerating the dishes with which Konrad, of the Third Part, might have restored his strength after wrestling with God and Satan in the

"Great" and "Small" Improvisations! The very idea is both absurd and shocking.

No, it would be highly improper to juxtapose such completely different works even though they were written by the same author. The beauty of *Pan Tadeusz* is a beauty per se and affects different areas of our sensibilities than does the beauty of the *Forefathers' Eve.* It is not meant to transform the reader's soul. The *Forefathers' Eve* clearly attempts to do just that. The author of this work was a moralist. He showed men who, like Prometheus, have challenged Heaven and pursue their fight in their own Slav fashion. Wars against Heaven in world literature have also their strategy and tactics, which are clamoring for a Clausewitz of their own.

The author of *Pan Tadeusz,* with incredible grace, turned angels into simple mortals. Romantic maidens and Byronic mistresses never possessed, in Poland, either body or sex. They had only souls. Summer or winter, in fair weather or foul, they trod the earth dressed in the same airy, lily-white raiments. Barefoot, of course. In *Pan Tadeusz* we have, at long last, real blood-and-flesh women. They dress in accordance with the season and with the fashion of the day. Indeed, they are very stylish. (Obviously Mickiewicz had an eye for feminine fashions.) To achieve their elaborate coiffures they resort to the use of curlers. They have definitely shaped bodies, and some of them, Telimena for instance, a definite weakness for sin. These ladies love and seduce, not ghosts, but normal, handsome, full-blooded young men. Were it not for *Pan Tadeusz,* anyone knowing Poland and Lithuania only from the previous works of Mickiewicz might have easily imagined that these lands were inhabited solely by Marylas, Aldonas, and Emilia Platers.[4] *Pan Tadeusz* is the book of the nation's life, just as its predecessors were books of the nation's death. Of death that was heroic.

One might think that there are no ghosts in *Pan Tadeusz*—gone are the spectres and apparitions from another world. Yet, it is not so. For has not all of Soplicowo, all that former Poland of "gentle-

4. Maryla, the love of young Mickiewicz, idealized in his poems; Aldona, a character in *Konrad Wallenrod;* Emilia Plater, a heroic leader in the Polish insurrection of 1830–1831.

folk," become to Mickiewicz, the Paris exile, an apparition from another world? A spectre of a world irrevocably gone? It is in this that I see a distant kinship between the aura of *Pan Tadeusz* and the aura of Proust's work. The emotional basis from which both writings spring is the irrevocable "bygone-ness" of their respective, completely different worlds. This "bygone-ness" throws into relief the past and with unearthly radiance traces its contours. *Pan Tadeusz,* too, was written "a la recherche du temps perdu." And not only "du temps" but also "de l'espace," since it was written by an exile. This, likewise, explains the meticulosity with which every vanished scent, every savor, every picture and sound, every form and name is evoked from the shadow of death. Mickiewicz finds intoxication in even the sound of bygone Lithuanian names. He is like the last Apparitor who every night before he falls asleep rereads aloud the Court Calendar:

> To common men the Calendar seems a mere list of names, but to the Apparitor it was a succession of magnificent pictures. So he read and mused: Oginski and Wizgird, the Dominicans and Rymsza, Rymsza and Wysogird, Radziwiłł and Wereszczaka, Giedroyć and Rodułtowski, Obuchowicz and the Jewish Commune, Juraha and Piotrowski, Malewski and Mickiewicz, and finally Count Horeszko and Soplica; and as he read, he called forth from these names the memory of mighty cases. . . .

It was not only the memory of mighty cases that Mickiewicz called forth from the past, but also the memory of matters that were small, idyllic or absurd, ominous or indifferent, every sort of matter of which life consists. It is this power of evocation which puts him in the ranks of the great epic poets of the world.

## 3

Before closing let us sigh nostalgically for the days when a literary work was, for its readers, not only a source of so-called aesthetic emotions or of moral shocks, but also a well of information. It satisfied curiosity, stimulated reflection, and entertained, while presenting in beautiful form the characters of people and the course of events. It made no difference if the people described really existed or if they were figments of the author's imagination, since there is sometimes more real truth in an artist's fancy than in accounts of "real life." In those bygone days it was also epic poetry, prose fiction, and personal accounts which spread gossip concerning prominent figures of the day, revealed what went on behind the scenes in royal courts and let the readers into the secrets of the world's great. Memoirs, chronicles, even simple letters turned into works of art, if their authors had the ambition to make them so. And ambitions, on the whole, aimed high. Even authors who gave no thought to the immediate or even posthumous publication of their writings clothed them in such form that later they became testimonials to the taste and style of their epoch.

There can be no doubt that today we are witnessing an impoverishment of literature. And that, in spite of desperate efforts from all quarters to renovate or to remodel almost every branch of poetry and prose. The reason is simply this: the growth of journalism, of photography, of cinema and radio, and, lately, of television, has forced the writers to abandon the surface of life and to seek its inner depth. It has compelled them to depict in words only those matters which cannot be presented in any other way. Except that, lately, we have been witnesses to a great confusion of the various fields of writing: combining journalism, for instance, with fiction.

The letters of the Marquise de Sévigné to her daughter, the Countess de Grignon, written with admirable perseverance over a period of more than twenty years, concerned, actually, only the addressee. Yet, today they are not only a classic of French prose; they also provide a vivid panorama of the era of Louis XIV. In these letters Madame de Sévigné told her daughter, who lived in the then distant Provence, all the news which Madame de Grignon would not otherwise have quickly learned; not even from the first newspaper which was just then being launched in France. In those days letters meant infinitely more than they do today. Today the art of letter writing is on the wane—not because people no longer know how to write but, more probably, because they have come to the conclusion that it would be hopeless to compete with newspapers and newsreels.

Do you want to know what goes on in London? Tune in the radio. Do you want to see what the ruins of Warsaw look like? Or how the reconstruction of that capital destroyed by the Germans is progressing? Don't ask for long letters from those parts; just glance through a photograph album or go to the movies and see the newsreels. Of course, if you insist, your private correspondent can always send you from some faraway place a picture postcard, or he can enclose in a short letter snapshots taken by himself. He can even send his own picture, taken against the background of the ruins.

Although the last war has spawned innumerable fat volumes of memoirs of its perpetrators, leaders and participants—some of them written by ghost writers especially engaged for that purpose—memoir writing as a separate form of literary art (which flourished once, particularly in the eighteenth century) now, actually, no longer exists. It would be useless to search among the best sellers of this branch of prose for new talents equal to Saint-Simon, Madame de Staal (not to be confused with Madame de Staël), Madame d'Epinay, or Madame du Deffand.

And yet, were it not for the many volumes of the memoirs of the Duc de Saint-Simon which in themselves are a work of art, the great cycle of Proust novels might perhaps never have been written. In both works, gossip has been, so to say, monumentalized, though by very different means. Where Saint-Simon describes a bare fact, providing it merely with a commentary, Proust, like a patient miner, burrows into the fact's most deeply hidden meaning. Formerly, events such as wars, conflagrations, plagues, and earthquakes reached the consciousness of the distant public only through the medium of individually colored, often distorted, accounts of writers. There were none of the syndicated visions of life and death which the press and the picture agencies and the radio networks are turning out in mass production today. Newsreels had not yet imposed upon the world their own brand of authentic or synthetic fragments of battles and catastrophies. The epic poet, the memoir and letter writer left much to the guesswork and imagination of the reader. He drew him into collaboration with his own creative fancy. The terrible earthquake which in 1775 turned practically all of Lisbon into a heap of rubble took its place in history and became memorable mainly through Voltaire and his *Candide.*

So, *Pan Tadeusz* for its time. All its charm as poetry apart, it can be considered simply as a well of information about the world and the times, unglimpsed by any camera eye, in which the poet's childhood had been spent. We will find in it quite a few gossipy tales about the authentic neighbors of the imaginary Horeszkos and Soplicas. It even contains several references to the Mickiewicz family.

We believe that the world of those days really looked just as the poet presented it. Indeed, the world always looks as poets, not reporters, present it. We believe that it is as it was seen by El Greco, Rembrandt and Cézanne, and not as it is seen by photographers.

*Translated by* RULKA LANGER

# A FEW WORDS ON *PAN TADEUSZ*

by GEORGE R. NOYES

IT WAS JUST a half century ago, in the autumn of 1898, when I was studying at the University of St. Petersburg, that I first made the acquaintance of *Pan Tadeusz*. Sitting in the classroom of Jan Łoś, later a scholar of rare distinction and, I am proud to say, a good friend of my own, I made my way through its opening pages. I read the poem also in company with three or four young Poles who were attending the University. One among them, Roman Morgulec, appealed to me by his glowingly upright personality, fine as that of Łoś himself. Thus memories of two loyal Poles are blended with my memories of a loyal poem. I promptly realized that that poem was a work worthy of affection and homage, that I had made no mistake in trying to learn Polish at the expense of time that would have made my Russian less imperfect. What charmed me first in *Pan Tadeusz* was the author's childlike point of view, mingled with his own consciousness that his point of view was childlike.

Let each man recall his memories of his mother as he knew her in the days of his childhood. Was she not the fairest of women? Was not all about her tingled with her own loveliness? Was not the lace that she wore on Sundays the rarest and most delicate of fabrics? Yes, even the china bowl that stood on her breakfast table was more shapely than a Grecian urn. Even the milk that she gave him with his porridge was a trifle whiter than that served in other houses. Each of us cherishes these childish self-deceptions, smiles at them, yet is proud of them; but he never speaks of them. For with our feeble powers of speech, if you or I should tell of these memories we would be ludicrous.

Yet some masters of expression have told of their wholesouled delight in the world that surrounded them as children. Here for example are words from Thomas Traherne, an English mystic of the seventeenth century:

> Certainly Adam in Paradise had not more sweet and curious apprehensions of the world, than I when I was a child. All appeared new, and strange at first, inexpressibly rare and delightful and beautiful. I was a little stranger, which at my entrance into the world was saluted and surrounded with innumerable joys. . . . The dust and stones of the street were as precious as gold: the gates were at first the end of the world. The green trees when I saw them first through one of the gates transported and ravished me, their sweetness and unusual beauty made my heart to leap, and almost mad with ecstasy, they were such strange and wonderful things. The Men! O what venerable and reverend creatures did the aged seem! Immortal Cherubims! And young men glittering and sparkling Angels, and maids strange seraphic pieces of life and beauty! Boys and girls tumbling in the street, and playing, were moving jewels. I knew not that they were born or should die; but all things abided eternally as they were in their proper places.

Even so, but with greater variety and with greater skill, Mickiewicz tells of the quiet manor of Soplicowo and the fields and forests about it. Zosia's garden, in which she plays with the village children, is more magnificent than a royal park. When she feeds the chickens she is as graceful as the Goddess of Love. The Judge's belt is more gorgeous than any ever woven in India. No frogs sing so sweetly as those of Poland. The forests of Lithuania are more mysteriously wonderful than those of tropical America.

Such is the charm that first captivates us in *Pan Tadeusz*. Yet three hundred pages of unalloyed childlike appreciation of beauty in the commonplace, even though clothed in the perfect verse of Mickiewicz and set forth with his complete mastery of expression, would become mawkish and tiresome. Hence that appreciation is only one of many sources of delight that Mickiewicz blends harmoniously in *Pan Tadeusz*. First of all he unites it with a sane and kindly humor, "the smile of Mickiewicz," a trait totally lacking, for instance, in the passage that I have quoted from Traherne. He praises the forests of Lithuania seriously, but he is aware that the Polish frogs and chickens are after all no better than those of other lands and that only the memories of his childhood endow them with any peculiar charm. The result is that the atmosphere of Mickiewicz seems childlike (as for similar reasons does that of Chaucer), but it never becomes childish.

This radiant humor pervades the whole poem. The actors in the epic of Mickiewicz are, with one exception, decidedly commonplace

POEZYE

ADAMA MICKIEWICZA.

TOM PIERWSZY.

WILNO.

DRUKIEM JÓZEFA ZAWADZKIEGO.

1822

TITLE PAGE OF MICKIEWICZ'S FIRST VOLUME OF POEMS

persons. The poet is amused by their weaknesses and their whimsicalities; but, again with one exception, he always views with kindness and affection the men and women whom he has created. Tadeusz is a gallant lad, but he is comically limited in his intellectual outlook. His uncle, Judge Soplica, is an upright soul who loves his country, but he has even more serious limitations of intellect and of character.

The sly, somewhat cowardly apparitor Protazy is made genuinely lovable by his loyalty to the Soplica family. Even the corrupt, ludicrous, Russified fashionable lady Telimena is a likable person; she has "a kind heart."

Yet childlike appreciation of beauty, combined with radiant, kindly humor, would not make *Pan Tadeusz* truly great were they not blended with stalwart courage and mature faith. *Pan Tadeusz* is childlike in its atmosphere and it is humorous, but it is far from being a comic poem. Mickiewicz describes a time that is dead and that can never be revived in quite the same form. But the spirit that animated that time, the spirit of old Poland—that is not dead nor can it ever die. From memories of his childhood Mickiewicz passes into courageous aspirations for a glorious future, to be gained by faith and consecration. He loves his country not only as a child but as an earnest, thoughtful man.

The one character in *Pan Tadeusz* whom Mickiewicz never finds in the least degree humorous is Jacek Soplica, the roistering village champion who has become an unselfish servant of his country, and who appears in the poem as Father Robak, "the worm," the man of vigorous energy who has been transformed from the incarnation of pride into the incarnation of humility. He is the embodiment of unselfish service to his native land and of cooperation with other men. Jacek is human; he has faults and he makes mistakes, but his ideals are those of loyalty and of service, and he is faithful to them. The scene at his deathbed has a high seriousness unmatched elsewhere in all Polish literature.

In *Pan Tadeusz* Mickiewicz expresses his patriotism through love for Poland, not through hatred for other lands. For small men it is easier, above all in times of strife, to hate the enemies of their country than to render unselfish service to that country. During the recent war too many people in the United States were busy cursing the Germans rather than in upholding the ideals that the Nazi government was trying to crush. So in 1832 Mickiewicz had written the third part of his *Forefathers' Eve* (*Dziady*), a poem inspired by the failure of the revolt of the Poles against the Russians; a poem which, one regrets to say, voices his hatred of Russia even more than his love for Poland. It is a work of genius, but not of the highest genius. Yet before the close of that same year he began to compose *Pan Tadeusz*. In that poem he is calm and serene. He can find good even in the Russians. Captain Ryków, the only Russian who plays a part in the epic, is an upright, kindly soldier, who respects the Poles and likes them, and the Poles regard him with similar feelings. Major Płut—the name means *rascal*—the basest figure in the poem, the only actor in it whom Mickiewicz regards with no gleam of kindliness, is a renegade Pole. A gardener's little girl does not envy her landlord's daughter for her gorgeous raiment; she is occupied by the interests of her own home, knowing few anxieties beyond it, and no hatreds. Her brother, when he fights for his country against its oppressors, hates his foes not as human beings, but as instruments of tyranny, as representatives of a wrong ideal. So in *Pan Tadeusz* Mickiewicz gives glowing expression to his love of Poland, almost unmixed with hatred for the Muscovites. This is true patriotism, patriotism inspired by love of one's neighbor and leading to love of all mankind. Mickiewicz has returned to childlike sympathy and childlike love for all men. "Whosoever shall not receive the kingdom of God as a little child shall in no wise enter therein." Mickiewicz has become as a little child; and, entering into the kingdom of God, the kingdom of love, beauty, and poetry, he has led into it, with him, all his readers, both Poles and Americans.

# MICKIEWICZ AS JOURNALIST

## SUMMARY AND EXCERPTS

Mickiewicz was engaged in journalism in two periods of his life, the first in 1833–1834 when he edited the periodical *The Polish Pilgrim* in Paris. Mickiewicz published in this paper a number of articles in which he discussed general and timely problems, Polish as well as European. They are characterized by emphasis on nationality, national traditions, and religious spirit, but at the same time by democratic and revolutionary convictions and an aversion to rationalist "program discussions," while, on the other hand, propagating concrete activity, *action* based on faith and intuition.

Sixteen years later Mickiewicz again devoted himself to journalism in entirely different circumstances. In 1849 he founded and edited in Paris the daily *La Tribune des Peuples,* a paper proclaiming republican, revolutionary, and socialist ideas. The paper's revolutionary character was manifested both by its ideology and by its selection of contributors, who came from among the French socialists as well as from among political exiles, fighters for democracy in various countries of Europe. The French contributors were: Jules Lechevalier, the well-known popularizer of Fourrier's ideas in France and editor of the Fourrierist paper *Revue du progrès social,* and who also published articles in Proudhon's daily *Le Peuple;* Charles Martin, editor of the socialist weekly *La Constitution républicaine du présent et de l'avenir;* Hippolite Castille, a popular novelist and journalist; Ange Pechméja, grandson of a well-known eighteenth century writer, Jean Pechméja, author of the famous socialist utopia *Télèphe* (1784); Eugène Carpentier, Alphonse Hermant, and Jean Julvécourt. The only woman on the editorial staff was Pauline Rolland, who was in charge of questions relating to the emancipation of women.

Except for the French, the Poles had the greatest number of representatives: Edmund Chojecki, a successful novelist known in France under the pseudonym of Charles Edmond; Franciszek Grzymała, former officer in Napoleon's army, later conspirator against Tsardom, one of the organizers of the Polish rising of 1830–1831; Ksawery

Bronikowski, leader of a revolutionary club in Warsaw and deputy mayor of the Polish capital during the rising of 1830–1831; Ksawery Godebski, historical writer; Kazimierz Kunaszowski, who translated Mickiewicz's lectures on Slavic literatures into German; Leopold Lew Sawaszkiewicz, a historian.

There were three Russians: Ivan Voinov, Sazonov, and Ivan Golovin, all followers of the program of the man who later espoused anarchism—Michael Bakunin.

There were two Italians: J. Ricciardi and J. Frappoli, both followers of Mazzini.

Spain also had two representatives on the *Tribune des Peuples.* They were Ramon de la Sagra, an outstanding leader of the revolutionary movement in Spain and a follower of Proudhon, and Francisco Bilbao, who, subsequently expelled from France, emigrated to Chile, carrying letters of recommendation from Mickiewicz to Ignacy Domeyko, a Pole who played a leading role in the life of contemporary Chile.

The Belgian Jean Collins was a particularly interesting figure. This officer of Napoleon's army, aide-de-camp of General Exelmans in the battle of Waterloo, emigrated to America after Napoleon's imprisonment. In the United States he successfully conducted agricultural research, and he also worked in Cuba. He carried on experiments in aviation and underwater navigation with the intention of liberating Napoleon from St. Helena. In later life he returned to Europe and was active in the workers' movement. He was the originator of the theory of the necessity of socializing landed estates, and through his pupils influenced the program of the Socialist International.

German socialism was represented on the *Tribune* by Hermann Ewerbeck, a personal friend of Marx and Engels, whom he energetically aided in their struggle against the utopian socialism of Weitling.

Among occasional contributors were Croats and Rumanians.

Thus this was an international team which saw the guarantee of the brotherhood of peoples in socialism. However, their socialism was not based on uniform theoretical foundations and the views of the individual contributors differed considerably. Mickiewicz himself combined his socialism with the Napoleonic idea. Consequently, the *Tribune des Peuples* was a periodical characteristic of Europe in the middle of the nineteenth century, when there existed among European peoples strong democratic and revolutionary tendencies which found expression in various doctrines directed against the established order, and when the word *socialism* signified a general tendency rather than a program. The majority of the paper's contributors remained within the orbit of Proudhon's ideas (whom Mickiewicz himself regarded very critically). The most extremist was Ewerbeck, who passed from under Proudhon's influence into the orbit of Marx and Engels. At any rate it was people like those writing for the *Tribune* and its readers that Walt Whitman had in mind when he wrote in the poem "To a foil'd European revolutionaire":

> Courage yet! my brother or my sister!
> Keep on! Liberty is to be subserv'd, whatever occurs;
> That is nothing that is quell'd by one or two failures,
> or any number of failures,
> Or by the indifference or ingratitude of the people,
> or by any unfaithfulness,
> Or the show of the tushes of power, soldiers, cannon,
> penal statutes.
> Revolt! and still revolt! revolt!
> What we believe in waits latent forever through all the
> continents, and all the islands and archipelagos
> of the sea;
> What we believe in invites no one, promises nothing, sits
> in calmness and light, is positive and composed,
> knows no discouragement.
> Waiting patiently, waiting its time.

*La Tribune des Peuples* appeared as a morning daily from March to November, 1849, with an interruption from June to September when it was suspended by the police; it ceased publication as a consequence of police measures. Mickiewicz published in it articles discussing timely problems of the revolutionary movement in Europe.

His journalistic activity, in the same way as his activity as a political leader in 1848 in Italy and in 1855 in Turkey, was an important fragment of his life. Since, according to him, poetry is only one of the releases for inspiration, which may also be manifested in practical activity and everyday life, he did not restrict himself to cultivating his art. It is noteworthy that he did not mix different spheres of effort. He started his professorial, journalistic, and political activity after concluding his creative phase with *Pan Tadeusz,* that is, with a work characterized by the purity of its artistic line and complete detachment. The "cyclic" character of Mickiewicz's life, his undivided devotion to one aim in each phase, constitutes one of the most interesting features of his personality.

The excerpts from Mickiewicz's articles given below furnish some idea of his views. The first two, "On the Tendencies of the Peoples of Europe" and "Our Program," though dating from different periods, are linked by the same concept of the solidarity and brotherhood of peoples. The article on "Socialism" shows Mickiewicz's own conception of the problem. The fragment called "Rome and Official Catholicism," written on the occasion of the proclamation of the Roman Republic in 1848 and France's armed intervention, then under consideration, discloses Mickiewicz's stand as a "non-official Catholic" opposed to the policy of the Vatican and of Pius IX. The last article, "Workers Settlements," shows his attitude toward reactionaries and capitalists.

## *On the Tendencies of the Peoples of Europe* (1833)

It has justly been said that the spirit of the age and the mass of peoples possessed by that spirit pose a riddle to government and statesmen and like a Sphinx devour those who do not know its solution. How many persons have been devoured, how many heads threatened since the time of the French Revolution! The riddle on which so much depends seems always to become so much more involved and obscure that there must be some common error in the methods that have been used to solve it. If the striving of the masses of the people is called the spirit of the age, why do proud statesmen detach their thought from these masses, and, instead of observing the general trend, shut themselves up with their own reason? If the spirit of the age is the spirit of the future, why do they seek to clothe this future, like a growing youth, in old, worn-out children's dresses and wonder that such a dress tears and shreds? If, finally, the feeling of the whole people, the heart of the whole people, speaks through the spirit of the age, how can one measure this feeling by personal calculation? If scholars had a little more political humility and were willing to observe what goes on around them, if they collected and summed up the conversations of the people, its clamorings, its prayers, they would perhaps learn more than from books and newspapers. The sounds that issue from the mouth of the people are a great petition which the spirit of the age in all humility submits to the cabinets, the houses of parliament, and the schools, before it attacks them with stones and bayonets from the pavements. Before the eruption of the volcano it is enough to observe the water in the wells and the smoke in the crevices of the mountain to foresee the danger; woe to those who then sit down to read up on the theory of volcanoes!

What is today the first, foremost, most vivid desire of peoples? We do not hesitate to say that it is the desire of reaching an understanding, uniting, combining their interests; without this it would be impossible to comprehend the general will, just as without calling together the members of a stock corporation it is impossible to guess their desires. Let us draw attention to a few symptoms which clearly show this great tendency of the spirit of the age.

During the French Revolution the memory of the brotherhood of nations, disrupted by the governments, was revived. In the Napoleonic wars a dim presentiment of European unity was more and more distinctly manifested in the fact that the people's parties joined hands with the French. But after the fall of Napoleon a political epoch is discernible. Who does not remember how after the outbreak of war in Greece collections for the insurgents were made, how young men hastened from everywhere to join their ranks? The revolutions in

Naples and Spain were also looked upon with favor. Often important discussions of local parliaments were silenced upon the arrival of news from the Levant or from Madrid. From Gibraltar to Moscow one could find homes making merry or in mourning at the news of the triumphs or defeats of the knighthood of freedom. This feeling of sympathy was not deduced directly from any theory, it was not referred to in any constitution. On the contrary, the French sophists argued that a constitutional king had the right to overthrow the constitution in neighboring countries. The sophists did not rejoice or laugh because no article prescribed it. What does this prove? It proves that none of the constitutions of that time expressed the needs of the age.

When after the July Revolution riots broke out in various sections, the people everywhere first attacked customhouses, frontier offices, passport offices. This attack was not caused, as some think, by revenge for the extortions of the toll collectors, because the toll collectors annoy mostly merchants and travelers who do not do much in revolutions; it was the result of the premonition of a greater and more extensive reform. The people felt instinctively that these customs and frontiers were contrary to the current tendency. Indeed, can there be anything more disgraceful than the old prejudice that a line drawn by the finger of kings through one country, often through one town, is to divide the inhabitants, even relatives, into natives and foreigners, into natural enemies? Things have gone so far that every European going from one place to another not only loses all political and civil rights, but is beforehand, as it were, suspected of theft, and must provide himself with descriptions and certificates. This custom has stunned many otherwise honest people; many cannot comprehend how in America, even in England, one may do without such restrictions.

We shall content ourselves with enumerating those two symptoms, leaving it to the future to trace others. Perhaps they will explain why Napoleon has evoked and continues to evoke such great sympathy in France, and even in Italy and Germany. Napoleon broke and overthrew the old governments which, like hothouses, previously helped the growth of nations but now oppress and choke them.

Napoleon felt that the cause of freedom is a European cause and that all Europe should be involved in it. Perhaps Europe expects such men today, too.

## *Our Program* (1849)

The condition of Europe is such that it is impossible that in the future any nation will be able to proceed along the road of progress in isolation from others unless it wishes to expose itself to ruin and thus threaten injury to the general cause.

The enemies of the people in Europe continue to act in solidarity; they confirm this solidarity by action at every step. More conscious of their common danger than anyone else, they have united themselves as never before. Their tactics consist of using all their government forces against each nationality that separately seeks liberation, and thus suppressing one after another and one through the other. Their plans, formed long ago, become evident when carried into effect; they are based on accurate data, according to which all the selfish interests of governments as well as of the individuals that exercise influence on them were calculated and the degree of their ambition, which is the motive prompting them all, was estimated.

. . . We are founding a European people's organ—*The Tribune of Peoples*. Determined to proclaim and defend the rights of France, provided they are in accord with the interest of the people's cause in Europe, we summon all nations to come to that tribune, each with its free word.

A group of foreigners who in their homelands have won popularity by their words as well as by their efforts and sacrifices have lent us their fraternal collaboration. Through them we shall have exact and accurate information on what concerns their countries. As men of the February Revolution we are also in full agreement with the tendencies of the Great Revolution and the Napoleonic period, in so far as these have been realized, because Napoleon actually put the revolutionary principles into effect when as an armed missionary he experienced the republican phase of his life.

The moment the First Consul abandoned this principle in order to negotiate with the old world and put the crown on his head, a series of misfortunes began from which the people still suffer today. In spite of this, it is still the revolutionary Napoleon who in the eyes of the people is the representative of the Great Revolution because he defended its ideas most perseveringly and most effectively. On the other hand, those who came after him became traitors on the very day they assumed power.

We shall seek the frontiers of the Republic even beyond the confines of Napoleon's power; we shall regard as reactionaries all those who, adopting the republican principle, measure its external activity according to their selfish interests, or who, admiring the spirit of action and strength of the Napoleonic epoch, would nevertheless like to exclude from it the spirit of sacrifice and republican expansion.

France, as we conceive her, is that very spirit which became the people and was embodied in the republican form.

That means that we shall defend the present Constitution, that we shall cooperate as best we can to accelerate its evolution toward a republic with all its consequences.

This is as far as internal affairs are concerned. With regard to foreign countries we shall courageously deal with matters directly concerning us: Italy, Poland, Germany, Denmark, Spain, the Slavonic countries, Hungary, the Danubian provinces.

Both internally and externally we shall be guided by the principles of Christian policy—the solidarity of peoples. In relation to the parties which struggle for power in Europe, in France and in the National Convention we shall always support those men who, faithful to the progressive instinct of the masses, will work to build a social order concordant with the new needs of the people. Only on this condition shall we recognize them as the true political representation of the people's interest in the whole world, the only true interest of France.

## *Socialism* (1849)

*Socialism* is an entirely new word. Who created this word? No one knows. Most terrible are the words which no one has created but which everyone repeats. Fifty years ago the words *revolution* and *revolutionary* were also neologisms, barbarisms.

"Socialism" first appeared officially in the people's programs in the days of the February Revolution. No one knows the names of the authors of those programs. An unknown hand put the word socialism in them, to the great consternation of all satisfied Balthasars of France.

The old society and all its representatives, though they did not grasp the meaning of this word, read their death sentence in it. . . . The old society feels itself attacked from all sides. What it lacks is certainly not prosecutors and gendarmes. It has at its disposal a larger supply of brute force than the Roman Empire ever possessed or than the Russian Empire controls. What it lacks is moral foundation, conviction, idea.

True socialism has never encouraged material disorder, riots, and all that which goes with them. It has never been an enemy of authority. It only demonstrates that in the old society there no longer exists any principle on which legitimate authority could be based, that is, an authority in conformity with the present needs of mankind.

Socialism would welcome power, but power that is new.

The old foundations of power no longer exist.

Religious dogma, formerly recognized and accepted by the vast majority of the French people, dogma which had created their religious and political life, is no longer officially referred to by theorists without force or practitioners without conscience. . . .

No, the socialist system is not negation. You may say that the inner idea of socialism has not yet acquired sufficient brightness to penetrate the eyes of men holding power, of representatives of society hostile to socialism, but you have no right to accuse socialism of being merely negation.

Modern socialism is only the manifestation of a feeling as old as life itself, a manifestation of sensing that which in our life is incomplete, cut off, abnormal, and consequently unhappy. The socialist feeling is the spirit's aspiration towards a better existence, not individual but common and solidary. We admit that this feeling was manifested with completely new force; it is a new sense which spiritual man managed to develop, it is a new passion. . . .

Socialism being completely new has new desires and new passions which people of the old society cannot comprehend, just as a young man's desires cannot be comprehended by children or doting old men.

Desires and passions are never negative; desires and passions are confirmations of the soul, just as problems are confirmations of the mind. A dogma is the confirmation of the soul in the past; an axiom is the confirmation of the mind, also in the past. Problem and desire are confirmations of mind and soul which aspire to the future. In dogmas and axioms society sinks into the grave; it is reborn in desires and problems. . . .

Social feeling will not become passion, action, and truth until it bursts forth in the souls of truly religious and patriotic people.

Religious and patriotic sentiments are the foundation of socialism. . . .

We agree with socialism always whenever it appears as the development of religious and patriotic feeling. We leave to theologians and professional philosophers the discussion of theories.

The theory of socialism should not be proclaimed by its spokesman in the National Assembly. Theories are published daily in books and periodicals. All deputies know them or at least must be assumed to be familiar with them. From the official spokesman of socialism, projects, draft resolutions, bills are expected.

The National Assembly is a great authority; it can give orders to the treasurers of the Republic and to the marshals of France. When one addresses such an authority he should draw his conclusions and should present clearly to it the items of the budget and the military route of march.

The National Assembly debated big international questions. Under discussion were Italy, Hungary, the spiritual and temporal power of the Pope, the principle of the Slavic and Magyar nationalities, questions epitomizing the religious and social conflict between the representatives of the old official church and of the old dynasties and the religious and socialist people of the new world.

In the most decisive moment of this debate the socialist speaker, leaving aside the most delicate matters—the only ones with which the members of the National Assembly were concerned—diverged into the sphere of general theory. The practical men in the Assembly, the leaders of parties, the most skillful enemies of socialism, were indeed very glad of this. They left the socialist speaker complete freedom to attack the principles of the old society, satisfied that this old society had secured the right of determining the fate of Italy, Hungary, and Poland.

## *Rome and Official Catholicism* (1849)

The party which in France officially assumes the name *Catholic* does not cease to proclaim through its organs, in the Chamber, and in the press, a crusade against the capital of Catholicism: in the opinion of leading members of this party Rome cannot exist religiously without the Pope, while the Pope would lose his spiritual existence if he were deprived of his civil list, his gendarmes, and his Swiss regiments. The godlessness of the Romans has recently deprived him of all these means of exercising his spiritual power! Rome is becoming a threat to the Catholic Church.

In the very name of religion and of the Church, *Univers religieux* and all official Catholics of France call for European intervention in Italian affairs. But since when has Rome become a seat of godlessness? We still have fresh in our memory the hymns sung by *Univers* in praise of the Romans. It presented this people to us as a model of religious fervor and political wisdom. What grave sin have they committed since that time that they have suddenly lost the treasures of their former merits and the gifts of grace—in a word, everything, even their faith?

Awaiting an answer to this question, we, unofficial Catholics, believe that the only sin of our Roman brothers, one which most of all scandalized the Pope, the Sacred College, the holders of large benefices, *Univers religieux* and its followers, is republicanism. An unpardonable sin! The Romans would probably be forgiven neglect of religious duties; they would be permitted freely to violate church discipline; their indifference in matters of religion would be tolerated and sometimes even supported; they would be permitted to proclaim today *atheism* from the height of the Capitol, provided the word republic is not pronounced in the Quirinal, provided the capacity of monarch is respected in the Pope.

This would suffice to put at ease the cardinals, in their capacity of princes of the Church, concerning the fate of their endowments, and would save the estates and families of the big holders of Church benefices. In the language of official Catholicism these very things are called the *splendor of the Church*. The Romans are required to sacrifice everything that in modern life is most essential, to sacrifice their human and civic dignity so that the auto-da-fé of their rights and liberties might resurrect the past splendor of the Church.

According to the views of official Catholics in France the Romans should be slaves attached to the ecclesiastic soil of the Pope's private estates; therefore, let them work to feed his court, let them pay for his army and diplomatic service, let them carry all the costs of the maintenance and improvement of this Church which should be splendid! And as far as the official Catholics of France are concerned, their sacred and sole duty is to admire these splendors from afar.

These are the mysteries of official theology which we do not understand at all.

## *Workers' Settlements*

They are trying to build workers' settlements in Paris. These are establishments of an entirely new kind for France. We owe them to the February Revolution and to the ideas which it began to put into effect. In these establishments the worker is assured the opportunity of breathing fresh air, of having lodgings and fuel, that is, advantages of which the proletarian has so far been deprived. Since nothing can be done without capital, it is said that rich people have appeared who are forming a company for building these settlements for the workers. Thus it is the result of the cooperative spirit. Therefore one cannot sufficiently encourage the building of such settlements.

However, the suppliers of funds and architects, seemingly yielding to the socialist idea, nevertheless make a deal among themselves to utilize it in the interest of expediency. It is an old tactical device of exploiters to take over from an idea perfect in itself only that which is profitable to them. Therefore, the reactionaries hastened to take the workers' settlements under their patronage. They hope to take advantage of this social institution as an army against socialism. According to what the reactionaries say, it is they who should be regarded as the inventors of those settlements, while, on the contrary, socialism is alleged to be the inexorable foe of the worker's welfare.

We have a right to ask the official representatives of reaction MM. Thiers, Fould, both Dupins,[1] why at the time when they were at the helm of authority and when they loudly proclaimed themselves conquerors of the Republic and of the socialist principle, it did not occur to them to set aside for the building of workers' settlements

1. Adolphe Thiers, French historian and statesman (1797–1877); Achille Fould, French politician and financier (1800–1867); André Dupin, French lawyer and politician (1783–1865); the other Dupin was probably André's brother, Charles.

the tremendous sums of money which they used for the building of a chain of fortifications, prisons, and other establishments of the same kind, whose sole purpose was the welfare of the royal crown.

We address these remarks to the workers, the future inhabitants of these settlements. They should be convinced that it was the revolutionary and socialist spirit, the spirit of July and of February, which forced the capitalists to recognize the necessity of concerning themselves at last with the proletarian's welfare. The help offered by the capitalists to the working class should be considered a concession wrested from selfishness by humanitarian progress, and not the work of Christian charity.

Therefore, it is in the interest of the worker to nurture in himself and to spread abroad the spirit which created these settlements: the more powerful this spirit becomes, the more means will be found to insure welfare to those who are its representatives. If the workers let themselves be bribed by the self-seeking concessions of materialists who take them under their patronage, if, resting content with an insignificant improvement of their situation, they separated from the general cause of the proletariat, they would be like those oppositionists who, having become salaried officials or ministers, renounce the sentiments and convictions which gained them the positions from which they now show such haughtiness.

Thus the fate of the workers' settlements depends on the workers themselves. Let them remain, as citizens, as they were during the February days. Let them not forget that by taking up arms in behalf of sufferings and general misery, that by exclaiming "Long live France, long live Italy, long live Poland!" they, who had no place to rest their heads, won the right to live in those settlements. Only when they had shaken the powers of all Europe, did they force the rulers of France to concern themselves with their lot.

*Translated by* LUDWIK KRZYŻANOWSKI

# MICKIEWICZ AND THE JEWISH PROBLEM [1]

by ABRAHAM G. DUKER

MICKIEWICZ'S significant but little-known synthesis of the ideas of Polish-Jewish rapprochement and Jewish emancipation found its final expression in his project to establish a "Jewish Legion" during the Crimean War.[2] This military unit was projected as part of the Ottoman Cossack regiment commanded by Sadyk Pasha, formerly Michał Czaykowski, a Polish Ukrainian nobleman and revolutionary, who became a Turkish military leader. The project of establishing "the Hussars of Israel," the term employed by Mickiewicz, was one of the poet's chief tasks, if not the central one, during the last months of his life. He viewed this idea and its execution as an "act of Providence" and referred to it as the "Cause."

Agreement on major policies of political action during the Crimean War drew the poet politically to Prince Adam Czartoryski's con-

1. This article is based on research done in connection with the preparation of a doctoral dissertation at Columbia University under the direction of Professor Salo W. Baron on the subject of "The Polish Political Émigrés and the Jewish Problem, 1831–1836," in which the topic of the present paper is treated more exhaustively. The author extends his thanks to Professor Baron for his interest and for his valuable guidance. Dr. Jacob Shatzky he wishes to thank for his contribution to the planning of this article, his kind perusal of the manuscript and valuable suggestions.

2. We have drawn heavily on Roman Brandstaetter, "Legjon Żydowski, Adama Mickiewicza," *Miesięcznik Żydowski, Łódź,* No. 1, January, 1932, pp. 20–45 (hereafter referred to as Brandstaetter I); No. 2, February, 1932, pp. 112–132 (hereafter referred to as Brandstaetter II); and No. 3, March, pp. 143–248 (hereafter referred to as Brandstaetter III). Brandstaetter based his researches on the manuscript collections in the Mickiewicz Museum in Paris and in the Czartoryski Museum in Cracow as well as on printed sources, references to which will be found in his work; regrettably it suffers from poor arrangement and some inaccuracies of dates. It nevertheless supersedes the earlier Franciszek Rawita-Gawrónski, *Adam Mickiewicz na Wschodzie,* Lwów, 1899, and Jacob Shatzky, "Hagdud Haivrishel, Adam Mickiewicz," *Hatzefira,* Warsaw, May 20, 27, June 3, 1921 (Hebrew).

servative wing among the Polish émigrés.[3] Mickiewicz willingly accepted the task of mediating in the dispute between Czaykowski and General Count Władysław Zamoyski concerning the leadership of the Cossack regiments then being recruited under Polish auspices for service on the Turkish side. Despite this sober political mission and his practical grasp of the state of affairs, the poet was in a mystic mood, perhaps more so than usual, when he set out on his journey to the Balkans. He inquired about the means of travel to the Holy Land.[4] The party, consisting of Mickiewicz, Armand Levy, Prince Władysław Czartoryski, Adam's son, and the émigré Henryk Służalski, stopped over at Smyrna, which reminded the poet of a Lithuanian Jewish town. Together with a local Polish Jew as interpreter, the group visited the rabbi.[5]

On the Sabbath (September 5, 1855), Mickiewicz and Levy attended the services at the Smyrna synagogue. The poet was greatly impressed with the mood of the worshipers, just as he had been ten years earlier when he brought his Towianist circle to the Tisha Be'av[6] rites in the Paris synagogue at 14 Rue Neuve St. Laurent. Following the services in Smyrna Mickiewicz told Levy that "God will eventually hearken to the prayers of this nation, whose sons know how to pray with such religious fervor and strong faith."

3. For general background see Adam Lewak, *Dzieje Emigracji Polskiej w Turcji (1831–1878)*, Warsaw, 1935, p. 131. For more details see Brandstaetter I, pp. 20–23, neither utilized nor mentioned by Lewak.

4. Józef Bohdan Zaleski to Zdzisław Morawski, in J. Kallenbach, *Adam Mickiewicz,* Lwów, 1923, II, 491–492, addendum.

5. Franciszek Rawita-Gawroński, *Adam Mickiewicz na Wschodzie,* Lwów, 1855, p. 18. Armand Levy was a Catholic of part Jewish descent who died a Jew. He was a participant in revolutionary and pro-Polish movements, the poet's intimate disciple and friend, and after Mickiewicz's death, the guardian of his family.

6. The Ninth Day of the Hebrew month Ab is the anniversary of the destructions of the Temples in Jerusalem in 586 B.C. and A.D. 70. Instructions for the visit, as dictated by Mickiewicz, were published in [Władysław Mickiewicz], *Współudział Adama Mickiewicza w Sprawie A. Towiańskiego,* Paris, 1877, pp. 278–279, which also contains (pp. 279–280) Mickiewicz's enthusiastic report on the visit. For French translations see Attillo Begey, *Towianski et Israel. Actes et Documents,* Rome, 1912, pp. 90–92. For partial Hebrew translations see A. Z. Aescoly, *Tenuat Towianski Bein Hayehudim,* Jerusalem, 1933, pp. 47–50.

He also confided to Levy his thoughts about the future of the Jews in Poland: "I would not want the Jews to leave Poland because, just as the Union of Poland with Lithuania, differing by origin and religion, brought our Polish state to its greatness and happiness, so I am certain that the union of Poland and Israel will assure our spiritual and moral strength." [7]

Upon his arrival in the Cossack camp in Burgas, Mickiewicz was enthusiastic about its martial atmosphere. He was particularly moved by the sight of the Jewish soldiers, numbering about two hundred at that time. This, according to Levy, was the incident that brought about the poet's decision to organize a Jewish Legion.

"The cause was conceived in a pure, disinterested way and was beyond any human calculation," stated Levy, in his mystic vein, emphasizing that "there is something in this cause that has to do with Providence. Mickiewicz always repeated: 'Believe that this cause is a Providential one: many irrational circumstances, which meet and are joined in their striving towards one aim, beyond any mental speculation, are the proof thereof.' " [8]

It is more likely, however, that this visit constituted merely the final catalyst that brought about the poet's decision to embark upon the formation of the Jewish legion, probably a culmination of his earlier ideas. Military service for Jews was viewed during the period of the March of Jewish Emancipation both as an essential and desirable condition for emancipation and its logical fruit. The idea of recruiting Jews for the Ottoman army was a recurrent theme in the French Jewish press.[9] In fact, the *Univers Israélite* reported in March, 1854, that the Istanbul rabbi "formed a legion of Israelites which he presented at the disposition of the Sultan," and that "Israelite notables of most cities are furnishing the necessary funds." [10] It is inconceivable that Levy was not acquainted with these rumors,

7. Jacob Shatzky, *op. cit.*, based on Władysław Mickiewicz, Żywot *Adama Mickiewicza*, IV, 426–427.
8. Brandstaetter I, p. 200.
9. For instance the *Univers Israélite* characterized as a fruit of tolerance the news that "youths of good families had solicited the Turkish government in favor of admission to the regular army" (July, 1853, p. 517).
10. P. 336.

or that he did not discuss them with the poet. Moreover, it is most unlikely that Mickiewicz was not told, in connection with his mission, about the significant successes achieved by the Poles in recruiting Jewish volunteers in England, France, North Africa, and among the Russian war prisoners for the Cossack military units in process of organization.

The utilization on Poland's behalf of the Jewish soldiers in the Russian army had been a steady subject of discussion in Polish *émigré* circles. During the Crimean War the strategists of Prince Czartoryski's camp felt that the time for action had come. In reporting his visit to the Plymouth war prisoners' camp, K. Lach Szyrma, the prince's agent, called attention to the presence among the 811 inmates of 51 Jews and 151 Catholic Poles.[11] Names of Jews among the war prisoners were usually entered upon the rosters compiled by the prince's agents under special rubrics entitled *Żydzi* (Jews). The Jewish war prisoners received from the prince the same financial aid as the Poles. In England, volunteering began in the Mill Bay prison in Plymouth, following Lach Szyrma's visit. A declaration signed November 29, 1854, requested Prince Czartoryski to secure for the prisoners permission to serve under Poland's banner and recognized his authority. At the end, under the heading *Żydzi,* appeared circles and other symbols in lieu of signatures of 16 persons. They evidently had not been permitted to sign their names in Hebrew, as they usually did, since they did not possess the knowledge of Latin characters and refused to make the mark of a cross. A later list included 53 names of Jews among the 200 Polish war prisoners who were to enter the Polish Legions.[12]

Names of Jewish volunteers appear frequently on lists of all

11. Czartoryski Museum, Cracow MS (Czar. MS) 5680; Report of Nov. 16, 1854.

12. A more extensive treatment of this problem will be found in my forthcoming book. Information on recruiting is based on the following, hitherto unpublished sources: Czar. MSS 4681, 5315, 5316, 5631, 5641, 5662, 5681; Rapperswil collection at the Warsaw Military Library, MS 751, Vol. XIV, letter 2019; Zamoyski collection in the Zamoyski Castle at Kórnik, Boxes, 1, IIa, 2, 3; as well as the émigré press and other publications. Not all the documents on recruiting among the war prisoners are extant or were made available to this writer.

kinds, including "actual" residents of French communities, Algiers, "Afrique," England. A roster of 50 volunteers from the United States includes the names Jacub Mets, Wais, and Julian Friedman.[13] The volunteers' motives were varied. But even taking into consideration such factors as unemployment, or the character of the professional soldiers who evidently knew of no other career but soldiering, there is no lack of evidence of idealistic inducements. In this respect there can be no question of the motives of the old-time *émigrés* or even the recent Jewish arrivals from Poland, who were Polish patriots and hated Tsarist oppression. Polish patriotism and the desire to return to the homeland cannot, however, account for the volunteering to the Polish Cossack troops of Jews born in France, England, Prussia, and Hungary, or of a Sephardic (Jew of Spanish origin) so anxious to serve in a Polish unit. The few biographical entries in the lists give evidence of hatred of Tsarist Russia and devotion to Poland's cause. We read of men of 19 and 20, some married, residing in London, who left Poland in order to escape military service, and of a 54-year-old *émigré* signing up for the Legions. We find the name of a 20-year-old saddlemaker born in Bydgoszcz, province of Poznań, as well as entries of Jews born in Moravia, Germany, Portsmouth, and Courland. Later we see their names as members of military units in Turkey, decorated for valor in action, with not a few of them on the lists of the wounded and killed.

It is, therefore, hardly likely that the poet had not been told of these developments prior to his sailing to the Near East, and it is therefore possible, as some historians have maintained, that Mickiewicz had harbored the idea of organizing a Jewish legion before his voyage to the Near East.[14]

13. Cf. Abraham G. Duker, "Polish Political Émigrés in the United States and the Jews, 1833–1865," *Publications of the American Jewish Historical Society,* No. XXXIX, Part 2, December, 1949, p. 151.

14. In fact, Władysław Mickiewicz and Zygmunt Miłkowski (Jeż) maintained that Mickiewicz came to Istanbul with the purpose of organizing the Jewish Legion. This is denied by Brandstaetter (I, p. 43, note 8) where the references will be found. Jacob Shatzky, *op. cit.,* similarly upholds the theory of the earlier decision, while Wacława Knapowska states that "Mickiewicz brought three ideas with him in connection with his mission, the desire to make peace between Sadyk and Zamoyski, the idea of the Israelite legion and

Levy emphasized the mystic element of the sudden and simultaneous encounter of Mickiewicz, Czaykowski, and himself with the idea of the Jewish Legion. There is sufficient evidence to prove that Czaykowski was quite skeptical about the "Cause" during its initial stage and that his mystic encounter was a pose, probably aimed to please Mickiewicz. The poet considered himself together with Levy and Czaykowski as the "instruments for this Cause, who were previously prepared by Providence." [15] The "Cause" was intimately connected with Poland's rise, in a much sharper way than in the poet's views expressed during his Towianist period. Of even greater significance is the omission, in the Jewish Legion stage, of assimilation or baptism as conditions for the solution of the Jewish problem.

An examination of Mickiewicz's statements and the testimonies of his co-workers in the new cause of the Jewish Legion reveals that he was an early advocate of the idea of the national group emancipation of the Jews, expressed later in such works as Hess's *Rome and Jerusalem* or Leo Pinsker's *Autoemancipation*. The Zionist element cannot be detected in Mickiewicz's expressions concerning the Jewish Legion. Some of the Legion's opponents made much of possibilities involved for the reestablishment of a Jewish state in Palestine. However, Levy was an early Zionist. Silence on this subject is understandable in view of the Turkish position. While Mickiewicz's early Zionism can at best only be surmised unless new documents are discovered, his views on Jewish emancipation are more in keeping with the twentieth century ideas of Jewish survivalist nationalism than with the nineteenth century position of assimilationist emancipation. They reveal the revolutionary changes in the poet's approach to the Jewish problem and its twin problem, that of Poland's restoration and future order.

Involved in this approach are Mickiewicz's view on Jewish nationalism and emancipation; his confidence in the usefulness of the Jews in the process of attaining Poland's liberation; and his belief in

---

the candidacy of Prince Napoleon (for Poland's throne)," *Kandydaci do tronu polskiego w czasie Wojny Krymskiej,* Poznań, 1927, p. 56. She bases her contention on Stanisław Szpotański, *Adam Mickiewicz,* III, 104–108.

15. Letter of Armand Levy to Bednarczyk, Brandstaetter I, p. 23.

the place of the Jews as a permanent and vital factor in the life of liberated Poland. As in all the other political activities of Mickiewicz, here too is to be found a mixture of mysticism and pragmatic attitude. And as in his other activities, it is impossible to separate the two elements.

A brief summary of Mickiewicz's views concerning the Jews in Poland during his *émigré* career is in order. Faced with the dilemma of the parallel of the two nations in exile, the Poles and the Jews, following the 1831 Insurrection, he rejected it outright at first by drawing in the *Books of the Polish Pilgrims* a distinction between the Poles and Jews. The latter he placed in the same category with the gypsies, who say "there is the fatherland where it is well," and contrasted them with the Poles, who tell "the nations: there is the fatherland where it is ill." [16]

This notion is not only in line with the typical contemporary stereotypes among the nobility but also with some liberal and early socialist views on Jewish "materialism" which prevailed at that period. It is also reflected in Mickiewicz's poems about Jan Czyński and Tadeusz Krępowiecki, radicals of Frankist descent.[17] Soon enough, this view seems to have been abandoned in *Pan Tadeusz*. Jankiel, the Jewish innkeeper, though at times treated jocularly and patronizingly, is the right hand of the revolutionary emissary, and one of the strongest personalities, sufficiently so to merit the poet Norwid's ironical comment that "the beloved national poem *Pan Tadeusz* is

16. This problem is dealt with more extensively in my forthcoming book.

17. Jacob Frank (1726–1791), a false Messiah, became converted to Catholicism together with many of his followers in Poland. The Frankists survived as a sect for several generations.

The quatrain, *Wpół jest Żydem,* was written in reply to Czyński's criticism of Mickiewicz's views in *Księgi Pielgrzymstwa.* One of the quatrain's effects was to label the democrat Czyński as Mickiewicz's "maligner" and later even as spy, a most unjust accusation against a leading figure in Polish liberalism. Cf. Mateusz W. Mieses, *Polacy chrześcijanie pochodzenia żydowskiego,* Warsaw, Vol. 1, 1938, pp. 83–92. An extensive treatment of Czyński's role in the emigration will be found in my forthcoming book. *Do Franciszka Grzymały,* the longer poem about Krępowiecki, came as a result of this democratic leader's critique of the aristocracy's role in the revolution. Cf. Mieses, *op. cit.,* II, 23–32.

a national poem in which the only serious figure is a Jew."[18] Perhaps Mickiewicz intended nothing more at that stage than to portray the typical village life with its Jewish innkeeper. Nevertheless, the obvious contrast between the patriotic Jankiel, possibly a historically authentic figure, and the remarks about the Jewish and gypsy souls cannot be passed off as accidental.

In the Towianist period Mickiewicz accepted Towiański's teachings concerning the position of the "Israel nations" chosen for historical greatness: the Jews, the French, and the Slavs, especially the Poles. According to this scheme Israel, the Jew, was destined for greatness, following his choice of the Towianist path to Christianity. Whether or not the theory of the poet's partial Jewish descent is accepted,[19] his marriage to the Frankist Celina Szymanowska served to stimulate his interest in the question of Polish-Jewish coexistence. Towiański's view of the solution of the Jewish problem in Poland through baptism and participation in the Towianist "Cause" added to his concern with the Jews, as testified by his contemporaries.[20]

Mickiewicz took a keen interest in the Koło's (Circle's) missionary efforts among Jews, and the greatest success in this respect was at-

18. We cite from Henryk Szyper, *Adam Mickiewicz, poeta i człowiek czynu.* Warsaw, 1947, p. 170. For the prototype of Jankiel, the innkeeper Jankiel Cymbalista of Podłuże, see note about Euzebjusz Łopaciński's researches in Pinchas Kon, "Z doby Berka Joselewicza na Litwie," *Album Pamiątkowy ku czci Berka Joselewicza,* pod redakcją . . . . . Majera Bałabana, Warsaw, 1934, pp. 122–123, note 19.

19. We refrain from entering into this discussion at present. Juliusz Kleiner's lengthy analysis of the problem which has led him to characterize the poet's alleged Jewish origin as a "rumor" (*Adam Mickiewicz,* Lwów, 1934, Vol. I, footnote on page 9) fails to answer some problems raised by Mieses, *op. cit.,* II, 119–126. The substantiation of Mickiewicz's partial Frankist descent would make more pertinent the application of psychological approaches to the problem of Mickiewicz's attitude towards the Jews.

20. To cite but one instance, the letter by the poet Józef Bohdan Zaleski to Michalina Dziekońska. The entry under August 5, 1851, reads as follows: "Adam came for dinner. During the dinner and after he was talkative and pleasant. He told interesting things about the Frankists whom he had the opportunity to meet through his wife." *Korespondencja,* p. 183. Other entries dealing with the poet's conversation about Jews, on July 29, 30, and 31, are to be found there on p. 182.

tained when he was the Circle's head.[21] In fact, Mickiewicz viewed the conversions of Jews to Catholicism as proof of the arrival of the new epoch.[22] He also became keenly aware of the parallel in the exiles of the Jews and the Poles, rejecting completely by this time his earlier notions expressed in the *Books of the Polish Pilgrims.*[23] This new approach is manifested not only in the poet's correspondence concerning Towianist matters, but also in his *Slavic Literature,* particularly in his defense of the converted Jews against the accusations in Zygmunt Krasiński's *Undivine Comedy.*[24] The new point of view is, in places, contradictory. Consistency, however, is seen on the subjects of the settlement and residence of the Jews in Poland as an act of Providence and the close similarity and tie between the fate of the Jewish people and that of the Polish nation.[25] The parallel of the two nations in exile also appears strongly in the instructions for the participation in the Tisha B'Av services in 1845.

Although the poet had to a large extent broken away from Towiański in 1848, he still adhered to his conversionist view of the solution of the Jewish problem. This can be seen in the emphasis on Israel's eternal welfare in the poet's 15-point *Skład Zasad* (Exposition of Principles) issued in connection with the recruiting for his Polish Legion in Italy. Not content with the general assertions of "freedom of speech, citizenship, and civil equality to all, freedom

21. The literature on the subject of Towianism and the Jews deals mainly with the conversion of Gerson Ram. To the sources cited in note 6, above, must also be added the following: Karol Drezdner, "Brat Gerszon," *Pamiętnik Literacki,* XXV, No. 2 (1928), 280–286, and Stanisław Pigón, "Z późniejszych lat J. A. Rama," *ibid.,* pp. 286–292. Our archival researches reveal more cases of conversions of Jews to Catholicism by Towianists.
22. He wrote to Domeyko on October 22, 1842, that "Israel is already beginning to unite with us, expecting the epoch of his return to Christ." *Dzieła,* ed. Pini and Reiter, XI, 334.
23. Mickiewicz recommended the reading of Exodus to Chodźko on two occasions in 1842. To B. Zaleski he wrote, "This book, always beloved by me, should always be before your eyes. What countless mysteries! I hope that it will strengthen you too." Szpotański, *op. cit.,* II, 130.
24. Lectures on January 18 and February 21, 1843.
25. Cf. Lecture of July 1, 1842, April 3, 1844, and *passim.* The Tishah B'Av instructions compared the destruction of Jerusalem to the Praga Massacres and Warsaw's capture. Cf. note 6, above.

to all confessions of God, to every rite and congregation," the poet proclaimed in Principle 10: "To Israel, our elder brother, respect, brotherhood, aid on the way to his eternal and terrestrial welfare, equality of rights for all." [26]

This emphasis on Israel's eternal welfare can be safely interpreted as signifying the solution through baptism. Equality for Slavs and Jews is in line with Mickiewicz's concept of a Poland that was to include all the historical peoples living in her territories.

Towianists like Chodźko reported to Mickiewicz that the behavior of the Jews who joined the Italian Legion was proof that "the new epoch of friendship with Israel is reflected in them." [27] Some Jewish soldiers attended Christian services, which, it can be taken for granted, served to encourage Mickiewicz.[28] The Jewish soldiers distinguished themselves in battle. Some were killed and others were wounded. Perhaps the demonstration of this valor might also have served as a contributing factor in the attempt to organize the Jewish Legion in 1855.

It is possible, however, that Mickiewicz's contact with the emancipated Jews in Italy served to change his opinion about Jewish emancipation. The poet proclaimed in his *Slavic Literature* that "it was in vain that heretofore attempts were made to tie the cause of this people (the Jews) with the cause of Poland, promising it land, properties and a better material existence. . . . Could it sell its past replete with glory for a piece of land?" [29] But he wrote from Livorno in 1849 in his discussion of the revolutionary situation in Italy that "many Jews there are devoted to the cause of this movement and are capable of serving it. They ought to serve as an example to their co-religionists in all countries." [30]

26. This is the generally cited text. Władysław Mickiewicz interestingly omits the adjective "elder" (*Legjon Adama Mickiewicza,* p. 30).
27. Referring to Michał Eisenbaum and Izydor Brunner, Chodźko wrote in addition that they "verify by their behavior the words of the Master about Israel." Letter, Marseilles, August 17, 1848, in Szpotański, *op. cit.,* Vol. III, Appendixes, p. 173.
28. Letter of Kamiński to Mickiewicz from Strassbourg in Władysław Mickiewicz, *Legjon,* p. 153.
29. Lecture of July 1, 1842.
30. *Tribune des Peuples,* March 29, 1849, cited from *Dzieła,* IX, 123. Perhaps

As was pointed out earlier, evident at this Jewish Legion stage of Mickiewicz's interest in the Jewish people is the poet's belief in their future beyond the Towianist solution through baptism. Although the elements of mysticism are there, the "Cause" itself is but one link in a projected series of events leading to the restoration of Jewish morale, a basis for emancipation of the Jews as a group, the retention of their national characteristics, their participation in the liberation of Poland, and to the coexistence of Jews and Poles in a liberated Poland organized on the basis of its historical multinational order. The organization of the Jewish Legion formed in Mickiewicz's belief the first stage in the restoration of Jewish morale by applying the military-psychological element. The Jewish Legion would serve both to win emancipation for the Jews and to aid the Polish military forces in driving out the Russian enemy—a preparation for the new charter of the Jews in a restored Poland.

The factor of military prowess in the attainment of emancipation was emphasized throughout the protracted negotiations with Rothschild interests, the High Porte, and the leaders of Turkish Jewry. In a letter to Czaykowski sent with the approval of Mickiewicz, who was ill at the time, on negotiations with the Istanbul Jewish banker Cammondo, Levy described the approach as follows:

I presented to him [Cammondo] the situation of his co-religionists in the camp of the Ottoman Cossacks, your personal feelings of sympathy for the Jews, the unusual importance of this question in the present war and in what way the personal participation of the Jews in it could affect their fate, especially the fate of the Jews found in such large numbers in Poland, and the situation of the people who are enjoying sympathy in Poland and who must suffer so much in Russia, particularly in recent times. I have told him that the ancient prejudices are slowly giving way, and that it

---

Mickiewicz's rude interruption of Juljan Klaczko's harangue at a social gathering in favor of a House of Lords in Poland can be traced to that period. The poet interrupted Klaczko by inquiring "whether there exists a Jewish school in some Lithuanian small town. Klaczko answered that he did not know and withdrew, and Wrotnowski asked why father [Mickiewicz] posed that question. 'In order to let him know that he would do better in thinking about advancing the Jews, rather than to worry about the House of Lords in the future Poland.'" Władysław Mickiewicz, *Pamiętniki,* I, 76–77. Klaczko was a convert to Catholicism.

was necessary to take advantage of this situation and form a union, so useful in the same cause for the Poles and the Jews. I pointed to the benefits which would accrue to the Jews following their organization for the first time in separate battalions, which would be for them the core of resistance, and which would permit them to prove that they were just as brave as the others, fighting on the side of those who considered themselves the bravest; as a result the Jews would eventually be able to gain everywhere religious freedom, guaranteed by the respect which they would have earned for themselves.[31]

The same reasoning is to be found to some extent even in the note dictated by Mickiewicz to Levy for presentation to high Ottoman authorities. Here the emphasis was understandingly on the direct effects of a Jewish Legion on Turkish Jewry, namely its role in popularizing military service. As a remedy the note suggested the organization of a separate Jewish military unit. Initially this was to be composed of a cavalry unit of 1,000 men to be recruited from and supplied by Turkish Jews, from the Jews of the Ottoman Cossack regiment, and Jewish war prisoners (who were to be permitted by the allies to join it), with Sadyk Pasha in command. "The Jews," continued the note, "forming a separate regiment, having the opportunities to attain every grade and by distinguishing themselves by their bravery and race in the eyes of the entire world, will consider themselves fortunate. At the same time the assurance that they will be able to retain their national customs according to their own ritual and to celebrate the Sabbath holiday, as long as this will not interfere with the needs of the service, will remove all religious scruples." [32] Levy also emphasized the same view in his conversation with Rustem Bey, whom he told among others that "we want to elevate ourselves as a race and we believe that the best means of attaining this aim is the submission of proof that we are not only as intelligent, but also as brave as the others." [33]

This argument is presented in its sharpest form in the note ad-

31. Brandstaetter I, pp. 35–37, letter dated October 20, 1855.
32. *Ibid.*, pp. 37–39, no date.
33. *Ibid.*, II, p. 115, no date; the terms "race" or "racial" are to be interpreted in the 19th century ethnic rather than 20th century racist sense.

dressed by Levy to Baron Alphonse Rothschild, after Mickiewicz's death. The note asserted the need for the restoration of Jewish morale and status through military service. Stressing that "in a warlike epoch such as ours the most valued virtue is bravery in combat" the note continued as follows:

When the Jews will prove today that they are not only as intelligent as the others but also no less brave, our religious and civil emancipation will be sealed throughout the entire world. The only means of showing our racial bravery is combat as a group, in Jewish regiments. It is a very good thing that the Jews have acquitted themselves bravely at Sebastopol. But it would have been much better, had they done so in a separate unit. Our bravery would have resounded throughout the world. Much is being done in our century to emancipate individual Jews, but today we must work above all for our racial emancipation, if we do not want our race to disappear. It is a good thing to possess civil rights, but it is necessary to be on guard lest this assimilation lead us to the complete destruction of our Jewish character, and lest this dispersion in foreign centers testify to our complete disappearance. While awaiting the day on which the Will of our Lord of Providence brings us together, let us make efforts that we should be more and more united as a race and that we should be increasingly safe in our observances, and in consequence increasingly more worthy of His mercy.[34]

Mickiewicz believed that the Jewish Legion would have a specific role to play in the attainment of Poland's independence. Like many *émigrés* he believed in the usefulness of the Jews, in the powerful influence exercised by them on the peasant population, and in the need of obtaining Jewish sympathy and understanding as the key to winning the masses to the cause of independence. Following the reading of a report that Jewish officers serving in the French army would seek permission to transfer to the Jewish Legion, Levy wrote:

Rejoicingly Mickiewicz told me: if upon our entry into Poland we shall be able to win to our side through the Jewish Legion the Jews of one synagogue, the peasants will not doubt our success, for knowing the foresight of the Israelites, they will say to themselves: "Our success is assured because the Jews are joining the Revolution." And we shall spread like

34. Brandstaetter I, p. 34. Letter of March 11, 1857.

lava with our continually growing Legion from synagogue to synagogue, village to village, into the very depths of Poland and Lithuania.[35]

Upon hearing that Czaykowski had been treating the idea of the Legion with levity and that he had in addition referred to Jews with the common opprobrium "scurvy Jew," Mickiewicz sent him a sharp reprimand.[36] Its text is not preserved. However, in another letter to Czaykowski the poet warned:

Please remember that our opponents are not joking; new things are attained only by gaining new forces. The Ottoman Cossacks, too, were spoken of in jest as long as they were not seen in body. The cause of the Israelites has been occupying many minds during the past two decades. In Poland they support our nationality and are considered to be a powerful element. Should this unit come into being, you would have support from the French government. Mr. Levy, the first physician of the French army here, enjoys the Emperor's great respect. There are also here in the army not a few well inclined officers; they can render effective help through their contacts in France. The Turkish Minister has reacted favorably to our attempt, and the local Israelites say they are ready to help.[37]

Thus can be surmised the poet's broad view as to the place of the Jewish Legion in obtaining support for Poland's cause by Jews everywhere and, through them, that of others.

The poet's view, evolving from mysticism to *Realpolitik,* turns back into mysticism at this point, the consideration of the Jews' permanent adjustment in Poland. We have referred earlier to Mickiewicz's mystic view of the Legion. He believed that "without the emancipation of the Jews and the development of their spirit Poland

35. Władysław Mickiewicz, *Żywot,* IV, 441, as cited in Brandstaetter I, p. 40.
36. Brandstaetter I, p. 40. This incident was recalled after the poet's death by Ludwika Śniadecka, in a letter to her husband Sadyk Pasha, as follows: "Perhaps Mickiewicz's origin, or his family's or his wife's, was such, for whence came such love for Israel. I never thought of it until, when I read your letter to him, I came across the scurvy Jew; how he shook, how he was excited, I don't know whether it is possible to love strange things so much, but perhaps he loved so much his own idea, wish and thoughts." Letter, January 16, 1856, cited in Brandstaetter I, p. 40, from *Rok Mickiewiczowski,* Lwów, 1898.
37. Letter, November 8, 1855, Adam Mickiewicz, *Korespondencya,* II, 130–131, as cited in Brandstaetter I, p. 41. Dr. Levy is not to be confused with Armand Levy.

cannot rise. Should she rise without the emancipation of the Jews, which I do not believe, she surely will not be able to maintain herself." [38] Indeed, Mickiewicz, perhaps lapsing into the mysticism of Polish-Jewish union as expressed in his *Slavic Literature,* visualized the Jews as forming a permanent part of Poland, destined to play a great historic role yet to be revealed. He told Levy that "I would not want the Jews to leave Poland, for the union of Poland with Israel is destined to strengthen our Republic morally as the union between Lithuania and Poland had strengthened her militarily in the days of yore." [39]

Mickiewicz's personal interest not only in the higher levels of negotiations but also in the day-by-day doings in the camp is therefore easily understandable.

After he had heard complaints about the lack of Jewish religious accommodations in the camp, the poet established and equipped there a synagogue under his own patronage. He was delighted with Czaykowski's order (following Levy's suggestion) that the Jewish Sabbath be made the day of rest for the Jews. "An occurrence of this kind," he told Levy, "has happened for the first time since the dispersion of the Jews, and a great deal of significance can be attached to it." [40]

Mickiewicz was pleased with the appearance of Lieutenant Michał Horenstein in the newly designed uniform of the Jewish Legion. To quote Czaykowski: "Mickiewicz poked fun at Horenstein, because he already had dressed himself up in the uniform of the Hussars of Israel, and had also dressed in the same uniform his young friend De Castro. Goliaths, Samsons, Holofernesses (said Mickiewicz) just look out that no Judith or Delilah crawl into your way, because

38. Levy to Bednarczyk as cited in Brandstaetter I, p. 24. Levy added to this: "Let us hold in seriousness these words of Mickiewicz; this is a source of a new policy, which we have already discussed many times, one that is based on intuition and enthusiasm."

39. Armand Levy in his preface to *Am Polones* (the Hebrew translation of the *Books of the Nation and the Books of Polish Pilgrims*), Paris, 1881, p. viii (French preface).

40. Brandstaetter I, p. 30, where the sources are also indicated for Czaykowski's humorous description of the ceremonial; the order is reprinted on pp. 30–31.

she will break up all the ranks, and it will be necessary to leave again the Hussars of Israel for *gescheft* and to become commission agents."[41]

There were many problems to solve. There was the question of the Legion's officers: several candidates had been suggested by different persons for commander-in-chief. There was the problem of Czaykowski, who was self-centered and viewed the Jewish Legion, at least in the beginning, only from the angle of personal benefit. At that time he ostensibly cooperated with Mickiewicz, but ridiculed the project behind the poet's back. He became more enthusiastic about it later, seeing its military and international values, but this enthusiasm was always tinged with suspicion of the Jews.[42] Turkish reluctance was a most aggravating factor, particularly the interminable red tape in the negotiations. An obstacle was the Turks' fear that a Jewish military unit might attempt to seize Palestine, and the rumors of Rothschild's ambition to rule the Holy Land did not help matters. Even more substantial was the fear of conflict with Catholic Powers.[43]

Levy's later audience with Prince Napoleon, a serious pretender to Poland's throne, brought no results because of the traditional French view on Jewish emancipation. Levy evalued the difficulties thus: "The Jewish question is looked upon more from the point of view of religious tolerance than from the racial standpoint. Here lies the greatest difficulty to be overcome by those who want to elevate the Jewish nation."[44]

41. *Ibid.*, III, pp. 123–124, based on Czaykowski's report. In a letter Czaykowski gave a detailed description of the proposed uniform. He thought it ought to be "lively in order to catch the eye—and even impress—and in this way destroy the ridiculous yet factually existing prejudice against a Jewish army." He also proposed that even the cavalry be equipped with carbines instead of lances: "a nation which had lost its military traditions should not revive them with cutting weapons" (*ibid.*, II, pp. 122–123).

42. For instance, he regretted later the failure of the Jewish Legion plan because "it might have been better for the Cossacks, they would have had credit and they could have caroused on credit from their comrades-in-arms (Brandstaetter I, p. 45, note 49, on basis of Czaykowski's memoirs).

43. Brandstaetter II, pp. 113–114.

44. *Ibid.*, III, p. 336.

Mickiewicz's illness seriously interfered with the negotiations. Nevertheless he "did not cease his work, but was wearing himself out and was losing his health." Czaykowski further reported that Służalski had told him "that before his death Adam Mickiewicz was sorry that he had not brought the matter to its conclusion, repeating more than once: 'When I am no longer alive, no one will even understand it.'"[45]

The poet's death in the midst of his work and worries marked the beginning of the end of the project. Levy's attempts and Sadyk Pasha's belated and not always natural enthusiasm were in vain. The proposed instructor, Colonel Emil Bednarczyk, clashed with Czaykowski and became involved in a false claim case with the Turkish government. The closing phase of the war presented an additional obstacle. A renewal of hope, roused by the Turkish government's consideration of a partial Jewish draft, turned out to be temporary. Through the efforts of Captain Michał Horenstein, temporarily in charge, Jewish war prisoners continued to be recruited as late as December, 1856.[46] However, in October, Levy was told that the Turkish government had no intention of carrying out the project, determined as it was to reduce its army. Levy's efforts to change the decision were of no avail, particularly after the Turkish Jewish leaders and the Rothschild representatives lost their interest in the cause.

Thus was the poet's idea relegated to an archival collection of documents, much neglected by historians. Interestingly enough, Count Władysław Zamoyski's rival outfit, which was supposedly organized as a Catholic and purely nationalist Polish military unit, also included a sizable number of Jewish soldiers.[47] Czaykowski later revealed that he had heard that Zamoyski had been aware of the negotiations concerning the Jewish Legion and that he had "desired to take this Jewish organization under his direction,"[48] testifying that

45. *Ibid.*, II, p. 123.
46. Brandstaetter III, pp. 234–236.
47. More information on these, based on documents in the Zamoyski archives in the ancestral castle at Kórnik as well as the Raperswil collection, will be included in my book. Some data are contained in Brandstaetter III, pp. 234, 247, note 149.
48. Brandstaetter III, p. 247.

the poet's idea found acceptance also among more "practical" people.

The Jewish Legion project was the culmination of Mickiewicz's evolution of thinking on the problem of the Jews in Poland. As such, it deserves closer attention on the part of Polish historical and literary scholars. In more than one respect it also presents the poet as a trail blazer in the history of the Jewish national renaissance. That can be taken for granted in the realm of the concept of group emancipation, a basis for later national minority status.

Mickiewicz's influence on Levy has even more far-reaching implications. "My friend Armand L., whose grandfather had already been converted," wrote Moses Hess in his classic *Rome and Jerusalem,* "is more interested in Jewish affairs than many a circumcized Jew, and he has preserved his faith in Jewish nationality more faithfully than our enlightened rabbis." [49] Again to quote Hess:

> My friend Armand Levy, who traveled for several years through the Danube Principalities, told me that the Jews were moved to tears when he announced to them the end of their sufferings with the words "The time of the return approaches." The more fortunate Occidental Jews do not know with what longing the Jewish masses of the East await the final redemption from the two thousand year exile.[50]

Indeed, Mickiewicz's influence is in need of evaluation also in the area of Jewish thought.

49. *Rom und Jerusalem, die Letzte Nationalitaetsfrage* (1862). Our citations are from the English edition, *Rome and Jerusalem, a Study in Jewish Nationalism,* tr. Meyer Waxman, New York, 1945, p. 47, where Levy's first name is cited wrongly as Armond, as also on p. 133.
50. *Ibid.,* p. 133, note 9.

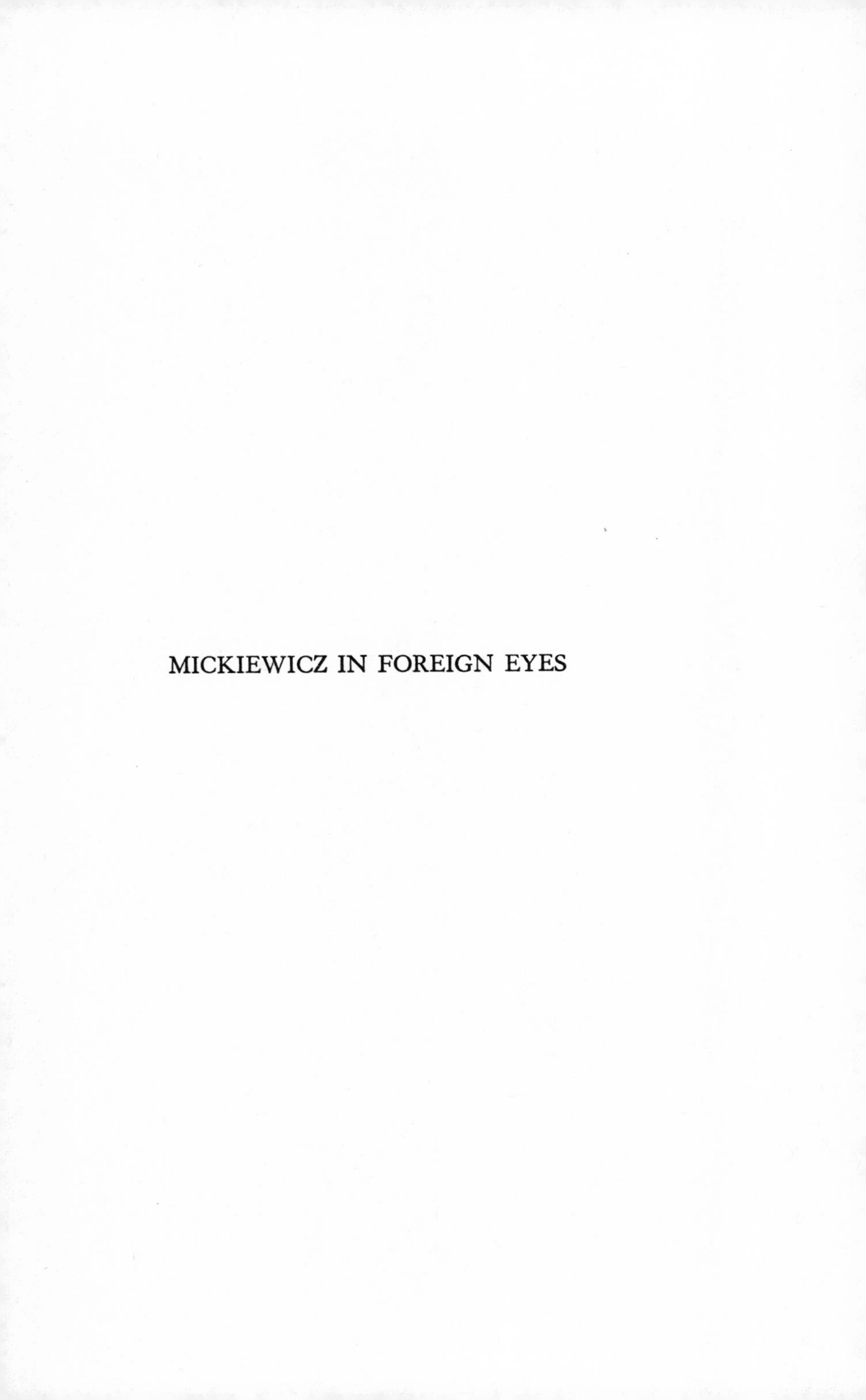

MICKIEWICZ IN FOREIGN EYES

# RUSSIA

## *Mickiewicz in Russia*

### by Czesław Zgorzelski

I

Professor V. Chernobayev closes his short study of the influence of Mickiewicz's work on Russian literature in the years from 1820 to 1830 with the following sentence: "On the contemporary Russian literary scene there was no one who could by his production equal Mickiewicz, there was not even anyone fully capable of understanding all the basic motifs of his poetry." [1]

This opinion, undoubtedly exaggerated if confronted with the level of Russian literature at that time (indeed, it was during that period that Pushkin wrote and developed), pertinently grasps the exceptional position that Mickiewicz won for himself among Russian literary society of the time. Moreover, it was by no means only a temporary position dependent on the poet's personal connections and friendships. Mickiewicz entered Russian literature to stay for good, and had already acquired in it the status of one of the world's leading writers. At one stroke, without the protests which he still encountered among his own countrymen, during his stay in Tsarist Russia Mickiewicz was received into the group of universally recognized classics as the author of works translated, imitated, and read with an admiration that was equaled a hundred years later in the thoroughly changed conditions of Soviet Russia.

This is evidenced above all by the concordant statements of Russian writers representing various literary epochs, camps, and trends, who always, and with the same reverence, praise Mickiewicz's poetry very highly and assign it a leading position in world literature. These utterances prove convincingly how quickly his renown was spreading. In 1827 P. A. Vyazemsky, well-known poet and friend of Mickie-

1. *Pamiętnik Literacki,* Vol. XXXI, Nos. 3–4.

wicz, had considered it necessary to introduce him to the Russian public. "Mickiewicz," he wrote in an article accompanying the translation of the *Crimean Sonnets,* "belongs to the chosen few who are given the happy right of representing the literary fame of their peoples." And only two years later, in 1829, another translator of Mickiewicz, V. I. Lyubich-Romanovich, began his collection of translations with the rhetorical question: "Who among educated Russians is not familiar with the name of the first of Poland's contemporary poets, and who has not heard about the works of his creative, independent genius?" From the very beginning a splendid future was predicted for him. "He should become a great poet," opines Zhukovsky. And Polevoi, bidding farewell to the poet on his leaving Russia, declares: "We shall await from afar his new songs, and we hope that we shall hear of his new masterpieces. Who knows to what heights Mickiewicz's poetry, lent added forcefulness by his uncommon knowledge of literature and his exceptionally enlightened mind, will soar." [2]

His fame spread rapidly. From the great poet of contemporary Poland, as he appears in Vyazemsky's article, he soon grows to the stature of one of the leading representatives of world literature. Quite a few examples are recorded by V. Chernobayev in the article cited above.[3] This recognition is perhaps most strikingly expressed by Ivan Kireyevsky, who, in his article on "Russian Literature in 1829," mentions Mickiewicz together with Goethe, Schiller, Shakespeare, Byron, and Moore as the six poets particularly popular among the Russian writers of the period.[4]

2. *Moskovsky Telegraf,* 1829, No. 6, pp. 200–201.

3. Cf. the opinion of the anonymous reviewer of *Galatea* in 1830, the words of *Severnaya Zvezda* in 1828, the view of the translator of *Farys* in *Syn Otechestva* of 1829, and others.

4. *Polnoye sobraniye sochinenii,* II (Moscow, 1911), 35. Similarly, V. G. Belinsky places Mickiewicz among the world's most outstanding poets. In an article written in 1835, "O russkoi povesti i povestyakh Gogolya," *Sobraniye sochinenii,* I (Moscow, 1948), OGIZ, 110, he enumerates some of the most outstanding examples of idealistic poetry, mentioning Mickiewicz's *Forefathers' Eve* among such works as Goethe's *Faust,* Byron's *Manfred,* Moore's poems, Jean Paul's fantasies and others. Belinsky's attitude toward Mickiewicz has not always been favorable. He also said sharp, unjust words distorted by

Thus, it is not strange that one of them, Baratynsky, addressing Mickiewicz in a beautiful poem, calls him a god who has no reason to humiliate himself before Byron, for he is the equal of the latter. These are by no means the manifestations of the preferences of individual poets or of the sympathies of some contemporary literary groupings. "The representatives of the most manifold literary trends," writes Chernobayev, "were united in their recognition of Mickiewicz. Periodicals opposing each other were in agreement when the publication of translations of *Farys* or of the *Sonnets* was involved. Not only Pogodin, Polevoi and Bulgarin printed translations of the poet's works in their publications, but so did Kachenovsky in *Vestnik Yevropy,* that is, in a periodical with strong classicist traditions, as well as the conservative *Galatea* or *Severnaya Minerva."* [5]

Not only the revolutionary Herzen bestowed his respect and sympathy on Mickiewicz, but also the Slavophile Khomyakov. In 1843, at a time when even the very name of Mickiewicz was prohibited, Khomyakov did not hesitate to offer a toast "in honor of the great Slavic poet who is not present," at a solemn banquet in Moscow.[6]

This was not the recognition of one generation or one epoch alone. Mickiewicz's fame as a poet continued to live for a hundred years virtually unimpaired—from Gogol, who declared that *Pan Tadeusz* was a "most astonishing thing," through Leskov, who even gave one of his tales a Polish heading—the first words of Mickiewicz's *Conversation:* "Beloved mine, what use is talk to us?" [7] to Bryusov,

---

the doctrinaire stand of his youth (cf. his article on Menzel). But later, when his views had undergone a thorough transformation, he regretted these words and wished to withdraw them. In a letter of December 10, 1840, he accuses himself as follows: "Now I am most sorry for my attack against Mickiewicz in my miserable article about Menzel. How could I have done it—to deny the great poet the most sacred right of lamenting the fall of that which is dearest to him in the world and in eternity—his homeland? . . . And I have in the press publicly called this noble and great poet a bawler, a poet of rhymed libels! . . ." (Pypin, *Belinsky, yego zhizn i perepiska,* Petersburg, 1876, II, 77).

5. *Pamiętnik Literacki,* Vol. XXXI, Nos. 3–4, p. 314.

6. According to Herzen's account; see M. Zhivov's introduction to Mickiewicz's *Izbrannoye* (Moscow, 1946, Goslitizdat), p. 33.

7. Leskov's attitude towards Polish poetry was in general one of close concern (cf. his opinions about Syrokomla, Korzeniowski, Kraszewski). For the in-

Bunin, and Balmont, whose translations from Mickiewicz prove eloquently how close his poems were to them.

For the sake of evidence let us cite a few more of the most significant utterances during the second half of the nineteenth century. Here is a fragment from the poet Polonsky's student reminiscences: "I remember the very strong impression made on me by the lyrical lines in Mickiewicz's *Forefathers* where the poet speaks of the nothingness of earthly life in the face of a past without a beginning and a future without an end, and of how insignificant is the span of our life in comparison with eternity." [8]

Another example is the statement of one of the leading critics of the time, A. Grigoryev. Discussing the poems of Pushkin that moved him most, Grigoryev affirms that "similar poems of the same force of heroic feeling, of such profound, poetic and human sadness, of the same passion and accessibility to all people may be found only in Mickiewicz." [9] And in a letter to Maikov, mentioning "Homer's, Dante's and Shakespeare's art of a new world" as a model, he writes: "Its earnests are Raphael's contours without colors; Pushkin and Mickiewicz are the water and fire, the sea and the mountains of the new world. We shall find all the fire of the Hebrew prophets in the singer of Wallenrod, and all that is wide, boundless, and at the same time feminine and tender, appears in Pushkin's nature." [10]

The same recognition sounds even more strongly in the words of V. Solovov. In an address on the anniversary of the poet's death he defined the essence of Mickiewicz's creativeness as follows: "His greatness lies in the fact that, rising to new levels of moral loftiness, he carried with him to these heights not proud and vain negation but love of that above which he was rising." [11]

---

formation on Leskov's short story I am indebted to Professor K. W. Zawodziński. Mickiewicz's *Conversation* seems to have enjoyed exceptional popularity at that time among Russian writers. Bestuzhev-Marlinsky quotes the last stanza of the poem as a motto for Chap. IV of his story *Fregat Nadezhda*. Ogaryov's translation of *Conversation,* entitled *Razgovor,* also dates from this period.

8. Quoted from M. Zhivov's introduction, *loc. cit.,* p. 37.

9. *Ibid.,* p. 36.

10. *Ibid.*

11. *Ibid.,* p. 37.

## 2

A survey of the unusually long list of Mickiewicz's works translated by the Russians may serve as a gauge of his importance in Russian literature. Not only second-rate pens, not only writers whose production is almost exclusively limited to translations, as is most often the case, take part in this work. Among Mickiewicz's translators are to be found almost all the most outstanding Russian poets of the nineteenth and twentieth centuries: Ryleyev, Vyazemsky, Pushkin, Lermontov, Fet, Benediktov, Kozlov, Mei, Shevyrev, Ogarev, Bunin, Bryusov, Balmont, Antokolsky, Aseyev—such is the by no means complete list, of which not many of the world's poets could boast. Even the old Dmitriev, representing a literary trend which was then drawing to a close, grasped his pen to try his hand once more, at the end of his life and after many years of inactivity, on the translation of one of the new poet's sonnets.

Many of Mickiewicz's works had several translations, and some had even a dozen or more. There are, for example, four complete translations of *Grażyna,* those of Lyubich-Romanovich, Benediktov, Alyabin, and Kovalevsky; five translations of *Pan Tadeusz,* two complete ones by Benediktov and Berg, and three fragmentary ones by Mei, Palmin, and Mar; and nine verse translations and one prose rendition of *Farys,* by Shchastny, Sayanov, Danilevsky, Manasein, and one anonymous translator (perhaps Bulgarin), Ikonnikov, Sokolov, Semyonov, Viskovatov, and Slutsky.

Exceptional popularity was enjoyed by the *Crimean Sonnets* and *Konrad Wallenrod.* People read and copied them as soon as they appeared in print. Ksenofont Polevoi speaks as follows of *Konrad Wallenrod*'s success before it had even been translated in verse: "A huge circle of the poet's Russian admirers knew this poem without knowing the Polish language, that is, knew its contents and fathomed its details and beauty. This is probably the only example of its kind! It was the result of the general interest of the St. Petersburg and Moscow public in the famous Polish poet. . . . People turned to Polish acquaintances and read with them Mickiewicz's new poem in a literal translation." [12]

12. *Ibid.,* p. 20.

Even Zhukovsky, to whom the poet himself read this work "in a poor French prose translation," confided to one of his feminine correspondents: "If I were writing now, or had time to write at all, I would at once take up the translation of this poem." [13] Indeed, the number of poets who translated it in part or in full exceeds fifteen writers of various periods of Russian literature. And about twenty poets translated the *Crimean Sonnets,* among them Lermontov ("View of the Mountains from the Steppes of Kozlov"), Fet (one sonnet), Bunin (three sonnets), Maikov, Benediktov, Kozlov, and the already mentioned Dmitriev.

In the history of Mickiewicz's reception in Russia several stages may be distinguished. The first and most active one coincides with the period of the poet's stay in Russia. It was then that each new work of Mickiewicz called forth a wide echo in Russian society, and translations were sometimes made even before the appearance of the originals in print, as was the case with the translation of *Farys* by Shchastny, who is said to have made his version directly from the author's manuscript.

The rise of the poet's popularity was not even hindered by the sentiments caused by the outbreak of the November Insurrection. At that time, in 1831, there appeared a complete translation of *Konrad Wallenrod* by A. Shpigotsky.[14] After the Insurrection had been crushed, Mickiewicz's name was for several decades expunged from pages printed in Russia as a result of the reprisals of censorship. But even reprisals did not succeed in ousting his works from Russian literature. Translations continued to appear, and not only in manuscript. They were printed with the general annotation "translation from the Polish," or giving only the first letter of the poet's name.[15]

Cancellation, in the second half of the nineteenth century, of the ban imposed on the printing of Mickiewicz's works was received

13. J. Tyc, "Pushkin's Translations from Mickiewicz," *Puszkin 1837–1937* (in Polish; Cracow, 1939), II, 16.

14. *Konrad Wallenrod,* Moscow, 1832; cf. Chernobayev, *loc. cit.,* p. 310.

15. As late as 1857 Mei indicated translations from Mickiewicz by "s polskogo" in his *Stikhotvorenia,* St. Petersburg, 1857. Cf. also the decision of the censorship office concerning the fourth edition of Kozlov's poems in 1853. This is mentioned by M. Zhivov, *loc. cit.,* p. 27.

with great satisfaction. Then a new stage in the reception of his poetry in Russia began. The first manifestation of this swelling wave was a collection of translations, including a full version of *Pan Tadeusz,* by N. Berg in 1865. However, the culminating point was not reached until 1880–1885.

In 1882 the first complete edition of Mickiewicz's works in Russian was published by the Polish publisher M. Wolff in St. Petersburg. The edition was made possible not only because the publisher had gathered abundant material heretofore scattered in periodicals and collections of poems, but also thanks to the indefatigable efforts of Mickiewicz's exceptional admirer and the most distinguished translator of his poetry, N. N. Semyonov.

By profession a lawyer, he only by chance had come across the works of the poet who was later to become his great favorite. Semyonov's biographer, S. Librovich, tells us that he acquired his Mickiewicz worship from a Polish prisoner whom he had met while serving as state prosecutor in Wilno shortly before the outbreak of the January, 1863, Insurrection. As translator he strove for accuracy in rendering not only words and thoughts, but also the rhythm and melody of the verse.

Neither the prosecutor's poetic inclinations nor their result in the form of translations from Mickiewicz were known to the general public for some time. Not until 1869 did Semyonov begin to publish fragments of his work. Many of his translations were among the collected poems of Mickiewicz published by Wolff. In 1885 Semyonov published the book entitled *Iz Mitskevicha.* It contained all his translations which he himself considered satisfactory. A year later he was given the Pushkin award of the Academy of Sciences for this book.

Semyonov's work was by no means the only manifestation of the tendency to popularize the works of Mickiewicz in Russia. Interest in his poetry continued and did not decline even during the difficult war years of 1914–1918. By way of example it is sufficient to cite K. Viskovatov's collection of translations *Iz zhemchuzhin polskoi poezii* (Pearls of Polish Poetry, Petrograd, 1915). Among the more than thirty specimens to be found here there are four items from Mickiewicz: the introduction to *Konrad Wallenrod,* "The Storm" from the *Crimean Sonnets, Farys,* and *Ode to Youth.* And a more striking indication of continued interest in Mickiewicz is the fact that in 1918, at the turning point between old and new Russia, there appeared in Moscow a second edition of a translation of the *Books of the Polish Nation and of the Polish Pilgrims.* The first edition had been sold out in less than eight months; the second appeared at the time of the revolution, and, in the Introduction, the editor stressed the exceptional significance which the wise words of the *Books* might have for the Russian people at such a moment.

In Soviet Russia interest in Mickiewicz does not wane. This is proved by popular "mass" editions of the poet's selected writings for young and adult readers, but its most significant manifestation is a collection of translations published a few years ago by the State Publishing House for Belles Lettres in Moscow.[16]

The significance of this volume may be compared with that of Wolff's edition and of Semyonov's book of translations. Like the other two it constitutes the summation of the efforts of many years. It includes forty new translations (by Antokolsky, Aseyev, Blaginina, Vinogradov, Gatov, Golodny, Zhivov, Zvyagintseva, Zenkevich, Karaban, Kovalevsky, Levik, Mar, Rumer, Turganov, Ushakov, and Tsvelyov), among them a complete translation of *Grażyna* (by A. Kovalensky), and of *Konrad Wallenrod* (by N. Aseyev), as well as an abridged version of *Pan Tadeusz* (by S. Mar).

The "Improvisation" of Konrad from the *Forefathers' Eve* has been printed for the first time in the Russian language, while in older translations passages formerly deleted by the censor have been restored. On the other hand, the Rome lyrics and the majority of the patriotic poems, including "Ordon's Redoubt" and "To a Polish Mother," have been completely omitted. Thus, on the basis of the present selection, the reader is unable to gain a complete picture of all the essential elements of Mickiewicz's creative art. The volume has been provided with notes (by N. Grekov) and a chronological

16. Adam Mitskevich, *Izbrannoye: Lirika-ballady-poemy,* perevod s polskogo, pod redaktsiyei M. F. Rylskogo i B. A. Turganova, Moscow, 1946, GIKHL, 603 pp.

Korybut Xiąże Nowogródka.
Poema
z Dziejów Litewskich.

Co raz to ciemniej świat pozłacany [illegible]
Na dole tuman a [illegible] wysoko,
Pośród [illegible] czarnych chmur [illegible]
W mgle zbielałe pokazywał oko.
Y świat był na kształt gmachu [illegible]
A niebo na kształt [illegible] [illegible]
Księżyc jak okno [illegible] [illegible] [illegible].

Zamek na barkach nowogródzkiej góry
Od miesięcznego brał postać obłoku;
10 Po wałach z darnu i po sinym piasku [illegible]
[illegible] olbrzymich stopach [illegible] się [illegible] bury
Spadając w łono, gdzie śród wieczornych ciemności
Dyszała woda spod zielonych pleśni.

Miasto już spało, w zamku ognie zgasły.
Tylko po wałach i po basztach stoją
Powtarzanemi [illegible] [illegible] hasły.
W tem się coś zdala na polu ozwie
Jakowiś ludzie biegą tu po błoniach
A [illegible] [illegible] na każdym się [illegible],
20 A biegą prędko, muszą być na koniach
A świecą mocno, muszą być pancerni
Zwiady konie [illegible] [illegible] [illegible]
Trzej to rycerze jadą w zbroi [illegible].
Zjechali stają a pierwszy z rycerzy
Trzykroć i w trąbę [illegible] uderzy.

Autograf »Grażyny«

MANUSCRIPT OF THE OPENING LINES OF GRAŻYNA

account of the poet's life and works (by A. Vinogradov); it also contains some introductory remarks by M. Rylsky and an interesting study by M. Zhivov entitled "Poezia Mitskevicha v perevodakh i otklikakh russkikh pisatelei." A considerable part of the facts and quotations of the present article has been taken from this extensive, though by no means complete, survey of Mickiewicz's reception in Russian literature and of the attitude of the various Russian writers toward the Polish poet.

## 3

Mickiewicz's position in Russian literature is demonstrated not only by translations and evaluations of his works by contemporary and later writers, but also by the influence which these works had on the formation of some of the poems of Pushkin, Lermontov, and others. Particularly significant in this respect are the echoes of Mickiewicz's creative art in the form of a discreet poetic polemic with *Konrad Wallenrod* carried out by Pushkin in *Poltava,*[17] and with the "Digression" of *Forefathers' Eve,* Part III, in *The Bronze Horseman.*[18]

These works, as well as the problem of Mickiewicz's influence on Lermontov, have been frequently discussed in Polish critical literature and do not require further elaboration.[19] However, not much attention has been devoted to the influence of Mickiewicz's works on the development of some of the poetic genres in Russian literature. A glance at Mickiewicz's influence as manifested in the evolution of the Russian ballad would be sufficient, merely by way of example, to give a very general indication of the problems in this field which still await a more detailed study.

Mickiewicz's first volume of poetry, *Ballads and Romances,* did not win such fame in Russia as his later *Sonnets* or *Konrad Wallenrod.* The debut of an unknown poet did not have the same possibilities

17. And perhaps also in *Gasub.* Cf. W. Lednicki, "Still Another Polemic of Pushkin with Mickiewicz," in the symposium *Puszkin 1837–1937* (Cracow, 1939), I, 227–247.
18. According to M. Zhivov (*loc. cit.,* p. 34) Ogarev's poem *Vyros gorod na bolote* is yet another reply to Mickiewicz's "Monument of Peter the Great."
19. See studies by Spasowicz, Zdziechowski, Tretiak, Lednicki, and others.

of attracting the interest of foreign writers as the works of the later exile who had already won fame in his own country. Nevertheless, even the ballads, soon after their publication, were bound to call forth certain echoes in Russian literary circles. Evidence of this seems to be furnished by Przecławski, who, as early as the beginning of 1823, reported to his Wilno friends from St. Petersburg that "the Russian writers were extremely interested" in Mickiewicz's little volume of poetry and that Zhukovsky "was growing enthusiastic" over "the ideas and external charm" of Mickiewicz's poems.[20]

Perhaps at the same time, if not later, K. Ryleyev, influenced by his personal acquaintance with Mickiewicz, tried to translate *The Lilies* in the unfinished poem "Zhena grekh tyazhky sovershila. . . ."[21]

However, those were only individual examples of interest in Mickiewicz's first fruit. The ballads did not win a wider circle of Russian readers until a few years later. From about 1825–1826 on, new translations kept appearing. In this connection it is an interesting fact that at first they were not (as was the case in Poland) regarded as a manifestation of the new Romantic school of poetry. Quite the contrary: the translators come mostly from the ranks of the "old" school, and in their versions they brought to light not the new, Romantic qualities of Mickiewicz's ballads, but above all the elements which corresponded to their own tastes nurtured on the sentimental predilections of the age or on the classicist poetics of the preceding century.

20. There is a clear contradiction between this report and what Zhukovsky wrote in a letter to Yelagina seven years later, after he had become personally acquainted with Mickiewicz: "As yet I know none of his works" (Tyc, *op. cit.*, p. 16). It is hard to imagine that during those seven years he should have completely forgotten his earlier enthusiasm over the ballads. It must rather be assumed that it was Przecławski who had given free rein to his imagination. Concerning Przecławski's account, cf. *The Correspondence of the Philomathians,* V, 40, Zan's letter to Mickiewicz of February 7, 1823.

21. P. A. Yefremov, *Sochinenia i perepiska K. F. Ryleyeva,* Petersburg, 1874, pp. 186–188. First published in an inaccurate version in P. I. Bartenev's collection *Devyatnadtsaty vek,* 1872, I, 371–372. M. Zhivov's account (*loc. cit.*, p. 14) to the effect that the translation was made as early as 1821, i.e., before Mickiewicz's volume was published, is obviously erroneous.

This is proved rather conclusively by the very selection of the poems translated. Thus, for example, J. Poznansky chose "Maryla's Grave," the most sentimental poem in the collection of Mickiewicz, called by him a "romance," but essentially not much different from the "pastoral" sentimentalities on the model of the idyls so prevalent at the time. Another translator of the same period (1825–1826), Michael Bestuzhev-Ryumin, translated "Lake Świteź" and "The Nymph of Świteź," but he adapted both ballads "entirely in the spirit of the descriptive poems of late classicism," as has been stated by V. Chernobayev.[22] In his version the fantastic-folkloristic elements of these poems were relegated to the background. Even four years later, in 1830, the very same Bestuzhev published in his periodical *Severny Merkurii* a translation of "This I Like," Mickiewicz's earliest ballad, a poem in which the influence of the sentimental elegy and of the mannerisms of its style was probably revealed most strongly. In this case also the translator's conservative tastes had obviously determined his choice.

This lack of understanding of the Romantic qualities of Mickiewicz's ballads becomes even stronger if one takes into consideration the fact that in the contemporary stage of the evolution of that genre in Russia these qualities by no means constituted the unusual revelation that they were in the history of Polish literature. At that time, not so much the result of the sentimental translations of Zhukovsky as of Katenin's *Olga* (1816) and the first ballads of Pushkin and his imitators, the Romantic ballad was beginning to strike deep roots in the soil of Russian poetry. However, it was growing in the halo of the glory of the German and Scottish ballad, and this glory probably prevented the Russian writers from noticing the qualities of the Romantic "primrose" of the closer Slavic poetry.

They were not brought to light until a few years later, and the path to them was not opened by the first and most Romantic ballads from the collection of Mickiewicz's Wilno-Kowno poetry, but by poems written by him in Russia, primarily "Czaty" ("The Ambush") and "The Three Brothers Budrys." This may not have been owing

22. V. Chernobayev, *op. cit.*, p. 295.

merely to the interest which at that time was called forth by every poem of Mickiewicz. Both these ballads presented certain new elements in Mickiewicz's poetry that were practically unnoticed by contemporary Polish literary criticism. Both introduced into his ballad technique a new epigrammatic principle of construction not employed in the Wilno-Kowno ballads, which represented primarily an epic, less concentrated type of plot development. It may have been this consideration—this specifically balladic method of presenting the story and effecting its denouement by means of a sharply indicated, epigrammatic point—that caused Pushkin to translate into Russian precisely these two out of all Mickiewicz's ballads.

Both "The Voyevoda" and "Budrys and His Sons" (the titles Pushkin gave to these two ballads) are clearly distinct from the contemporary Russian ballads, gravitating, like the Polish ones, to that variety of this genre characterized by an epic sweep or diffusion. They constitute a considerable step forward in the evolution of the compact, concentrated type of balladic story. The unusual popularity of both these poems increased the power of their influence on later poets even more, thereby enabling Mickiewicz to play a rather significant role in the development of the Russian ballad.

Thus, only after about 1835 did Mickiewicz's ballads win a place among the most highly appreciated European models of this genre, exerting a creative influence on its further evolution in Russia. Time and again new translations appeared. "The Ambush" found a second magnificent translator in Fet, whose version, entitled "Dozor," soon reached (thanks to the melody added to it) the broad masses of the population, just as "The Voyevoda" had done before.[23]

Soon translations of Mickiewicz's other Wilno-Kowno and later ballads also began to appear. Fet rendered into Russian "The Nymph of Świteź," as did Mei in addition to "Twardowski's Wife" and "The Renegade," while Benediktov translated "The Fish," "Alpuhara," and "Father's Return." "Father's Return," the last of the Wilno-Kowno ballads and perhaps closest to the two translated by Pushkin, also found a sizable number of translators: besides Bene-

23. Later both these ballads ("The Ambush" and "The Three Brothers Budrys") were also translated by Danilevsky.

diktov's version, it was put into Russian by J. Pozharsky ("Vstrecha ottsa") and Surikov ("Vozvrashcheniye tyati").

The influence of the plots of the ballads of Mickiewicz is also considerable, exceeding even the sphere of the ballad, as is proved by Pushkin's unfinished fantastic drama entitled *Rusalka* (1832), based perhaps on a motif borrowed from Mickiewicz's "The Fish." To the already known examples could be added Koltsov's "Naiad," a ballad whose story shows an indubitable similarity to "The Nymph of Świteź," while its expressive and suggestive description of water and sky may have its genealogy in the descriptive stanzas of the first part of "Lake Świteź." Also significant is the resumption of Mickiewicz's unfinished plots and their further development according to the writers' own poetic invention, as, for example, in the case of the continuation of "The Renegade" by J. Polonsky.[24]

Therefore, the opinion of W. Neumann does not seem to be lacking foundation. This German scholar stresses Schiller's and Mickiewicz's influence as the main cause for the appearance of new artistic tendencies in the development of the Russian ballad after 1830.[25] On the other hand, it is difficult to agree with his thesis that Mickiewicz's influence tended to make itself felt in stressing the ideological, socio-political content of the Russian ballads, especially when he tries to link these tendencies with the meaning of such poems as "The Ambush" or "The Three Brothers Budrys." Apparently the German scholar found it hard to grasp the real meaning of Mickiewicz's ballads. For example, he tries to reduce "The Three Brothers Budrys" to the role of a poem serving the idea of Lithuania's union with Poland, endeavoring to explain the fact that, although the brothers set out in three different directions, they all bring home Polish girls as an underscoring of Poland's greatness with frontiers "from sea to sea." Probably only the strength of the universal conviction that after the loss of independence each work of a Pole must contain a hidden political idea could have led Neumann so far astray from the real meaning of the poem.

24. See M. Zhivov, *loc. cit.*, p. 37.
25. See *Geschichte der russischen Ballade,* Königsberg, 1937, pp. 156–157, 163–165.

Mickiewicz's influence on the Russian ballad after 1830 seems indisputable. It appears, however, not in the strengthening of its ideological tendencies but is manifested either in the form of plot borrowings or as a stimulus to seek new technical solutions which would bring about a fuller realization of the ballad form for story presentation.

4

Mickiewicz has penetrated deeply into the tradition of Russian literature. He has become an important and continuously living factor in its development. The knowledge of his works was obligatory in the same way as that of the basic works of Goethe, Schiller, Shakespeare, or Byron.

Perhaps the most significant manifestation of Mickiewicz's high place in Russian literature is Pushkin's sentence in *Dubrovsky* in which, describing the heroine's work on the loom, he makes an allusion to Mickiewicz's Aldona. These are Pushkin's words: "She did not tangle up the silk threads like Konrad's sweetheart, who in amorous distraction embroidered a rose in green silk. . . ." Zhivov rightly observes that these words not only prove how well Pushkin knew and remembered Mickiewicz's works, but also what wide popularity the Polish poet enjoyed among the Russian readers, since it was unnecessary to explain which Konrad was meant and since it was sufficient to refer to the then (1832–1833) apparently general knowledge of the poem.[26]

Within only a few years the young poet-exile won a magnificent triumph, which he could not have expected, when through the Pointed Gate of Wilno he left his native land carrying with him a weighty burden of nostalgia and anxiety. Indeed, he had expected that before news of him would reach his loved ones "eternal snow may have swallowed up the traveller." However, the power of his talent was to transform the land of exile into a field for his poetic triumphs.

*Translated by* Ludwik Krzyżanowski

26. Cf. M. Zhivov, *loc. cit.*, p. 29.

## *The Russians on Mickiewicz*

by JOHN N. WASHBURN

POLISH SCHOLARS like Lednicki, Spasowicz, and Tretiak have done outstanding work in clarifying the relationship between Mickiewicz and Pushkin during the first half of the nineteenth century. Poland's interest in Pushkin is indicated by the fact that more translations of the great Russian poet's works have appeared there than in any other country. And, to reverse the process, it is Russia which leads the world in the number of translations of Mickiewicz's literary production. Moreover, Russian scholars have not slackened their efforts to set forth more clearly the role of Mickiewicz in the literary history of Russia.[1]

The numerous Russian translations of Mickiewicz's works and the extent to which his works were reflected in Russian poetry, taken together with the enthusiastic response given by Russian critics and writers to his literary creation, constitute the base upon which the fame of the poet Mickiewicz was built up in Russia. Russian scholars always stress the significance of Mickiewicz as a poet, and devote much less attention to Mickiewicz the man, and to Mickiewicz as an influential political and religious figure.

### THE MAN

There is an amazing unanimity in Russian source material bearing on Mickiewicz the man—he was loved and respected by all cultured

1. D. Blagoi, M. Zhivov, N. Aseyev, and other literary figures in Soviet Russia have given a new impetus in the last decade to the study of Mickiewicz's influence on Russian literature. An example of the work being done is N. Aseyev's article "Perevody iz Adama Mitskevicha" (*Novy Mir,* No. 1–2, 1946, pp. 148–154), showing the influence of *Konrad Wallenrod* on some of Pushkin's lesser known works.

and talented representatives of literature and art in Russian society of the 1820s, a list which extends from the Decembrists K. Ryleyev and A. Bestuzhev and which includes Pushkin, Zhukovsky, Baratynsky, Venevitinov, Sobolevsky, Shevyryov, Kozlov, Griboyedov, Delvig, and many others. Vyazemsky's description of Mickiewicz's personal charm and graciousness is typical: "His whole personality was attractive and aroused sympathy. He was highly educated and well-bred, lively in his conversation and extremely courteous in his deportment. . . . He was at home everywhere, whether in the study of a scholar and writer, in the salon of a distinguished society lady, or at table with a merry company. . . . Only the very few people acquainted with the Polish language could esteem Mickiewicz the poet, but all esteemed and loved Mickiewicz the man."[2] And Ksenofont Polevoi echoes Vyazemsky when he writes that everyone who met Mickiewicz at the Polevoi home came "to love him not as a poet (for very few could read his works), but as a man," being attracted by "his great intellect, fine education, and a kind of open-hearted naïveté and amiability that he alone possessed."[3] Thus Mickiewicz was at first loved as a man, and personal admiration for him tended to increase his popularity as a poet.

One side of Mickiewicz's character which Russian friends admired was the straightforward and vigorous manner in which he stated his opinions on things literary. Ksenofont Polevoi tells how Mickiewicz reacted when someone praised a French critic who had referred disparagingly to the Italian poet Petrarch's poetry. After observing that the Frenchman's article was but an extract from Sismondi, who had judged Petrarch's poetry in a cold and unfavorable light, Mickiewicz came to the defense of that "most affectionate and passionate of poets." He concentrated his remarks on the power and variety

2. M. A. Tsyavlovsky, "Mitskevich i yego russkiye druzya," *Novy Mir,* No. 11–12, 1940, p. 305.

3. Ksenofont Polevoi, "Zapiski o zhizni i sochineniyakh Nikolaya Alekseyevicha Polevogo (1855–1865)," in *Nikolai Polevoi,* redaktsia V. Orlova, Leningrad, 1934, p. 206. Mme Kern also mentions Mickiewicz's graciousness. See "Vospominania A. P. Markovoi-Vinogradskoi (Kern)," in L. N. Maikov, *Pushkin: Biograficheskiye materialy i istoriko-literaturnye ocherki,* St. Petersburg, 1899, p. 254.

in the sonnets of Petrarch and on the inimitable feeling and genuineness in the poet's expressions. After quoting in French some of Petrarch's sonnets, Mickiewicz exclaimed: "If this isn't poetry, then poetry does not exist!"[4] Vyazemsky relates an instance in which Mickiewicz manifested his ready wit and used it with telling effect. "In Moscow someone began to quarrel with him about the spelling of a Polish name: Mokronowski. The Russian declared that it was spelled Mokronoski. Mickiewicz insisted, and perfectly correctly, that it was spelled Mokronowski. 'It is possible,' he added, 'that this name was shortened as a result of a new partition of Poland about which I have not yet heard.'"[5]

The sincere feeling of friendship which bound Mickiewicz and the Russian *literati* during the entire period of his stay in Russia was exemplified by the farewell dinner arranged for him by his Moscow friends in April, 1828. He was presented with a beautiful goblet on which the names of those present were inscribed. Ivan Kireyevsky read a poem he had written for the occasion, and Mickiewicz replied with an improvisation in French. Mickiewicz was deeply moved by this farewell celebration given in his honor.

After Mickiewicz's departure from Russia in 1829 the friendships he had made there did not "wither away," as it were, from lack of personal contact. Years after he left Russia it was learned in Moscow that the Polish poet, then living near Paris, needed funds. Five thousand rubles were collected through the efforts of Khomyakov, and contributors included Khomyakov, Baratynsky, and Shevyryov. Mickiewicz, in tears, gratefully accepted the money sent him by his Russian friends.[6]

An even more striking example of the durability of Mickiewicz's

4. Ksenofont Polevoi, *op. cit.*, p. 210.

5. *Polnoye sobraniye sochinenii Knyazya P. A. Vyazemskago,* Izdaniye S. D. Sheremeteva, St. Petersburg, VII (1882), 327.

6. P. I. Bartenev, who tells this story, says that he got his information from the very person who took the money from Khomyakov to deliver it to Mickiewicz in France. See *Russky Arkhiv,* 1874, Book 2, pp. 223–224. Among the articles in which this story is included are: W. Lednicki, "Mickiewicz en Russie," *Revue de l'Université de Bruxelles,* No. 3, 1929, pp. 330–331; and M. A. Tsyavlovsky, *op. cit.*, p. 315.

friendship with individual Russians involves M. P. Pogodin. Upon learning of the death of Mickiewicz he drew up a four-paragraph letter to the Tsar, urging that financial assistance be given regularly, yet in an unofficial way, to the widow and children of "our famous enemy, the poet and favorite son of the whole Polish people." [7] That Pogodin's daring suggestion was composed in good faith and in a spirit of magnanimity is not to be doubted.

### THE POLITICAL AND RELIGIOUS FIGURE

"Mickiewicz, like Byron, like Pushkin, could not be an active political figure. He was both above and below that role." [8] This statement by Vyazemsky is based on his conviction that the three above-mentioned poets, once they left the soil native to them and on which they were recognized as masters, became "on the foreign scene pawns and slaves of often petty and self-seeking politicians or impresarios." [9] Vyazemsky also wrote about the effects of Mickiewicz's aberration into mysticism under the influence of Towiański. As a result, states Vyazemsky, Mickiewicz "created a dreamy and (however painful it is to admit) nonsensical teaching about some sort of Napoleonic Messianism." [10] In his comments on the necrology of Pushkin written by Mickiewicz for the Paris newspaper *Le Globe,* issue of May 25, 1837, Vyazemsky noted various places in the text where the Polish poet had interpreted Pushkin erroneously, and attributed these errors to Mickiewicz's Messianic concepts.[11]

V. G. Belinsky, engaged on the side of the *Sovremennik* in that journal's polemic against *Moskvityanin,* the organ of the Slavophiles, wrote an article in which he flatly rejected the contention that all Europe was terribly concerned with the Slavic question. This article, published in 1847, was mutilated by censorship and a passage dealing with Mickiewicz's role in connection with the Slavic question in

7. Nikolai Barsukov, *Zhizn i trudy M. P. Pogodina,* St. Petersburg, Book XIV, 1900, p. 448.
8. *Polnoye sobraniye sochinenii Knyazya P. A. Vyazemskago,* Izdaniye S. D. Sheremeteva, St. Petersburg, VII (1882), 307.
9. *Ibid.,* p. 307.
10. *Ibid.,* p. 308.
11. *Ibid.,* pp. 315 ff.

Europe was deleted. Belinsky had written that Mickiewicz's "really eloquent though also scatter-brained voice" had drawn attention to himself but had aroused no interest in the Slavic question. Belinsky brought in the figure of Towiański in his concluding remarks about Poland's great poet: "Mickiewicz believed in this charlatan, which proves that he had a passionate and enthusiastic nature, and an imagination that was fervent and inclined toward mysticism, but a weak head." [12]

The Russian Slavophile Khomyakov represents a diametrically opposed view to that of Belinsky on the question of Mickiewicz's political and religious activities during this period of his life. Khomyakov's fraternal feeling for the Polish people and his desire to build a bridge over the deep chasm that separated the Poles from the Russians enabled him to find common ground with Mickiewicz on matters such as moral regeneration of the world and religion's fundamental role in life. Mickiewicz in a lecture given at the Collège de France in January, 1843, praised one of Khomyakov's poems very highly, declaring that the Russian poet had "embraced all mankind in his verses." [13] And it was Khomyakov who, in 1843, at a time when the very name of Mickiewicz was forbidden in Russia, proposed a toast to "the great Slavic poet who is not present" at a public dinner given in honor of Granovsky.

Alexander Herzen's diary contains several references to the Slavophile tendencies of Mickiewicz. In the entry of February 12, 1844, he refers to the lectures of Mickiewicz at the Collège de France as follows: "Mickiewicz is a Slavophile, like Khomyakov and Co., with the sole difference that he is a Pole and not a Russian, that he lives in Europe and not in Moscow, that he talks not about Rus alone but also about Czechs, Illyrians, etc." [14] About a month later, having finished reading these lectures of Mickiewicz, he notes in his diary: "There is much that is beautiful, much that is prophetic, but he is far from a solution to the riddle; on the contrary, it is sad to see on

12. *V. G. Belinsky,* Vol. III, Stati i retsenzii: 1843–1848, Moscow, Goslitizdat, 1948, p. 760.
13. Andrei Sirotinin, *Rossia i slavyanye,* St. Petersburg, 1913, p. 77.
14. *Sochinenia A. I. Gertsena,* Izdaniye F. Pavlenkova, St. Petersburg, 1905, VI, 105.

what he bases hope for Poland and the Slavic world. . . . No, not Catholicism will save the Slavic world and will call it to life, and (the truth forces me to admit this) not the Poles will capture the future. . . . Poland will be saved apart from Messianism and *Pan-ism.*" [15]

Herzen met Mickiewicz for the first time at a dinner held in Paris at the home of the Polish writer Chojecki on February 24, 1849. The dinner was to usher in the official beginning of the new paper *La Tribune des Peuples.* The carefully laid plans of the host were disrupted when the paper's editor-in-chief, Adam Mickiewicz, in a short speech dealing with the future policy of *La Tribune des Peuples,* digressed so far into the Napoleonic aspect of his Messianic beliefs that Herzen became very angry and sullen. The lack of unity among the members of the editorial board was made plainly evident at this inauspicious inaugural meeting, and Herzen's prejudices against Polish Messianism as interpreted by Towiański and Mickiewicz became even more deep-rooted.

Another famous Russian exile in Western Europe during the middle of the nineteenth century—Bakunin—also came into contact with Mickiewicz. In the period from 1844 to 1846 he made the acquaintance of both Lelewel and Mickiewicz. In his autobiographical *Ispoved* (Confession) he writes as follows: "I also occasionally saw Mickiewicz, whom in the past I respected as a great Slavic poet, but for whom I was sorry at the present time, as a half-duped and half-deceiving apostle and prophet of a new nonsensical religion and a new Messiah. Mickiewicz tried to convert me . . . but he was unable to." [16]

Of the Russians who met Mickiewicz personally in the period

15. *Ibid.,* p. 112. The preponderant political, economic, and social position of the Polish nobility (*szlachta*), together with the frame of mind and attitude of the *szlachta* that derived from possession of such extensive influence in Polish affairs, is what Herzen has in mind when employing the word "Pan-ism," which he has fabricated by adding a suffix to the genuine Polish word "Pan" meaning Sir, gentleman, master.

16. *Materialy dlya biografii M. Bakunina,* redaktsia Vyacheslava Polonskogo, Vol. I (Gosudarstvennoye Izdatelstvo, Moscow-Petrograd, 1923), p. 118. It must be remembered that *Ispoved* was written while its author was incarcerated in Petropavlovsk prison in 1851.

1840–1850 the least-known figure is probably Fyodor Vasilevich Chizhov.[17] Chizhov's memoirs reveal the close bonds of friendship that existed between Mickiewicz and himself during the summer of 1844 in Paris.[18] In June and July of 1844 they had frequent meetings and talks, their Slavophilism constituting the basis for mutual respect and sincere affection. Chizhov thought so highly of his Polish confrere that late in June, 1844, he wrote Mickiewicz a letter in which he said that always upon leaving his presence he felt sad and hence requested Mickiewicz to indicate to him "the path of purification." [19] There is no doubt whatsoever that Mickiewicz, on his part, also thought a great deal of Chizhov. One letter to him, written early in July, 1844, begins as follows: "Mon cher Monsieur. Vous êtes de ceux à qui il m'est permis de parler de la vérité sans detour, ni ménagement. Les hommes de cette sorte sont encore peu nombreux. C'est une consolation pour moi d'en rencontrer un seul." [20]

Mickiewicz's Messianism and his views on the role of Napoleon and of France in the struggle for the freedom of Poland are mentioned in several places in Chizhov's memoirs; what impressed him most when Mickiewicz expounded on such subjects was his "ardor and the purity of this ardor." [21] Chizhov states that his own convictions differ from those of Mickiewicz and considers certain views of the Polish poet to be erroneous; and yet he believes that there is

17. F. V. Chizhov (1811–1877) began his career as a mathematics professor in St. Petersburg, became interested in art and literature during the period 1832–1840, and, after abandoning the teaching profession in 1840, traveled for several years throughout Europe (including the Balkans) studying the history of art. Returning to Russia he was arrested because views he had expressed abroad and his activities in *émigré* circles had made the Tsarist government suspicious of him. Released shortly thereafter he embarked on a career as industrialist, banker, financier!

18. The material on F. V. Chizhov's relationship to Mickiewicz is to be found in the article "Wspomnienia Czyżowa o Mickiewiczu," in Samuel Fiszman's recent work *Mickiewicz w Rosji,* Państwowy Instytut Wydawniczy, Warsaw, 1949, pp. 75–92. Chizhov saw Mickiewicz for the first time at the Collège de France, where he attended Mickiewicz's last lecture, on May 28, 1844.

19. Samuel Fiszman, *op. cit.,* p. 86.

20. *Ibid.,* p. 89.

21. *Ibid.,* p. 90.

something infallible in this man.[22] In the "lofty, holy purity" of Mickiewicz's soul Chizhov found refuge in times of bitterness and despondency; it was a "sanctuary to which he came to pray" while in Paris.[23]

One of Mickiewicz's Moscow friends, M. P. Pogodin, tried continually to persuade the Polish people and their leading representatives to forget the past and to put themselves under the protection of the Russian Tsar. Back in June, 1839, Pogodin came to Paris and paid the Polish poet a visit. In describing the visit, he reveals his own feelings at that time in the following passage: "Oh! How I would have liked to throw myself on his neck and to tell him to deliver himself up to the magnanimity of the Russian Sovereign. . . ." [24] It should be noted that the appeals Pogodin made to the Poles many years later, during the 1850s and 1860s, often contained the following phrases: "As one close to Mickiewicz as far back as 1828, and on friendly scholarly relations with Lelewel from the year 1824, I ask you to receive my words affectionately." [25]

How is the Russian opinion of Mickiewicz the political and religious figure to be reconciled with his reputation as a poet among the Russians? Vyazemsky has given perhaps the most satisfying answer to this question. Declaring that Mickiewicz remains a brother to all cultured members of the human family, he adds: "Politics is usually a disuniting force: poetry must be always a reconciling and consolidating force. The political prejudices, rancors and sympathies of Mickiewicz died with him: for us they are of no concern. But that which was created by the inner spirit and talent of the poet outlives the endeavors of the one-sided and alarming activity of Mickiewicz the exile." [26]

22. *Ibid.*, p. 92.
23. *Ibid.*
24. Nikolai Barsukov, *op. cit.*, Book V, 1892, p. 279.
25. *Ibid.*, Book XVIII, 1904, p. 111.
26. *Polnoye sobraniye sochinenii Knyazya P. A. Vyazemskago*, Izdaniye S. D. Sheremeteva, St. Petersburg, VII (1882), 306–307. The Russian sources cited in this section of the article may give the mistaken impression that Mickiewicz was simply a mystical dreamer, reduced to a state of passive inactivity and fettered by his own Messianic beliefs. It should not be forgotten, however, that

## THE POET

The clearest indication of the high esteem in which Mickiewicz has been and is still held by Russian poets is the list of those who have translated his works, a list crowned by Pushkin and Lermontov. Russians have been translating Mickiewicz for more than 125 years, and, during that lengthy period, virtually every Russian poet has directly or indirectly come into contact with his literary creation.

The Decembrists K. Ryleyev and A. Bestuzhev were among the first Russian friends of Mickiewicz. Their friendship, which began in November–December, 1824, was undoubtedly based on literary and poetic interests primarily, but kindred views on ideological and political matters also played an important role.[27] An indication of the high regard in which the budding poet Mickiewicz was held by Ryleyev and Bestuzhev is to be found in their letters written in January, 1825, to the poet V. I. Tumansky, then living in Odessa.[28] Ryleyev wrote: "Love Mickiewicz and his friends Malewski and Jeżowski: they are fine fellows. Moreover, in feeling and pattern of thought they are already our friends, and Mickiewicz is, in addition, a poet—'the favorite of his people.' " And Bestuzhev wrote: "I recommend to you Mickiewicz, Malewski and Jeżowski. You know the first one by name, and I vouch for his soul and talent." Mickiewicz retained fond memories of his friendship with Ryleyev and Bestuzhev. The tribute he pays them in the poem *"To My Russian Friends"* in *Forefathers' Eve,* Part III, is evidence of this.

---

Mickiewicz's work in the field of politics and religion also had a positive and practical aspect, as exemplified by his role as a leader and organizer of Polish legions in Italy (1848) and in Turkey (1855).

27. Not only did Ryleyev and Bestuzhev know the Polish language, but they were also well versed in Polish literature and each had started translating Polish literary works before they made Mickiewicz's personal acquaintance. See Mark Zhivov's article "Poezia Mitskevicha v perevodakh i otklikakh russkikh pisatelei," in *Adam Mitskevich: Izbrannoye,* pod redaktsiyei M. F. Rylskogo i B. A. Turganova, Goslitizdat, Moscow, 1946, p. 14.

28. For the text of the Ryleyev and Bestuzhev letters to Tumansky, both of which were written on one and the same sheet of letter-paper, see the short article "Tumansky i Mitskevich," in *Kievskaya Starina,* LXIV (Kiev, March, 1899), 299–300.

P. A. Vyazemsky and Nikolai Polevoi, editor of the *Moskovsky Telegraf,* helped to interest the Russian public in the poetry of Mickiewicz.[29] In his editorial footnote to an article on Polish poetry translated from a Warsaw journal Polevoi stressed the deplorable fact that "Polish literature is almost completely unknown in Russia," and expressed the hope that Russian readers would in this article make the acquaintance of Poland's new poets, especially Mickiewicz "whom all Poland is reading with delight and who . . . deserves European renown for his powerful, fervent poetry."[30] Reviewing Mickiewicz's *Sonnets,* published in Moscow in 1826, Vyazemsky also bewailed Russian ignorance of Polish literature and urged that a Polish-Russian literary rapprochement be effected.[31] The very warm welcome he accorded the *Sonnets* in this review set the tone for their reception by Russia's literary society. Vyazemsky began his review as follows: "Here is an unusual and satisfying phenomenon. An exquisite work of foreign poetry, the work of one of the foremost poets of Poland. . . . It may be positively asserted that the place of honor in the generation of poets contemporary with us belongs to him." Vyazemsky lauds not only "the powerful and vivid poetic feeling" which is ever present in these sonnets, but also Mickiewicz's ability "to insert within the limited framework of the sonnet pictures in all the fullness of their diverse and often gigantic beauty." In the conclusion of the article Vyazemsky presents a Russian translation (by the poet Dmitriev) of one of Mickiewicz's *Crimean Sonnets* and then expresses the hope that this effort on the part of Dmitriyev "will stimulate competition among our foremost young poets also, and that Pushkin and Baratynsky will consecrate by their names the desired friendship between the Russian and Polish Muses."

E. A. Baratynsky greatly admired Mickiewicz. When hostile articles appeared in Warsaw criticizing the *Crimean Sonnets,* the

29. This was in line with the general policy of the *Moskovsky Telegraf,* which rendered great service to the cause of Russian enlightenment by its practice of informing the reading public of outstanding successes of European literatures.

30. *Moskovsky Telegraf,* 1826, Chast X, Otdeleniye pervoye, pp. 183–184.
31. *Ibid.,* 1827, Chast XIV, Otdeleniye pervoye, pp. 191–222.

irritated Baratynsky wrote a poem entitled "K . . ." ("To . . ."), which was printed in the *Moskovsky Telegraf* early in 1827. The first four lines of this poem were:

> Do not fear caustic condemnations,
> But rapturous compliments:
> Often in their fumes a powerful genius
> Has fallen into the sleep of enfeeblement.[32]

In 1828, having become a close friend of Mickiewicz while the Polish poet was in Moscow, Baratynsky wrote a poem which shows how highly he valued the talent of the author of *Konrad Wallenrod* and the *Crimean Sonnets.* This poem, first published in 1829, ends with the following tribute:

> When thee, inspired Mickiewicz,
> I find at Byron's feet,
> I think: humble worshipper,
> Arise, arise and remember: thou art thyself god.[33]

Pushkin's respect for the poetic gifts of Mickiewicz was deep and sincere. Ksenofont Polevoi relates that Pushkin, usually the dominant figure in Russian literary circles of his time, was very modest in Mickiewicz's presence, made the latter speak more than he spoke himself, and turned to him with his opinions as if wishing the Polish poet's approval.[34] In 1828, when both Mickiewicz and Pushkin were living in the same place in St. Petersburg, K. Polevoi and Pushkin started talking about Mickiewicz. Among other things Pushkin told him the following anecdote: "Recently Zhukovsky said to me, 'You know, don't you, brother, that he is sure to eclipse you.' 'Don't say it that way,' I replied; 'he already has eclipsed me.' "[35]

32. M. A. Tsyavlovsky, *op. cit.,* pp. 306–307. Tsyavlovsky does not doubt that this poem was dedicated to Mickiewicz, whereas M. L. Gofman, who edited *Polnoye sobraniye sochinenii E. A. Baratynskago* (St. Petersburg, 1914), is not positively sure of this. W. Lednicki is of the same opinion as Gofman; see *Przyjaciele Moskale,* Cracow, 1935, pp. 223 ff.
33. M. L. Gofman, *op. cit.,* I, 104.
34. Because of the unfriendly relationship that existed between Pushkin and the Polevoi brothers their statements must be accepted with reservation. See W. Lednicki, *Przyjaciele Moskale,* p. 171, note 7, and p. 203.
35. Ksenofont Polevoi, *op. cit.,* p. 207.

The Pushkin-Mickiewicz poetical union is exemplified by their translations of one another's works. In 1833 Pushkin translated two of Mickiewicz's ballads, and Mickiewicz, before he left Russia in 1829, translated Pushkin's poem "Vospominaniye" ("Reminiscence"). The genetic ties between the poetry of Pushkin and Mickiewicz, together with the competitive and polemical elements contained therein, distinguish Pushkin's *Poltava* and "Gasub" and Mickiewicz's *Konrad Wallenrod,* and also Pushkin's "Bronze Horseman" and Mickiewicz's cycle of poems comprising "The Digression" in *Forefathers' Eve,* Part III.

The Polish Insurrection of 1830–1831 brought on Pushkin's trilogy of anti-Polish poems, but such chauvinistic poems did not impair his respect for Mickiewicz's genius as a poet.[36] Evidence of this is the short poem Pushkin wrote in the summer of 1834, which has become the most famous Russian poem about Mickiewicz. It reads as follows:

He lived among us, amid a people alien to him; in his soul he harbored no malice toward us; and we loved him. Gentle, kindhearted, he attended our discussions. We shared with him both pure dreams and songs (he was inspired from above and from on high he gazed on life). Often he spoke of future times when nations, having forgotten their discords, would unite in a great family. Eagerly we listened to the poet. He departed for the West, and our blessings accompanied him. But now our gentle guest has become our enemy—and he, in order to please the turbulent rabble, imbues his verses with venom. The voice of the spiteful poet reaches us from afar, familiar voice! . . . Oh God, illumine his heart with thy truth and restore peace to his soul.[37]

Mickiewicz's own poetic image of the relationship between Pushkin and himself is that which appears in the following lines of the poem "Pomnik Piotra Wielkiego," in *Forefathers' Eve,* Part III:

36. The best work in connection with Pushkin's anti-Polish trilogy is that by W. Lednicki, *Pouchkine et la Pologne,* Librairie Ernest Leroux, Paris, 1928. The trilogy is comprised of the following poems: the odes "To the Calumniators of Russia" and "The Anniversary of Borodino," and the poem beginning "Before the sacred tomb."

37. *A. S. Pushkin—Polnoye sobraniye sochinenii,* pod redaktsiyei Yu.G. Oksmana i M. A. Tsyavlovskogo, Vol. II (Academia, Moscow-Leningrad, 1936), p. 78.

Though their acquaintance was of short duration,
Already they are tied in friendship close.
Their souls soared high o'er earthly obstacles;
Like kindred peaks atop the granite Alps,
Though cleft forever by a surging stream,
They scarcely hear the hostile element,
Each to the other his lofty summit bending.[38]

Not only Mickiewicz's published works but also his improvisations won him fame in Russia. His amazing ability to improvise poetry is described in reverential terms by the Russians who were present at dinner parties and soirées in Moscow and St. Petersburg, where Mickiewicz demonstrated his genius at oral creation on any given theme. Perhaps Vyazemsky, who once wrote of his own poetry that it was "improvisation in fits and starts," is the best man to quote in order to obtain a full appreciation of Mickiewicz's talent as an improviser. Writes Vyazemsky: "His improvised poem freely and rapidly gushed from his lips in a sonorous and sparkling torrent. In his improvisations there were thought, feeling, images and expressions poetic in the highest degree. One would have thought that he was in inspired fashion delivering from memory a poem he had already written." [39] Vyazemsky tells of an improvisation by Mickiewicz so brilliantly done that those present, including Pushkin and Zhukovsky, were enthralled by the "fiery outburst of poetry," even though it had been given not in the poet's native tongue, but in French, and in prose besides! [40]

Many Russians prominent in the literary milieu of Moscow and St. Petersburg during the first half of the nineteenth century ranked Mickiewicz among the world's foremost poets. Ivan Kireyevsky, in his article "Survey of Russian Literature for 1829," declares: "Mickiewicz, having concentrated in himself the spirit of his people, first gave Polish poetry the right to possess a voice of its own among the intellectual spokesmen of Europe, and also gave it the opportunity

38. *Adam Mickiewicz—Dzieła,* Wydanie narodowe, Vol. III ("Czytelnik," Cracow, 1948), p. 281.

39. *Polnoye sobraniye sochinenii Knyazya P. A. Vyazemskago* (Izdaniye S. D. Sheremeteva, St. Petersburg, 1882), VII, 328–329.

40. *Ibid.,* p. 329.

of influencing our poetry as well."[41] V. G. Belinsky, writing ten years after the appearance of Kireyevsky's article, takes note of the high development attained by poetry in the nineteenth century and lists its great poets: "Byron, Walter Scott, Cooper, Thomas Moore, Wordsworth, Pushkin, Gogol, Mickiewicz, Heine, Beranger . . . and others."[42]

Perhaps the most striking statement as to the greatness of the Polish poet in comparison with other poets of his time is that made by his Russian friend Nikolai Polevoi in March, 1829. Reviewing the new edition of Mickiewicz's poetry which had just been published in St. Petersburg, Polevoi, having listed the poet's creations included therein, exclaims: "These are Mickiewicz's claims to fame, great claims if one compares his works with the works of other contemporary poets. We should be proud that Mickiewicz is not only the *first* poet of Poland but also, now that Goethe is silent and Byron is no more, perhaps the *first* among poets now living. *Wallenrod, Forefathers, Sonnets, Farys* are products of a creative imagination which cannot be equalled by any poet of England, Germany, France and Italy now living."[43]

In the following epochs of Russian literary history Mickiewicz's stature as a poet of world renown was unreservedly accepted by poets, prose writers, critics, and other famous Russians. Gogol, Herzen, Ogaryov, Dobrolyubov, Chernyshevsky, Leskov, Korolenko, Saltykov-Shchedrin, Leo Tolstoy, Bryusov, Bunin, Balmont, and other major Russian figures manifested a high regard for the poetry of Mickiewicz.

In 1856 the eminent critic Apollon Grigoryev, while commenting on Byronism, twice affirms that Pushkin, Mickiewicz, and Byron were equally great poets. In the case of Grigoryev equating Mickiewicz with Byron and Pushkin had more than ordinary significance,

41. *Polnoye sobraniye sochinenii I. V. Kireyevskago* (redaktsia M. Gershensona, Moscow, 1911), II, 35.

42. V. G. Belinsky, *Stati i retsenzii: 1834–1841* (Moscow, Goslitizdat, 1948), I, 465.

43. *Moskovsky Telegraf,* No. 6 (March, 1829), pp. 199–200. The review quoted from was unsigned, hence it is logical and natural to assume that the editor of the journal was its author.

for of Pushkin he once had said: "Pushkin—nashe vsyo" ("Pushkin is our everything").

Vladimir Solovyov, a penetrating literary critic in his own right, wrote an article in 1899 in which he made some cogent remarks about Pushkin, Byron, and Mickiewicz—"by the grace of God poets of genius." Singling out the "religious loftiness" of Mickiewicz, he declared that the Polish poet was "greater than Pushkin by the depth of his religious feeling, by the seriousness of his moral demands on personal and national life, by the loftiness of his mystical notions."[44] But Solovyov also saw the detrimental effect which the central feature of Mickiewicz's personality—"religious mysticism"—had on his poetry. "The dominating tendency of Mickiewicz was lofty and beautiful; but when it obtrudes too clearly in his poetry it destroys its beauty; and surely *Pan Tadeusz* is justly recognized to be the very best, if not the most characteristic production of Mickiewicz, because of the fact that here the poet hardly ever moves away from his purely poetical task."[45]

Two of the most important figures in Soviet Russian literature—A. V. Lunacharsky and A. M. Gorky—have expressed an opinion about Mickiewicz. Lunacharsky had this to say about Mickiewicz in 1929: "He belongs to the small group of Polish writers who have entered into the pantheon of world literature, and, moreover, he occupies a very honorable place in this pantheon. It is already essential to make the acquaintance of Mickiewicz's works because he is in full measure a world classic. . . . Adam Mickiewicz is one of the revolutionary poets. . . . The combination in one person of the poet of world significance and the revolutionary poet is rarely encountered."[46] A. M. Gorky, the father of Soviet Russian literature, indicated the significance of Mickiewicz in a picturesque way in the following short passage: "Every man strong in heart constitutes, as it were, a tightly rolled-up scroll, containing in writing the impres-

44. *Sobraniye sochinenii Vladimira Sergeyevicha Solovyova,* pod redaktsiyei S. M. Solovyova i E. L. Radlova, Vtoroye izdaniye, Vol. IX (1897–1900), St. Petersburg, 1913, p. 297.
45. *Ibid.,* p. 298.
46. Cited in Mark Zhivov, *op. cit.,* p. 44.

sions of the historical life of his nation and his forebears. Under fortunate circumstances this scroll, being unrolled, enriches us with joyous phenomena such as Shevchenko, Pushkin, Mickiewicz—men who embody the spirit of their people with the greatest beauty, power and completeness." [47]

Vladimir Solovyov perhaps best epitomized Mickiewicz's nature in a speech that he delivered on December 27, 1898, at a dinner in honor of the Polish poet. His concluding words on this occasion were: "He was truly a great man and could gaze upon life from on high, because life raised him up. Grave ordeals did not crush, did not weaken, did not lay waste his soul. The wrecking of his personal happiness did not leave him as a disenchanted misanthrope and pessimist; the wrecking of national happiness did not change him into an indifferent cosmopolite; and the struggle for inner religious conviction against external authority did not make him an enemy of the church. He is great because of the fact that, rising to new levels of moral loftiness, he carried with him to these heights not proud and vain negation, but love of that above which he was rising." [48]

## *The Origin of Pushkin's Poem about Mickiewicz*

## *A New Hypothesis*

by Marian Jakóbiec

The November insurrection of 1830 exerted a powerful influence on the further development of Pushkin's attitude toward Poland and her affairs. From that time on Poland becomes an important national, political, and, above all, cultural problem for him. On the one hand,

47. *Ibid.*, p. 44.
48. *Sobraniye sochinenii Vladimira Sergeyevicha Solovyova*, p. 264.

his intimate acquaintance and friendship with Mickiewicz, who had revealed to him hitherto almost unknown areas of Polish culture and the progressive ideology of a nation so far known to him from a different aspect, and on the other, the Poles' stand in the struggle for freedom, make him look upon these matters, so important for a Russian patriot, in a different light. The poet buys new books dealing with Polish history. He reads the history of Poland by Fletcher which had just been published in Paris (1832), and familiarizes himself with works on Poland by Claude Rulhière, Salvandy, Schnitzler, Solignac. Finally, he seems to have studied the Polish language very intensively. He listens intently to Polish echoes in the West after the defeat of the Insurrection. At that time, on August 22, 1833, Sergei Sobolevsky returned from abroad. He had just spent a few months in Italy and France. From there he probably brought plenty of news about the political sentiment among the Polish *émigrés* and about Mickiewicz. Indeed, he had in Rome helped the Polish poet depart for Poland, then enveloped by the flames of war. He had even taken care of him during the first half of the journey.[1] He knew in detail the poet's every step and the patriotic sentiments of his environment. He was the first to bring to Russia news about *The Books of the Polish Nation and of the Polish Pilgrims*. For Pushkin he brought a valuable gift: the four-volume Paris edition of the works of their mutual friend.[2] These books have been preserved in Pushkin's library to this day. On the fourth volume is to be seen the donor's humorous dedication: "To A. S. Pushkin, for diligence, success, and good behavior, S. Sobolevsky." In addition to *Forefathers' Eve,* Part III, Pushkin found in that volume "The Digression" ("The Road to Russia," "The Suburbs of the Capital," "St. Petersburg," "The Monument of Peter the Great," "Review of the Troops," "Oleszkiewicz") and finally the dedication of these poems—"To My Russian Friends" —in short, everything that directly defined Mickiewicz's attitude toward Russia.[3]

1. A. K. Vinogradov, *Mérimée v pismakh k Sobolevskomu,* Moscow, 1928, p. 201.
2. *Poezye Adama Mickiewicza,* Paris, 1828–1832, Vols. I–IV.
3. This group of poems depicts various aspects of Russian scenery and life.

Pushkin apparently had no time to read these poems immediately. Three weeks after Sobolevsky's return to St. Petersburg he went on a long journey to Orenburg province to collect material concerning the history of the Pugachev revolt. He took the slender volumes with him. On his return trip he stopped at his father's family estate in the village of Boldino near Nizhni Novgorod. He spent the time from October 1 to the middle of November, 1833, in feverish work.

In Pushkin's biography, that fall may without exaggeration be called the Polish autumn. In the remote solitude he started to read the inspired and pain-saturated poems of his Polish friend. It is hard to say what induced him to transcribe the Polish text of poems included in "The Digression" into his work copybook. Was it indeed, as Russian and Polish Pushkin scholars suppose, the intention to translate them? This does not seem very probable. In the notebook, published fifteen years ago by M. A. Tsyavlovsky,[4] Pushkin copied the following texts: "Z Mitskevicha" [sic]; "Oleszkiewicz. The Day before the Petersburg Flood of 1824" in its entirety (144 lines!); "To My Russian Friends" (in its entirety, 36 lines); and from the beginning of "The Monument of Peter the Great" (31 lines). In a careful, extremely legible hand he put down word after word in a language he knew only from having heard it. He systematically wrote *l* instead of the letter *ł*, *c* often instead of *z*, *i* occasionally instead of *y*, *ź* instead of *ż*, and so on. Finally, he very often makes mistakes by confusing Russian and Polish characters and using *b* instead of *w*, *y* instead of *u*, even *Л* instead of *L*. As Tsyavlovsky rightly observed, Pushkin showed by these mistakes that he took over the Polish language through the intermediary of the Russian, succumbing to their mutual resemblance: he writes *kriknall* for *krzyknął*, *razumial* for *rozumiał*, *otkryta* for *odkryta*, and so on. On the other hand, he also yielded to the suggestive influence of the

Epic description is mingled with sharp satirical elements directed against official Russia, the Tsar, the bureaucracy, despotism, and oppression. On the other hand, warm and sympathetic words are devoted to Russian revolutionaries who are praised also in "To My Russian Friends." Pushkin appears in the poem "The Monument of Peter the Great" as the Polish poet's intimate friend and sharing his views. [Ed.]

4. *Rukoyu Pushkina*, Moscow-Leningrad, 1935, pp. 535–552.

French language. In any case, the analysis of the mistakes made by Pushkin in transcribing "The Digression" attests that passively, from hearing it, Polish was not unfamiliar to him, and that he read it, if not correctly, at any rate with some understanding. Thus it is difficult not to share the opinion of the Soviet scholar that Sękowski, the best authority on this question, was right when he wrote in a biographical sketch of the poet [5] that Pushkin "as a grown-up, learned Polish only to such a degree as was indispensable for the reading of the great models of poetry and literature." Nor is there any doubt that he knew that language to a greater extent than was thought by the poet's father, who maintained that he understood the Polish language only as it is understood by Russians in general.

Consequently, Pushkin did not transcribe excerpts from "The Digression" in order to translate them. As will appear later, he understood them as a bitter reproach directed against himself and his patriotic environment. If he conceived any poetical intention with regard to these poems, it was only the plan of a reply, a plan carried out very quickly and on a level worthy of Mickiewicz's criticism. Tsyavlovsky's [6] arguments notwithstanding, a poetic translation of those poems was not necessary either to Pushkin himself or to the Russian reader. He transcribed the Polish text simply in order to understand it better and more accurately. He selected the passages which interested him most for personal and creative reasons: "Oleszkiewicz" attracted him because of the description of the St. Petersburg flood which soon he was to describe himself; the poem "To My Russian Friends" directly concerned his closest Decembrist friends; and purely personal allusions to himself induced him to copy the beginning of "The Monument of Peter the Great." It can hardly be supposed that he used auxiliary books in familiarizing himself with the Polish text. He actually had in his library [7] all four volumes of S. B. Linde's *Dictionary of the Polish Language,* three dictionaries

5. *Portretnaya i biograficheskaya gallereya slovesnosti, khudozhestv i isskustv v Rossii,* Vol. I (*Pushkin i Bryullov*), St. Petersburg, 1841.
6. *Rukoyu Pushkina.*
7. B. Modzalevsky, *Biblioteka A. S. Pushkina,* Bibliograficheskoye opisaniye, Pushkin i yego sovremenniki, Materialy i izsledovania, Vypusk IX–X, St. Petersburg, 1910.

by Michal Abraham Trotz (Polish-German, Polish-French and French-Polish), a Polish *Grammar for the Second Grade of the National Schools,* published in Cracow in 1794, and finally *Theoretisch-praktische Grammatik der polnischen Sprache mit Übungsaufgaben, Gesprächen, Titulaturen und den zum Sprechen nötigsten Wörtern,* von Karl Pohl, Lehrer der polnischen Sprache am königl. Friedrichs-Gimnasium zu Breslau, Breslau, bei Wilhelm Gottlieb Korn, 1829. He probably did not take them on the long trip to the Urals.

Nevertheless, at Boldino he started to translate Mickiewicz, not "The Digression" however, but poems incomparably easier, namely "The Three Budrys" and "The Ambush." [8] The manuscripts of both translations bear the date of October 28, 1833. He rendered the former with almost exemplary accuracy, and the latter poem is a free adaptation. He published them within a short time, as early as March, 1834, in the periodical *Biblioteka dlya chtenia.* He provided "The Three Budrys" with the significant subtitle: "A Lithuanian Ballad—From M—cz." At that time it was dangerous to mention or write the name of Mickiewicz in Russia. But this cryptogram was deciphered without difficulty not only by his Russian friends but also by the reading public.

During this fertile Boldino autumn Pushkin replied to Mickiewicz's *Forefathers' Eve* and "The Digression" with the most beautiful and most profound poem that he ever wrote—"The Bronze Horseman." He worked on it between October 6 and October 31, that is, simultaneously with the translations of "The Three Budrys" and "The Ambush." [9] After a long discussion that has been going on for a century about this enigmatic work, in which on the Russian side such outstanding scholars and literary critics as Vissarion Belinsky, Shevyryov, Eichenvald, Ovsyaniko-Kulikovsky, Ivanov-Razumnik, Lunacharsky, Blagoi, and on the Polish side Włodzimierz Spasowicz, Józef Tretiak, Aleksander Brückner and Wacław Lednicki participated, one thing may be stated: apart from its patriotic

8. See the French translation of both poems by Paul Cazin, pp. 214–219 of this publication. [Ed.]

9. Pushkin, *Sochinenia,* Redaktsia, biograficheskу ocherk i primechania B. Tomashevskogo, Leningrad, 1936, p. 830.

and revolutionary content "The Bronze Horseman" was a reply to Mickiewicz's "Digression." It was perhaps the conclusion of the discussions which he had once had with his Polish friend in St. Petersburg "having clasped each other's hand under one cloak." [10]

In the second half of November, 1833, Pushkin returned to St. Petersburg. He was preoccupied with historical studies and the busy, enervating life in very close contact with the imperial court; he had worries about material existence and was in a state of constant anxiety about the good name of his wife. In the summer of 1834 he again turned his mind to Mickiewicz. He writes a poem devoted to the Polish poet. Judging from the preserved rough drafts he worked on it feverishly as if struck by some poetic enunciation of his. One of the redactions of the text bears the date of August 10, 1834. This poem, today universally known, translated and commented upon, bears the simple title "Mitskevich" or is designated by its initial words: "On mezhdu nami zhil (He lived among us)." [11] It was neither completed nor published in the poet's lifetime. It is broken off in the middle of a sentence. It was published only in 1841 by Zhukovsky in Volume XI of the posthumous edition of Pushkin's works in a form which at once raised doubts as to the authenticity of its text. Therefore, it is not surprising that the rough drafts of the poem preserved to this day were the object of most thorough research and of various interpretations. These manuscript materials were first published in 1924 by the well-known Pushkin scholar M. L. Hofman in the Paris almanac *Okno*. On the basis of photostatic copies of the texts Wacław Lednicki also studied them extensively.[12] The Soviet Pushkin scholar M. Tsyavlovsky once again turned his attention to these rough drafts, examined and read them in their entirety, established the final text of the poem, and in 1939 published, together with facsimiles, an interesting study about them.[13]

10. Quotation from Mickiewicz's poem "The Monument of Peter the Great." [Ed.]

11. See the translation of the whole poem on p. 155 of this book. [Ed.]

12. *Aleksander Puszkin, Studia,* Cracow, 1926, pp. 162–212; "Z historii poetyckiej przyjaźni, I: Wiersz Puszkina do Mickiewicza."

13. *Rukopisi Pushkina,* Fototipicheskoye izdaniye, Albom 1833–1835 g., Tetrad

For the time being we are not interested in the variant texts of the poem or in the problem of the retouching made by the original editor, V. Zhukovsky. Tsyavlovsky, contrary to the opinion of Hofman and Lednicki, believes that Zhukovsky introduced no changes himself, but that he had in his hands still another variant of the text unknown to us today.

Let us consider the last words of the poem:

> . . . But now our gentle guest has become our enemy—and he, in order to please the turbulent rabble, imbues his verses with venom. The voice of the spiteful poet reaches us from afar, familiar voice! . . . Oh God, illumine his heart with thy truth and restore peace to his soul.

These words are strikingly timely, current, actual. They are written on the spur of the moment as if in answer to some new utterance of Mickiewicz, open and impassioned, and touching the Russian poet's patriotic feelings, already inflamed by recent political events. It is difficult to imagine that he would still react so sharply to the recollection of poems which he had read and answered at Boldino ten months previously. However, among the Poles and Russians the belief was long current that the poem was a direct reply to "The Digression" and to the message "To My Russian Friends." Often such opinions are expressed even today, especially in journalistic articles. Lednicki rightly observed that the statement should not be made in this form because, although there indubitably is a connection between it and Mickiewicz's "Digression," "On mezhdu nami zhil . . ." was not Pushkin's reply to Mickiewicz. Pushkin had given his reply in "The Bronze Horseman" and had no need to return to this subject.

In more recent times all Pushkin scholars without exception are looking for some other stimulus which might have induced the poet to concern himself with his Polish literary colleague. This viewpoint is so significant for Pushkin-Polish relations in general that it is worthwhile to recall it.

In the diary which Pushkin kept in 1833–1835 he put down under

---

No. 2374 Publichnoi Biblioteki SSSR imeni Lenina, Kommentarii, Moscow, 1939.

the date of April 11, 1834, the following fact: "I just got from Count Stroganov a page from the Frankfort Daily where the following article was printed. . . ." Here he quotes the widely known, tendentious and unpleasant article relating how Joachim Lelewel, in an address on January 25, 1834, in Brussels on the anniversary of Tsar Nicholas' removal from the Polish throne (and in commemoration of the Decembrist uprising and in honor of its executed heroes),[14] mentioned a young Russian poet (Pushkin) who had devoted his talent to the revolutionary cause and had not hesitated to send the Tsar a certain fable denouncing his tyranny. Lelewel's words were inaccurate. Pushkin's revolutionary poems actually reached the Tsar's hands, but the adaptation of Ségur's fable, which was involved here, was erroneously ascribed to Pushkin. As has been proved, the article was inspired by Tsarist agents; it derided Lelewel and at the same time struck at Pushkin, denouncing him in the eyes of the Russian government and reactionary circles both in Russia and abroad. Count Grigorii Aleksandrovich Stroganov (a Tsarist diplomat and a distant relative of Pushkin's wife), who had sent the poet the unpleasant newspaper clipping, most probably wanted in this way to warn him of possible unpleasantness which Lelewel's incautious words and the denunciation of the Tsar's foreign agents might bring upon him. Pushkin found himself in a difficult situation. He had somehow to excuse himself before the ultraloyal Stroganov. Willy-nilly, he wrote him a letter in the first half of April, 1834, explaining how he disliked the memories of his youthful fancies and stating that exile to Siberia would be more pleasant to him than Lelewel's embrace. It is hard to agree with Lednicki that the poet did not act as civil courage would have demanded. It was a step of self-defense in relation to a powerful dignitary who was influential in the famous Third Section (secret police) of the Tsar's chancellery.

All modern Pushkin scholars are inclined to consider the incident with Lelewel the stimulus which directed the poet's mind to Polish

14. J. Lelewel (1786–1861), outstanding Polish historian and leader of the Polish democratic party in exile. The removal of Nicholas from the throne of the Polish "Congress Kingdom" (founded in 1815) was voted by the Diet in Warsaw in 1831, during the uprising against Tsarist Russia. [Ed.]

problems, and hence to Mickiewicz. Such a genealogy of Pushkin's poem about Mickiewicz does not seem justified. Why did Pushkin reply to Mickiewicz and not to Lelewel? Why did he undertake the polemics just then? Why does the poet bring his Polish friend's stand so vividly up to date? Unfortunately, the chronicle of Pushkin's life and works [15] does not reveal any personal contacts, conversations, or readings which would suggest to him the Polish poet.

Traces of Pushkin's contemporary Polish interests are to be found elsewhere. In the catalogue of the poet's private library, edited and published in 1910 with meticulous care by Boris Modzalevsky, supplemented by his son Lev Modzalevsky,[16] we find only books of Mickiewicz which the Russian poet had received, and with which he became familiar, before 1834: The St. Petersburg edition of *Konrad Wallenrod* of 1828, *Poems,* the new enlarged edition in two volumes published in St. Petersburg in 1829, and the Paris edition of 1832. However, the catalogue includes a valuable *polonicum* which by a strange coincidence has so far escaped the attention of scholars: *Kordian—Part I of a Trilogy, The Coronation Plot,* Paris, At the Author's Expense, The Polish Bookstore, 1834.

This work of Julius Słowacki appeared anonymously.[17] The author of the catalogue of Pushkin's library, not familiar with Polish literature, did not solve the anonym and so placed the book under the letter K, between Kobelstein and Kotzebue. The name of Słowacki does not appear in the catalogue's index of personal names, from which Polish Pushkin scholars seem to have started their investigations.

Unfortunately, it is difficult to establish when and how a copy of *Kordian* found its way into Pushkin's hands. It obviously does not appear in the bills rendered the poet for books bought at the Bellisar and Dickson bookstore.[18] The book is not mentioned in the poet's

15. N. Lerner, *Trudy i dni Pushkina,* St. Petersburg, 1910.
16. *Literaturnoye Nasledstvo,* Nos. 16–18, A. S. Pushkin.
17. J. Słowacki (1809–1849) one of the greatest Polish poets, contemporary of Mickiewicz. His *Kordian* is a romantic drama depicting a young man (Kordian) searching for his life's goal. He finally becomes a member of an underground patriotic organization and makes an attempt on the Tsar's life. [Ed.]
18. B. Modzalevsky, *Biblioteka A. S. Pushkina,* p. xviii.

diary or correspondence. It was prohibited in Russia; therefore, he must have received it from someone who was abroad. It may have been brought by somebody from Paris, as in the case of Mickiewicz's poems a year earlier. When? By whom? No one knows.

As we know, *Kordian* appeared before March 24, 1834.[19] On that day Słowacki wrote to his mother: "My fourth child has come into the world." Today it is also known that immediately after its publication its authorship was ascribed to Mickiewicz. This is attested by the words of Słowacki himself, who in a letter to his mother as early as April 27, 1834, wrote as follows:

> Many in Paris ascribe my poem to Adam; here is an excerpt from a letter written to me: "I was present when Ogiński attacked Adam and when the latter denied being the author of the work saying he did not know anything about it; Ogiński replied: 'At least we know that you want this to be a secret.'" . . . In another letter [the poet informs his mother] one of my friends writes me: "From Memel, where I have sent copies, they write me about *Kordian* with great approval and take it for a work of Adam." From these two reports it is evident that my anonymously published work is in many places ascribed to another; knowing our countrymen's prejudice in this respect, such a mistake is not unpleasant to me.[20]

If *Kordian* was regarded as Mickiewicz's work not only in Paris, but also in nearby Klaipeda (Memel), the transfer point of illegal foreign literature to Russia, this version might have circulated in certain Russian circles close to Pushkin. Consequently, it is not excluded that it reached his hands, too, as a work of Mickiewicz. Let us not deceive ourselves in thinking that Pushkin, reading the text of the tragedy, would have been able to realize that its style and atmosphere was foreign to Mickiewicz, when this difference was not felt even by Słowacki's own countrymen. Apparently Pushkin read it rather thoroughly. According to Modzalevsky the entire volume is cut throughout, which the poet was not wont to do with books he did not read. The history of his library practically excludes the possibility that somebody in the poet's immediate circle became in-

19. Cf. introduction to *Kordian* by Józef Ujejski; Juliusz Słowacki, *Dzieła wszystkie,* pod redakcją Juliusza Kleinera, II (Lwów, 1926), 198.
20. *Dzieła wszystkie,* II, 198.

terested in this inconspicuous little book after his death. It is also difficult to resist the impression that the reading of *Kordian,* like "The Digression," could stimulate him to a reply, no longer a historiosophical one in the highest poetic spheres, as in "The Bronze Horseman," but open, sincere, and personal.

Between the appearance of *Kordian* and the writing of the poem about Mickiewicz five months elapsed. Thus there was sufficient time for the tragedy to reach Pushkin, for him to read it, and to react to it as a poet. The poem was broken off in the middle of a sentence and left in rough drafts. Perhaps, while finishing it, Pushkin had learned who was the real author of this book which pained him so.

The hypothesis of *Kordian* as a work supposed to have been created by Mickiewicz, and to which Pushkin replied with the poem "On mezhdu nami zhil . . . ," will become plausible if it is established when its text reached the poet and whether, and if so when, he occupied himself with it more closely. Perhaps Soviet Pushkin scholars who have so thoroughly examined the poetic heritage of their national poet, and who have at their disposal the inexhaustible treasures of the archives of the poet and his environment, will be able to give an answer to these questions.

*Translated by* LUDWIK KRZYŻANOWSKI

# GERMANY

## *Visit to Goethe*

ANTONI EDWARD ODYNIEC (1804–1885), Mickiewicz's fellow student and friend in Wilno, a poet and writer, accompanied Mickiewicz on his trip abroad and described it in *Listy z podróży* (Letters from a Journey, 4 vols., Warsaw, 1875–1878). His letters are sometimes naïve and not wholly reliable. We give one of them (Vol. I, pp. 153–157) as it is the only description of Mickiewicz's first visit to Goethe.

*Weimar, August 20, 1829*

[To Julian Korsak]

Yesterday, precisely at noon, Madame Ottilia's [1] smart cabriolet stopped in front of our hotel, and a quarter of an hour later we alighted from it at the garden gate of Goethe's country house. An old servant who had been waiting for us conducted us through the garden, opened the door to the drawing room, let us in, and left. It is a small, two-storey house and must be of stone, for it is white and covered with vines. The drawing room in which we waited is spacious, furnished modestly, in country style, not with a parquet but with a board floor painted red. In the fireplace, swept clean as if there had never been a fire in it, lay a piece of paper torn in two. I picked up one half; Adam recognized Goethe's handwriting which he had seen in Madame Szymanowska's [2] album. We saved it as a souvenir; it was a fragment of something about physics. We waited almost a quarter of an hour talking in low tones. Adam asked me whether my heart was not beating. Indeed, this was like waiting for a supernatural phenomenon. He himself recalled how he had once envied Madame Szymanowska for having seen and talked with Goethe.

1. Goethe's daughter-in-law.
2. Mary Szymanowska, famous Polish pianist, known both in eastern and western Europe.

Suddenly we heard steps upstairs. Adam gravely quoted Kiszka Zgierski's [3] poem "Walking and treading is to be heard aloft." As we were laughing at this quotation, so apropos at this moment, the door opened and enter—Jupiter! I got hot all over. And without exaggerating there is something Jove-like in him. The tall stature, colossal frame; serious, imposing face; and the forehead!—it is precisely there that his Jove-like dignity rests. Without a diadem it shines majestically. The hair, not yet overly white, thins out noticeably over the forehead. His brown, bright and vivid eyes are moreover distinguished by a singular, light-gray, as if enameled border which surrounds both irises of his pupils. Adam likened it to a ring of Saturn. We have never before seen anything like this on anyone.

He wore a dark-brown coat buttoned from top to bottom. On his neck he had a white kerchief, without a collar, fastened crosswise with a gold pin. Like a ray of the sun from behind a cloud a surprisingly pleasant, kind smile brightened the severity of this physiognomy when, hardly having entered, he greeted us with a bow and a handshake, saying at the same time: "Pardon, Messieurs, que je vous ai fait attendre. Il m'est très agréable de voir les amis de Mme. Szymanowska, qui m'honore aussi de son amitié." For you must know that Goethe had once been a great admirer of Mme S., and continuing, he said about her: "Elle est charmante, comme elle est belle, et gracieuse, comme elle est charmante." Then, after we had sat down, he turned to Adam and said he knew that Adam was at the head of the new trend which literature was assuming in Poland as well as in the whole of Europe. "I know from experience," he added, "what a difficult thing this is; it is like going against the wind." "We also know from Your Excellency's experience," answered Adam, "that in their progress great geniuses turn this wind to follow them." Goethe nodded his forehead slightly as if to indicate that he understood the compliment, and went on to say that he regretted that he knew very little about Polish literature and that he was not familiar with any Slavic language. "Mais l'homme a tant à faire dans cette vie." He added, however, that he had known about Adam

3. Count Wincenty Kiszka-Zgierski, a notorious Polish rhymester of the beginning of the nineteenth century.

from the newspapers and was familiar with some excerpts from his new poem (*Wallenrod*) which Mme S. had been good enough to send him in a German translation (by Miss Karolina Jänisch, Adam's friend in Moscow), or which he had later read in *Leipziger Jahrbücher*. Turning to me he said that it was also from there that he knew about the almanac (*Melitele*) edited by me, containing works of all living Polish poets, and that he had read there a translation of my *The Lithuanian's Captive*. He praised the vividness of its plot and style "autant que je peut en juger par la traduction." I grew terribly red, whether from modesty or joy I do not know myself, but certainly from profound emotion. In the meantime Adam added a few words about my translations from Bürger. Raising my eyes I met Goethe's glance, in which I seemed to notice an expression of friendly kindness. And when Adam, at his request, told him in a wonderfully concise and clever manner the whole course of Polish literature from the oldest to the most recent times, linking and comparing it with historical epochs, you could see in Goethe's eyes fixed on Adam not only deep attention but also keen interest which this account roused in him. The motion of the fingers of his hand resting on his knee also seemed to prove this. Incidentally, I forgot to mention that at the beginning of this conversation Goethe had started to speak German; but when Adam, also in German, told him that even though he knew this language he would not dare to speak it in his presence, he at once returned to French. During further conversation Goethe maintained that in view of the increasingly clear striving everywhere for universal truth, poetry and literature in general must and would become more and more universal; he agreed, however, with Adam's opinion that it would never lose its distinctive, national characteristics. Hence we came to talk about folk songs, and Goethe asked with lively interest and listened to what Adam, and partly I myself, said about the variety and difference, in character and tone, of our provincial songs. Later on, at dinner, he repeated this to others. This concluded our literary conversation.

Then, addressing in turn Adam and me, he asked us about plans for our future journey. He tenderly recalled Italy and Rome, envying us, as he said, that we were going to places from which he had in his youth brought back most pleasant memories. Next he talked with

Adam about his acquaintances in Berlin, whom Adam had met while passing through, and particularly about Professor Gans. Then he returned again to Mme Szymanowska and mentioned a few other Poles he had known before, namely Jan Potocki and Princess Lubomirska, whom he praised highly. When we rose to take leave of him he declared he was very sorry that because of the rain which was then falling he could not show us his little garden (son petit jardin). "Mais j'aurai le plaisir de jouir encore de votre societé à diner chez ma belle-fille." And turning to me with a smile he added: "Et nous aurons quelques jolies dames et demoiselles; j'espère que ça vous fera plaisir." We both laughed and he, laughing also, turned quickly to Adam and asked as if confidentially: "N'est-ce pas?" Then he again shook hands with us, and, when we were already on the stairs, he opened the door of the drawing room a little and repeated "Au revoir."

"My, but he is clever!" was Adam's first exclamation when we had come down the stairs.

*Translated by* LUDWIK KRZYŻANOWSKI

To this report of Odyniec it may be added that Goethe offered Mickiewicz a pen and the following distich, written especially for him:

Dem Dichter widm' ich mich, der sich erprobt
Und unsere Freundin heiter gründlich lobt. [Ed.]

## *Voices of German Poets and Scholars*

LUDWIG UHLAND (1787–1862) was one of the most distinguished representatives of late German romanticism ("Spätromantik"), and leader of the so-called "schwäbischer Dichterkreis" (Poetic Circle of Swabia). His poem "Mickiewicz" was probably written around 1831–1833, at a time when there was in Germany great enthusiasm for the Polish cause.

### MICKIEWICZ

An der Weichsel fernem Strande
Tobt ein Kampf mit Donnerschall,
Weithin über deutsche Lande

Rollt er seinen Widerhall.
Schwert und Sense, scharfen Klanges,
Dringen her zu unseren Ohren,
Und der Ruf des Schlachtgesanges:
"Noch ist Polen nicht verloren."

Und wir horchen und wir lauschen,
Stille waltet um und um,
Nur die trägen Wellen rauschen,
Und das weite Feld ist stumm;
Nur wie Sterbender Gestöhne,
Lufthauch durch gebroch'ne Hallen,
Hört man dumpfe Trauertöne:
"Polen, Polen ist gefallen."

Mitten in der stillen Feier
Wird ein Saitengriff getan.
Ha, wie schwillet diese Leier
Voller stets and mächtiger an.
Leben schaffen solche Geister,
Dann wird Totes neu geboren;
Ja, mir bürgt des Liedes Meister:
"Noch ist Polen nicht verloren."

ANNETTE VON DROSTE-HÜLSHOFF (1797–1848), regarded as the greatest of Germany's women poets, was especially noted for her epic and lyric poems. Her remarks on *Pan Tadeusz* are taken from *Die Briefe der Annette von Droste-Hülshoff* (Jena, 1944, Vol. I, p. 202).

To Chr. B. Schlüter

*Rauschhaus, on Maundy Thursday,*
March 23, 1837

. . . *Pan Tadeusz* returns with this, I was thoroughly delighted with it. Though it could be more beautiful in places, it certainly couldn't be more original, this is a genuinely native strain. The translation is sometimes clumsy but still the book gave me great pleasure —a true classic. . . .

JOHANNES SCHERR (1817–1886) was professor at the "Politechnikum" in Zurich, historian, literary historian, and novelist. In his *Allgemeine Geschichte der Literatur* (Stuttgart, 1880, Vol. II), we find the following remarks on Mickiewicz.

He [Adam Mickiewicz] performed for Polish poetry the same service that Oehlenschläger, Atterbom, Geiger, and Tegnér did for Scandinavian, but as a poet he leaves all four behind him. He is without question the greatest poet yet to appear in Poland or in any Slavic country. . . . His real [reform of Polish literature] consisted in the fact that he fused Romanticism—in Byron's sense, not Fr. Schlegel's—with the national element in an incomparably satisfying manner. He is a Romantic and at the same time a modern poet. Besides old Slavic popular poetry, Shakespeare, Schiller, and Byron influenced him, the last named in particular. It was not without reason, and certainly in covert reference to himself, that Mickiewicz once said Byron was the secret bond which tied all Slavic literature to that of the West. . . .

. . . But even though the poet of *Childe Harold* revealed to our Pole the "secret of his own mission," Mickiewicz is no blind imitator of Byron. And why not? Because in Christianity, or rather in Catholicism, the Pole found for himself the reconciliation of the antithesis between Ideal and Life, which the more deeply burrowing skepticism of Byron failed to find. Also because he was a Pole from top to toe, because he was a patriot. "My native land" —that is the chord which always sounds in Mickiewicz' writings.

FRIEDRICH NIETZSCHE and his friend Franz Overbeck comment on *Pan Tadeusz* in their correspondence (*Friedrich Nietzsches Briefwechsel mit Franz Overbeck*, ed. by Richard Oehler and Carl Albrecht Bernouilli, Leipzig, 1916). We quote the following interesting remarks.

Overbeck to Nietzsche

*Basle, April 3, 1884*

. . . Do you know Mickiewicz' *Pan Tadeusz* in Lipiner's translation? I must admit that I am amazed that such a poem should appear in our times. I couldn't think of anything in the literature of our century to match it in richness, power, and simplicity of mood and real poetic magic, and besides I feel the translation is splendid. Last night my wife and I were most enjoyably exalted and cheered by the 8th canto.

Nietzsche to Overbeck

*Nice, April 7, 1884*

Thanks very much, my dear friend. Even your tip about Mickiewicz came just at the right moment. I am ashamed to know so little of the Poles (who are, after all, my forebears!)—how I have longed to find a poet that belonged to Chopin and did me as much good as he!

JOHANNES VOLKELT (1848–1930), professor at the universities of Jena, Basel, Switzerland, and Leipzig, was the author of the fundamental *Aesthetik des Tragischen* (1897), *System der Aesthetik* (1905–1914), and many other works. We give below excerpts concerning Mickiewicz from "The Aesthetic of the Tragic" (third edition, 1917), from a chapter dealing with "Arten des Erhebend Tragischen" (Types of Sublime Tragedy).

An interesting example [of sublime tragedy] is afforded by the beggar-monk Robak, that touchingly tragic figure in Mickiewicz's *Pan Tadeusz,* an epic imbued with a mighty and glorious stream of festive joy, and translated by Siegfried Lipiner into German poetic in its own right. Scornfully dismissed by the proud Pantler whose daughter he loved, Robak had treacherously assassinated him in a vengeful fury. After vain attempts to soothe his agonies of conscience, he decides to adopt a life of humble poverty in toil and danger. As a matter of fact, in the perilous obligations he has taken on himself he finds death. Here crime is followed by inner annihilation and a hard life of toil dedicated to moral purification. Because it is earnestly and unswervingly devoted to the goal of reparation, even a shattered man's pain-wracked continuation of existence here produces an overwhelmingly sublime impression.

Mickiewicz is able to stimulate both our sympathy and anxiety to the utmost when in *Forefathers' Eve* he paints with vindictive ardor, burning hate, and matchlessly holy wrath the fiendish abuses which the Czar inflicts on the Poles.

Gustav in Mickiewicz's *Forefathers' Eve,* too, with his almost insane excess of feeling and dreaming on the one hand and his lack of factual perception on the other, with his acute conflict of spineless weakness and scornful bravery, of loving and cursing, of self-deception and discernment, is portrayed so that one easily heeds the compulsion of a remarkable individual case. By contrast, in the same great work Konrad is an eminent representative of the typically human sort of tragedy. The feelings of God, World, and Self have hardly been expressed elsewhere with more ardently superhuman power.

JOSEF NADLER (1884–), outstanding German literary historian, Professor at the universities at Freiburg, Switzerland, Königsberg and Vienna, was the author of *Die Wissenschaftslehre der Literaturgeschichte* (1914), *Literaturgeschichte der deutschen Stämme und Landschaften* (1912), and other works. Below are excerpts from his article "Adam Mickiewicz, Deutsche Klassik, deutsche Romantik," which was published in *Deutschland und Polen* (ed. by Albert Brackmann, Munich and Berlin, 1933).

. . . It seems that Adam Mickiewicz in his two greatest poetic works has been much too one-sidedly linked to Goethe. . . .

The dramatic poem *Forefathers' Eve* was written about 1823. This was Mickiewicz's fateful year, the year in which he was arrested at Wilno and then deported into the interior of Russia. The first three parts appeared before this year; the fourth, after it.[1] Leaving out of consideration the abandoned numbering of the original, the parts assume the following order according to inner meaning: 1) The prelude, 2) The conjuration of the dead, 3) Gustav's appearance in the parsonage, 4) The scenes at Wilno. The first three groups make the first main part, while the fourth is the second part. The poem is constructed with meticulous beauty around the basic idea of a Lithuanian folk custom. Once a year about the time of All Souls'

1. The dates cited by Nadler are not quite exact. The "first three parts" (according to his enumeration, which is not that of the poet) appeared in 1823, the "fourth" (in reality, the third), in 1832. [Ed.]

Day, the peasants prepare, in a secluded spot, a banquet for the dead, so as to refresh the returning ones and to hear their requests and warnings. The prelude sounds the main theme. Then the conjuration of the dead begins. It is carried out by the Wizard in a dialogue with the chorus of peasants and is achieved in the holy number of all rites, three times. First, a child appears; "Whose earthly bliss had no alloy Ne'er shall taste of heavenly joy." Next, a cruel landowner: "Who never felt for human kind, human help can never aid." Then a maiden: "He who never touched the earth may not join in heavenly mirth." The fourth time, the conjuration fails. A shadow appears, but cannot be forced to speak, by any means. The height of dread is concentrated in this moment. It is expressed in the dying away of the final choking question: "What will appear?, What will appear?" Change of scene, third group. A hermit appears in the parsonage, mysteriously indistinct. He acts out the last hours of a man crazed with love, blazes up bright as day in the form of Gustav, the hero of the prelude, stabs his dagger into his breast without killing himself, and disappears again like a ghost. It is the silent shadow of the fourth conjuration. And his last word fits with the other three: "He who glimpsed heaven on earth will not find it so easily in the next life." Now did he really return from the dead like the other three, or did he die the death of hopeless love only in his sinful thoughts?

Change of scene to the fourth group, from the first to the second main part. Konrad, the hero of the second part, is born in Gustav's death. Konrad awakes in the dungeon of the Basilian monastery in Wilno. The two groups of scenes in the second main section surge up with terrible force toward heaven. In this overpowering framework are three monologues: Konrad's outrageous indictment of God's loveless omnipotence; Peter the monk's vision of the sufferings of Poland on the cross of three nations; Eva's child-pure prayer for the poet Konrad, whom she knows only from his songs. Before and after these three monologues, couched in despair deep as hell and in heaven-storming prayers, all man's misery on this earth is portrayed in scenes of shocking reality. Before the monologues the dungeon scenes of the Polish political prisoners take place, and Peter the monk drives the devil of blasphemy out of Konrad. After the monologues come the dreadful scenes of Novosiltsev, the Russian torturer of the Poles. Peter the monk steps into this dance of death as a herald of divine justice. Change of scene and return to the conjuration of the dead. Meanwhile we have become acquainted with the silent unconjurable shadow in both his forms. The Wizard and the women who interrogated him see the banished ones wandering eastward in the distance. The shadow is living. The wound in his breast was of the soul. This can probably be healed only by death. But the wound on his forehead burns into his brain. This is the one he inflicted on himself and not even Death's hand can heal it.

The construction of Goethe's *Faust* appears unmistakably in this poem. A double poem has been built around a hero in a dual role: before and after the crisis in his life. The musical composition of the whole and the choruses are in the style of *Faust,* and also among other things, Konrad's monologue in the second part and the Easter hymn which is heard during Friar Peter's monologue. But the poem received Faustian style only in the second part, the fourth group of scenes. When Mickiewicz wrote the first three groups of his poem he was not thinking of the first part of Goethe's *Faust,* which was, after all, the only part he could have known. Only when he transformed Gustav into Konrad and conceived the idea of adding a fourth group of scenes to the three previous groups, did the great fragment attract him. The fact that he undertook, on his own foundations and in his own way, to continue what was as yet incomplete in Goethe's poem, makes this point important as well as fascinating. In the Germany of the 1820s everyone was trying to guess how Goethe would solve the Faust problem. Seen in this environment the work of the Polish poet is clarified and given significance. All that is Faustian in the style of *Forefathers' Eve* is concentrated in the fourth group of scenes. Here Mickiewicz remembered the first part of Goethe's *Faust* and "continued" it in his own fashion. Only in general outline is the construction like that of *Faust.* The first three groups of scenes cannot be connected either with Faust's conjuration or with the Walpurgis Night. They are completely within Lithuanian folk custom. And if, in an attempt to characterize spirit and atmosphere, one looks for related German material, one must turn his gaze far from Goethe. It is the spirit and style of Bürger, whose *Lenore* Mickiewicz certainly knew. It might be Hölty's dreamy graveyard melancholy. Here are the horrible sepulchral chimeras of the young Schiller. It is the death poetry less of German Romanticism than of the general German post-Romantic period. Here, too, the mysterious hermits and God-fired monks are at home. And if one studies Konrad's great monologue more closely, one hears Hamlet rather than Faust, and the wild accusing eloquence of Schiller's heroes sounds more clearly than the stylized despair of Goethe's seekers after truth. And if we, once again, wish to review the style of this Polish poem as a whole and look for the place where it might perhaps belong in Germany, then we recall Bertold's first and second lives in Arnim's novel *The Guardians of the Crown* or his *Halle and Jerusalem.* But as to his older German contemporaries, Mickiewicz's artistic purpose is especially clear if he is compared with the Prussian dramas of Zacharias Werner. Even from the point of view of artistic form, the components of the Faustian style yield to Romantic traits. And the climax of the parsonage scene can hardly be called anything but Romantic irony. Therefore *Forefathers' Eve* cannot be thus unequivocally linked to Goethe's *Faust.* And the consonance is entirely lost when we concentrate on the poem's content. The only comparable point is that the hero is transmuted from one existence to another. Neither is Gustav in the situation of the first Faust nor does Konrad strive for the goal of the second. The way of the Polish hero does not lead from perception to deed. The first main group of *Forefathers' Eve* turn on the original idea: no heavenly consummation without earthly perfection. On this earth one must live a full, pure, and well-rounded human life. Consciousness of an unconsummated life on earth holds the soul fast at the border between heaven and earth, being nothing to the world although still in it, and, once again in the world, being nothing for it. Every one of these four apparitions has failed this law of consummation in one way or another, some innocently and some knowingly. Of these four the poet selects one, Gustav, so as to expose the whole problem with his case as an example. Even Gustav has lived only a shadowy existence, a short life of fruitless and corrosive revel. And he knocked wantonly at death's door, either in thought or deed. But this Werther-like plot is not the real subject of the poem. The hero's shadow rises only to give warning and to announce the moral. This hero undoubtedly gets his speech of passion from Goethe's Werther; but the connection with Werther himself is very incidental. Goethe's book is mentioned only among others of the same sort. The character of the poem comes from Mme Juliane von Krüdener's novel *Valeria.* The essential events in this poem have nothing to do with either Werther or Goethe. Here Mickiewicz and his hero complete the mystic rite of self-immolation, the obliteration of sensual and personal ego, so as to be reborn to a new life. And this rebirth occurs in the last part. Goethe's Faust slumbers easily on a bed of roses through the transition from his first to his second life. What happens here is no more than the natural psychological phenomenon of relaxing, resting, and forgetting. Mickiewicz's Gustav becomes Konrad through repentance, atonement, and a mystical transfiguration of soul. With Goethe it is spiritual hygiene; with Mickiewicz it is a work of grace. Goethe's hero remains what he was. Mickiewicz's hero receives as a token of death and resurrection a new "name" as a Christian in baptism. Konrad's struggle with God in the great monologue of the last part is not Faust's striving for the secret of the world's creative energy. Mickiewicz in unequivocal words sets his work in contrast to Goethe's. Konrad violently rejects Faust's passionate will to perceive. Heart against heart he struggles with God. And it is not for human wisdom that he breaks into God's sanctuary. It is by love, rather than by the perception of Goethe's Faust, that he wishes to share in God's creative power. It is the blind terror of Goethe's conception of God which he condemns. His last sacrilegious devil-poisoned thought sees a merciless Tsar rather than a loving father on the throne of the world. So the Polish poet's hero undergoes a double transformation: from sensitivity of feeling to the titanic strength of heart and to heroism of pain. The selfishness of his eroticism turns on the one hand to altruistic love and on the other to renunciation for society. And since it seems that he is to be denied unity with God in love of creation, he takes on himself the communion of suffering with his people. Through a mystical union Poland becomes for him the crucified savior of the world. And so Gustav, the shade of his sweetheart wandering between heaven and earth, becomes Konrad's *imi-*

*tatio Poloniae crucifixae.* But these are waves of feeling and trains of thought which Reinhold Lenz and Zacharias Werner have experienced and dramatized. In all German literature there is no counterpart to Mickiewicz and his Messianic idea except in the East Prussian Romanticist Zacharias Werner. But the cosmopolitan German has all mankind in view, while the nationalistic Pole is thinking of his people. . . .

When Mickiewicz, relieved of the intolerable strain of his *Forefathers' Eve,* began to write his epic poem *Pan Tadeusz,* his delight recalled Goethe's gaily serious small town idyl *Hermann und Dorothea.* But when Mickiewicz had finished his poem, for which the German people may well envy the Poles, what had it become? Is this, seen and described with eyes moist but smiling, the small world of the fathers on the Lithuanian farm? It is more than this, and something greater. . . . The form and style of this poem, too, may be referred back to Goethe. But it is outside the scope of Goethe's world. Unique of its kind, there is nothing in German literature to match this poem in kind and rank. In Josef von Eichendorff's novel *Presentiment and the Present* one experiences the same sultriness of the same coming events. In the novels of Johann Paul Richter one meets similarly upright eccentrics and dusty lawsuits. And Mickiewicz was acquainted with Richter's books. But what does all this prove in the face of Cervantes, Tasso, and Scott, whose spirit completely governs this wonderful poem? . . .

. . . In the spiritual history of the Polish people Mickiewicz occupies a position which, in their own literature, the German people cannot fill by a poet of equal rank. For not one of the great German poets was as helpful to the German people in bearing its cross as was Mickiewicz to his people. . . .

## *Mickiewicz As Professor*

THE AUGSBURG periodical, *Beilage zur Allgemeinen Zeitung,* printed in its issue of March 9, 1843, the following vivid report written by an unidentified L.A.Z. who attended Mickiewicz's course in the Collège de France.

*Paris*

. . . France, always magnanimous to foreigners if their sufferings are in any measure honorable, turned over to this profoundly learned man the professorship for Slavic literature at the Collège de France in Paris. Here, then, he teaches, surrounded by a throng of Polish and French youths and by foreigners from all the countries to which his fame has penetrated. The large audience which hangs on the words of the celebrated master reminds one of the picture by the Polish painter Stattler [1] showing Mickiewicz reading *The Book of the Polish Pilgrims* to a crowd in front of the Church of Our Lady in Cracow. Yes, these are the noble features which the sculptor David immortalized at Goethe's behest,[2] these are the dreamy eyes that reflect the glow of a heart fired with pure love. But these eyes shine only momentarily, as did the star of Poland when her people took up arms under Kościuszko, when it spoke with Kołłontay's [3] eloquent tongue and dipped into the spring of knowledge with Lelewel's [4] hand. The gravity of the time is expressed in every line of its representative's face. The furrows recount to the observant eye the oppressive days outfaced. The damp breath of the dungeon vault at Wilno may have bleached your hair, O worthy friend of the noble Thomas Zan,[5] but neither Senator Novosiltsov's [6] cross-questioning nor the flattering promises of the affable courtiers in St. Petersburg could compromise your true heart's steadiness. There is something of marble in this famous Pole's expression. His voice is hoarse. He pronounces French very harshly, almost brokenly. There

1. Wojciech Korneli Stattler (1800–1882), Representative of the Classic school in Polish painting, known in France chiefly for his "Maccabees" which in 1841 won him the highest prize in Paris.
2. David d'Angers (1788–1856), French sculptor, did a beautiful bust of Mickiewicz.
3. Hugo Kołłątaj (1750–1812), prominent Polish statesman and writer.
4. Joachim Lelewel (1786–1861), the most outstanding Polish historian of the nineteenth century.
5. Tomasz Zan (1796–1855), Mickiewicz's fellow student and friend in Wilno, poet and writer.
6. Russian Senator Novosiltsov, who persecuted the student organization of Philomats in Wilno.

is no insinuation in his delivery, no expressive pantomime, no lively gesticulation. Here one sees nothing of the carefully chosen costume of the younger French lecture-desk heroes, none of that striving for effect, that seeking for applause. Completely enveloped in his simple dark brown coat, the earnest man sits motionless before the closely packed crowd of listeners, only now and again smoothing back from his forehead his bushy gray hair, grown low and thick, whose former shining black still appears in places. The words that struggle from lips so expressive of energy and steadfastness lose none of their spirit for all their simplicity. Often he is at a loss for the precise expression and must search for it—but he finds it. The listener feels how the thoughts develop in the speaker's mind as they are spoken. Captivated, he follows their frequently bold flights and soon forgets the form in the content. Mickiewicz is treating Slavic literature in his lectures, but in a completely original way. . . .

. . . He traces with a marvelous thoroughness the earliest history of this very ancient people. . . . He points out the ancient home of this [the Slavic] race and indicates the probable limits of its expansion. In contemplating its fate and its spiritual and political situation in those days he more than once bursts into complaints, so melancholy from his lips, that this people has apparently been destined of old to bear the yoke of slavery, that in most eras of history nothing is comparable to its moral humiliation unless it be its own limitless sufferings. Such views are usually reconciled by solace in religion, in which the heritage of the Polish nation, a faithful and fervent adherence to strict Catholicism can be easily discerned. The samples he gives from different periods of Slavic literature he has himself skillfully put into French. In reading them he often interrupts himself with short but comprehensive comments. These interesting lectures are now the Parisian *rendez-vous* for the fashionable literary world of both sexes. One frequently meets celebrities there, for example George Sand, who on more than one occasion has thus sacrificed her long-cherished love of strict seclusion to her reverence for Mickiewicz.

L.A.Z.

*Translations from the German by* ALDEN HAUPT

# BOHEMIA

## *Mickiewicz and Bohemia*

by Karel Krejči

Few foreign poets have met with such response in Czech literature as Adam Mickiewicz. This is shown by the great number of translations made by generations of Czech poets, from Mickiewicz's contemporaries to the poets of today. In this connection, however, it is most important to note how the conception of Mickiewicz underwent changes from generation to generation, always under the influence of that part of his immense and complex work which best suited the spirit of the generation and the need of the moment. It it this fact which proves that we are dealing with more than the mere academic respect and deference to an author who enjoys world fame and who belongs to a related Slavic nation.

Mickiewicz's direct contacts with Bohemia were not numerous, but were nevertheless significant. He visited Prague only once, in 1829, when stopping over on his way to a northern Bohemian spa. He stayed in Prague for just a few days, which barely sufficed to make the most superficial contacts with some of the Czech patriots. Among others he met the Czech Slavophile Václav Hanka, who was famous at that time for his "discovery" of supposedly ancient Czech poems (later found to have been forged). In his office at the Czech Museum, Hanka was visited by almost all Slavic cultural leaders passing through Prague, and he tried to use his contacts to propagate the Czech cause. He attempted to induce Mickiewicz, who already enjoyed world fame, to write an epic about the leader of the Czech Hussites, Jan Žižka, and his warfare with the Teutonic Knights. Basically, this idea was a very good one, as Mickiewicz had at that time already written two epic poems, *Grażyna* and *Konrad Wallenrod,* taken from the history of the struggles of Poles and Lithuanians with the Teutonic Order, so that Hanka's topic might have been quite suitable. It seems that Mickiewicz did not refuse Hanka, but still he did not write the epic about Žižka. One of the main reasons for this must have been, as is generally believed, his reverting to Catholicism, linked with an unfavorable opinion of the Hussite movement, which was later expressed in his Parisian lectures. However, there was another reason, no less serious; this lay in his creative development. It is evident that the type of epic proposed fades from Mickiewicz's work around that time. His *Forefathers' Eve* and *Pan Tadeusz* are of a literary type entirely different from *Grażyna* and *Wallenrod*.

During the latter part of his life, the Polish poet-prophet no longer visited Bohemia. It can be said with certainty that while he was in western Europe he occasionally met some Czechs, but without coming into closer personal contact with them. He did not, however, cease to occupy himself with Czech problems as well as with cultural progress in Bohemia, and lectured about these topics quite extensively in his Slavic lectures at the Collège de France. As for the Slavic literature covered in his program, Mickiewicz was, understandably, more familiar with Polish and Russian writings; only such Czech literature as found its way to Paris was known to him. It is for this reason that Mickiewicz's survey of Czech literature appears to be strongly distorted and represents the "cosmopolitanism" of the period of the Czech Revival, a movement which broke through the confining borders of the then still rather provincial Czech society. It is not at all difficult to understand that only those Czech works written in German by members of the highest society—the aristocracy—had readily penetrated abroad, as these authors had family and social ties with the rest of European aristocracy. Hence it is understandable that as the Polish poet-professor was in contact with Prince Czartoryski and his circle at the "Hotel Lambert," he knew and somewhat overrated two German publications by Czech aristocrats, Count Kinský and Count Lev Thun, and that he also overestimated the importance of the role which aristocracy played in the Czech Movement. Besides these two works, which were pushed to the foreground by the then existing social structure of European intellectual society, Czech literature was introduced to the world by works which were sensational in their external circumstances, or which complied with the vogue of the moment. Czech literature had at that time two such sensational works. One consisted of the so-called *Queen's Court* and *White Mountain Manuscripts.* These were "discovered" in the decade between 1810–1820 as presumably authentic poetic works of the tenth and thirteenth centuries and, of course, evoked considerable enthusiasm in a Europe already charmed by the songs of Ossian, a Europe which saw true art in everything presented in the romantic style of the ancient past. These "Old Czech" ballads were translated into many languages at the time—one of the translators was J. W. von Goethe—and they gained acclaim in the whole intellectual world. Not until much later was it discovered that they were not authentic.

Another such work was a great epic, or rather, a collection of sonnets, connected in content as well as in ideology, published by the Slovak poet Jan Kollár under the title of *Slávy dcera,*[1] a great poetic manifesto voicing the striving for Slavic unity then called Panslavism.

Kollár's work enjoyed considerable favor among all Slav nations, and even with non-Slavs, because of its full and energetic manifestation of tendencies shared by nearly all Slavic nations.

In addition, Bohemia had aroused Europe's interest with a chapter of its cultural and political history, the Hussite movement, which the liberally minded in Europe considered the first manifestation of true liberalism in history. Its originators and defenders were praised as pioneers of a new European ideology. Even many French writers close to Mickiewicz, such as J. Michelet, George Sand, and Louis Blanc, wrote about the Hussite movement from this point of view.

In professional circles Czech science and literature were well known, particularly the works of Dobrovský on Slavic philology and the archeological writings of Šafařík, both of which gained world fame. A few other names from the past were known. They were then, of course, not evaluated as they are today. In his very first lecture Mickiewicz mentioned in conclusion the great discoveries which

1. Double meaning, can be translated as "Daughter of Fame" or "Daughter of the Slavs."

Slavs had contributed to European science. Next to Kopernik he mentioned the Czech physician and natural historian of the sixteenth century, Adam Zalužanský, who, not entirely correctly, was considered the discoverer of the bisexuality of plants and thus a predecessor of Linné. On the other hand, Mickiewicz expressly declared that "Europe has forgotten Komenský," who was in fact one of the greatest educational philosophers and thinkers of the seventeenth century.

To these facts, knowledge of which was fairly general abroad, we may add those which Mickiewicz acquired by his own special research. He had, of course, to rely on the sources available to him and the opinions expressed therein, as he did not have an opportunity to study other works of Czech literature directly. In general he acquainted himself with the main facts of older Czech literature, evaluating them most likely on the basis of information received from Czech sources. With the exception of Kollár's works he hardly mentioned the newer Czech literature. Of course these writings did not reach the European public of the time and were probably not available to him. The fact that he did not know the greatest Czech poet of the period, Karel Hynek Mácha, can be explained by the standpoint of contemporary Czech critics who themselves for long did not realize Mácha's true significance. However, it is doubtful whether Mickiewicz would have given more thought to Mácha than to the Polish poet, J. Słowacki, whom he knew thoroughly and whose writings were similar to those of Mácha.

We must be sure to understand the basis on which Mickiewicz built if we want to ascertain and properly characterize his relation to Czech literature. Mickiewicz did not content himself with a mere informative survey of facts, but strove for a personalized interpretation of them and especially for their inclusion in his ideologically and philosophically directed system of Slavic literature.

Mickiewicz liked the Czechs. In his first reference to the Czech Zalužanský, he speaks of him as "our author." Further on he combines Bohemia and Poland into a western Slavic unit as opposed to the eastern (Russian) one. Both of these facts testify that even in the narrower circle of the Slavic family he linked the Czech people closely with his own people. He spoke with heartfelt sympathy of the Czech Revival and admired the vital strength of the Czech nation, which succeeded in surviving so many obstacles and the attacks of its enemies; he calls the Czechs "the most moral and artistic of all Slavic nations." Any negative criticism he had to offer concerned individual phenomena, or tendencies which he considered unhealthy from a national as well as a Slavic point of view.

In the first part of his lectures he gave much thought to the forged manuscripts, which he considered to be the oldest monuments of Slavic literature. He evaluated them favorably, not extravagantly, mentioning Dobrovský's doubts as to their authenticity, but leaning toward the opinion of the majority of Czech literary men, who, led by Palacký and Šafařík, firmly believed in them. Moreover, the manuscript fraud was in itself important for one of Mickiewicz's own theses. These documents, which were supposed to have stemmed from the tenth century, making them the very oldest of Slavic writings, were written in Roman characters, and this proved that the Western or Latin culture which had also served as the basis for the culture of Poland was, among the Slavs, actually no less ancient than Eastern culture.

Mickiewicz accused more recent Czech literature of lack of national feeling, of submission to foreign influences. This judgment was based not only on the knowledge of ancient Czech literature prevailing at that time, but also on its evaluation in Czech circles. One of the most popular works of ancient Czech literature during the Czech Revival in Prague was a chronicle written in verse at the beginning of the fourteenth century, the so-called chronicle of Dalimil, which in a spirit of opposition of the lower Czech gentry passionately revolted against the Germanizing tendencies of the Royal House of Přemysl and of the high aristocracy, that is to say, against their activity in spreading alien, German culture in Bohemia. This nationalistic bias of the ancient annalist was not unlike the feeling of the patriots of that time, and it became one of the basic factors in their evaluation of national history, concurring with the judgment of Mickiewicz.

In essence, Mickiewicz evaluated the Hussite movement negatively. If we wish to understand his point of view, we must consider that even at home the leaders of the Czech Revival had to fight inch by inch for recognition. Two hundred years of the Catholic counter-reformation had blackened the Hussite movement considerably, and its reinstatement was therefore difficult. Even liberal influences in Western Europe which led to a deep appreciation of the Hussite movement were slow in penetrating into Bohemia and succeeded in so doing only in the 1840s. Czech authors soon recognized in Jan Žižka a great warrior who had brought the glorious past of their nation to the foreground, but they neither fully appreciated nor understood the fundamentally revolutionary importance of the doctrine for which he had fought, or that of the social change which followed it. The Hussite movement was fully evaluated only upon publication of the third volume of Palacký's *History,* devoted to the Hussite period. This history was published in 1845, that is, after Mickiewicz's lectures. Because of his standpoint regarding Catholicism, Mickiewicz must have found the anti-Catholic Hussite movement alien, but from the ideological point of view he was not against it. He accused it of stopping cultural development by instigating religious warfare and thus preventing the Czech nation from freeing itself from the foreign dependence into which it had been forced long before.

Mickiewicz considered the defeat of the Protestant estates by the Habsburgs in the Battle of Bílá Hora (White Mountain) a catastrophe and good reason for the downfall of the Czech national spirit and culture; this is in accord with the current conception. He expressed admiration for the Czech Revival of the late eighteenth and early nineteenth centuries and believed in its future, but he also pointed out what he considered its shortcomings. Mickiewicz claimed that the Czechs had lost national distinction in their literature; further he was disturbed at the expansion of their overdeveloped rationalism, which, in the eyes of a poet who stressed the emotional factor, was definitely a shortcoming. Although Mickiewicz felt that in this instance rationalism was a drawback, at other times he praised Czech literary circles for it. He arrived at this conclusion because the worthiest fruits of Czech culture of that time were scientific works, with which he was thoroughly acquainted. In his lectures he mentioned

Dobrovský and spoke in detail of the archeological endeavors of Šafařík, and in his chapter on Slavic philology he quoted the relatively little known Czech author Amerling. He called the Czechs a nation of philologists, admitted their primacy in the scientific sphere, and, when classifying Slavonic languages as to their function in national life, he defined Czech as the Slavonic language of science. In spite of this recognition he considered the predominance of rationalism in the Czech character as a one-sidedness which he would like to have seen supplemented with Polish emotionalism.

He chose the work of Kollár for careful analysis; he gave it his approval, but in conclusion he argued against Kollár's Russophilism which he considered to be a manifestation of one-sided belief in the predominance of materialism. He confronted this belief with the Austrophile standpoint of Count Thun, who opposed Czarist Russia, and who believed in the future of the Czechs within the bounds of the Austro-Hungarian Empire. In both cases Mickiewicz advised the Czechs to follow the romantic slogan, "Measure your strength according to your intentions, not your intentions according to your strength," and to emancipate themselves from their intellectual dependence on material forces, to lean toward the Poles' emotional view of revolution and thus cultivate within themselves the ability to attain complete liberty even from Austria, and to fight their way toward a completely national school of thought, entirely free of foreign influences.

The analysis of and objections to Kollár's and Thun's opinions closed the Czech chapters of Mickiewicz's lectures. It is known that in his very last lectures Mickiewicz concentrated almost entirely on the interpretation of Towiański's theories, so that he no longer had time to dwell on Slavonic literature itself and in fact later left the Chair under pressure from the French government.

Mickiewicz even attempted to implement his idea of winning the Czechs over to a romantic revolutionary struggle against Austria with a view toward their liberation. He used to this end the stormy events of 1848, when he organized a Slavic Legion in Rome. The core of this Legion consisted of a few young Polish enthusiasts and was intended to be supplemented by Slavic soldiers from Austrian garrisons stationed in Italy. This army was to destroy feudal Austria, bring freedom to "Brother Czech and Brother Russian" and, of course, liberate Poland also; thus a union of Slavic nations would be formed and led by the freedom-loving revolutionary spirit of Poland. Mickiewicz's plan failed, of course, as it lacked practical strategy; it nevertheless testifies to the fact that the poetic fancy of this great man was closely linked with the reality of his life.

As mentioned before, Mickiewicz's works found rewarding and varied response in Bohemia. When considering his contemporaries, we can distinguish between several fields of his influence. He proved primarily effective as a poet of folk ballads. One of the main sources from which the literature of the period of Czech national resurgence tried to draw was folk poetry, highly praised by Herder, Goethe, and almost all of Romantic Europe. With his ballads Mickiewicz presented an example of how to rework folk poetry, extracting from it all the qualities which attracted poets of romanticism; at the same time he incorporated these popular elements formally and ideologically into a progressive development of fine literature. Thus a special genre which captured the inner beauty of folk poetry was created, purged, of course, of primitivism. This genre was very prolific in Czech literature, where it produced, among others, the classical ballads of František Ladislav Čelakovský and Karel Jaromír Erben.

The group of poets surrounding the Byronic Romanticist Karel Hynek Mácha drew from Mickiewicz and other Polish poets the very ideals which Mickiewicz sought to instill into the Czech nation: revolutionary enthusiasm and courage. The generation which led the nation to barricades in 1848 in Prague was reared on Mickiewicz's poems, just as were the Polish revolutionaries of 1830.

The most important translator of Mickiewicz's works at that time was Václav Štulc, a Roman Catholic, a poet of average ability and an eminent ecclesiastical politician, who derived from Mickiewicz his optimistic view of life, based on moral principles coupled with service to the nation and to God. Though, by his firm and dogmatic confidence he was a complete contradiction of Mickiewicz, who sought and struggled painfully, still, influenced by his Polish model, Štulc was sympathetic to the Polish uprising of 1863. This was rather unusual in the light of his essentially conservative politics.

The generation succeeding Mickiewicz found something quite different in his works. Mickiewicz became almost a model for the poets of the so-called National School of the 1860s and 1870s, who were carried away by the vigor with which Czech society of that period progressed. They encouraged this vigorous development with their poems influenced by the *Ode on Youth,* and created for it a new type of patriotic epic which on one hand, in its Byronic hyperromanticism did not contradict the current striving toward realism, but on the other hand served their national mission with its mildly idealizing optimism. One of their examples of this type of epic was *Pan Tadeusz,* which was translated by an eminent poet of the school, Eliška Krásnohorská, and became the spirit by which Svatopluk Čech, a leading poet of that group, was guided.

Another generation, younger still, which strove to make Czech literature cosmopolitan by emancipating it from the confining borders of national themes and enriching it by the fruits of world literary tradition, included Mickiewicz's works in its enormous production of translations. It is not mere accident that a translator of Shakespeare, J. V. Sládek, chose to translate *Wallenrod,* and that Jaroslav Vrchlický, the translator of Goethe's *Faust* and one of the greatest of Czech poets, translated *Dziady* (*The Forefathers' Eve*).

The generation of 1890 was strongly influenced by new ideas, primarily socialism, and took notice of Mickiewicz as a politician and social thinker. From its midst stems a monograph by L. K. Hoffman; this was one of the very first works illuminating Mickiewicz's relationship with ideological currents of his time, particularly socialism and Marxism. At this time, too, Professor T. G. Masaryk, a leading spirit of this generation, turned attention to Mickiewicz's works.

Finally, there is the last stage of Mickiewicz's influence in Bohemia, the German occupation during World War II, which led one of the most prominent *avant-garde* Czech poets to a new, modern translation of Mickiewicz's most important writings. Several briefer translations by other authors are now being published. All these facts testify how vital and stimulating for Bohemia was Mickiewicz's influence and how deeply it has penetrated into Czech cultural development.

# FRANCE

## *Literary and Personal Acclaim*

Felicité de Lamennais (1782–1854), first apologist of Catholicism, afterwards revolutionary democrat, was in close touch with Mickiewicz in the years 1830–1834. The Catholic writings of Lamennais, especially *Essai sur l'indifférence en matière de religion* (Paris, 1817–1823), were studied by Mickiewicz during his stay in Rome and contributed to the formation of his Catholic faith and conception of life. The situation was reversed when Mickiewicz published his *Books of the Polish Pilgrims* (1832) which in turn influenced Lamennais's *Paroles d'un croyant* (1834). Lamennais became acquainted with the *Books* through a French translation edited with a preface by his friend Count Charles Montalembert. Lamennais's letters to the latter from January to May, 1833, are full of questions about the progress of the translation and demonstrate his eagerness to read it. Finally in May, 1833, he received the proofs. His appreciation of the work is illustrated by the following excerpts from his letters.

To Montalembert

*May 2, 1833*

I have received in yesterday's mail thirteen leaves of the book by Mickiewicz. . . . One cannot read anything more touching and more original. This little work will do immense good not only to the Poles, but to the French and all nations into whose languages it will be translated. It should be sent to England, to Germany and to Italy. If you are too busy, print my opinion without waiting.

*May 4, 1833*

I am becoming more and more convinced of the immense good that this little book can do. Would it not be possible to think of some way to spread it especially among the youth and among the people?

*May 5, 1833*

Don't neglect any means to spread the *Books of the Polish Pilgrims.* It is the book of all mankind. . . .[1]

To the Marquis de Corioli

*May 6, 1833*

There will shortly appear a little volume entitled *The Books of the Polish Pilgrims,* by Mickiewicz, undoubtedly the first poet of our epoch. It contains enchanting things; without forgetting all the distance which separates the word of man from the word of God I should almost dare to say: this is as beautiful as the Gospel. Such a pure expression of faith and liberty joined together is a miracle in our age of servitude and disbelief.[2]

A letter to Countess Senftt of May 9, 1833, contains remarks about the "general evil" which affects everybody and at the time especially the Poles. "Their great poet Mickiewicz," writes Lamennais, "wrote for them an enchanting work . . . one of the most beautiful written in recent times." [3]

Charles de Montalembert (1810–1870), French Catholic writer and politician, closely related to Lamennais, was one of the prominent representatives of liberal, progressive Catholicism. We give below his Preface to the French translation of Mickiewicz's *Books of the Polish Pilgrims* (*Livre des pèlerins polonais,* traduit du polonais d'Adam Mickiewicz, par le Comte Ch. de Montalembert; suivi d'un *Hymne à la Pologne,* par F. de La Mennais, Paris, 1833).

The work which we offer here to the friends of Poland is that of a poet who has been famous for a long time in his own country. Although he is still little known in ours, it would seem that he must become so more and more, in proportion to the development among

1. *Lettres inédites de Lamennais à Montalembert* par Eugène Forgues (Paris, Perrin, 1877), pp. 124, 127, 129.
2. E. D. Forgues, *Oeuvres posthumes de Lamennais* (Paris, Didier, 1863), II, 290.
3. *Ibid.,* 291.

Frenchmen of a feeling for really regenerative principles, in proportion to the strengthening of the bonds that should unite forever two undying friends, a nation that has been victimized and a nation that avenges injustice.

When he was quite young Adam Mickiewicz experienced both glory and its noble comrade, persecution. His *Crimean Sonnets,* sparkling with patriotism and poetry, have already been translated into French, as well as *Konrad Wallenrod,* an historical poem which takes its subject from the wars of Lithuania against her Teutonic oppressors and which provides a modern comparison, veiled but animated, with the cruel fate of Poland since the crime of partition. The popularity that this poem enjoys in Slavic countries has made it into a sort of national epic.

When the July revolution broke out, in the interval which elapsed between the glories of Paris and those of Warsaw, he composed an elegy, "To a Polish Mother," in which, while lamenting the fate which he believed was to be in store for a long time for his countrymen, he seems to us to have stirred the deepest emotions of humanity and patriotism.

November followed July.[1] Poland gave to a stupefied and sorrowing Europe the most sublime demonstration of modern times; ten months of unequaled glory were crowned by a martyrdom that still goes on.

Since then the soul of Mickiewicz, wedded to the fate of his country, seems to have grown with her misfortunes. . . . That admirable drama of *Forefathers' Eve,* of which one part, composed since the latest catastrophe, is destined to rescue from oblivion the persecution of Wilno, in which he was one of the victims. We know nothing in modern literature that is superior to this work, in which a genius at once so catholic and so national has spanned the entire range of poetry, from the bitterness and vindictive power of satire to a piety so impassioned and so exalted that it might be said to have been borrowed from the legends of the primitive Church or from the choirs of celestial spirits.

1. Allusion to the Polish uprising in November, 1830. [Ed.]

But at the same time, always guided by his sorrow and his patriotism, he has not been afraid to attack the greatest problems of the religious and social future of humanity, and their solution has not evaded him. He has probed the most painful evils of modern society, and we believe that he has understood the remedy for them; he has advanced still farther into the bosom of a positive and universal religion, and he no longer feels the self-pity that possesses those who have no hope.

*The Books of the Polish Pilgrims* is the first revelation of the new direction of his mind; here he renounces the forms and the traditional dignity of poetry, so that he may expound to his fellow countrymen, in a biblical and popular prose, the outstanding mission which the Creator has, according to him, assigned to Poland in both the past and future of Europe. He preaches to them the sanctification of their majestic adversity through a humble and implicit confidence in divine mercy, through the most perfect solidarity, through the avoidance of all recrimination about the past, as well as of all participation in the trifling and ephemeral struggles of day-to-day politics, and finally through an imperishable faith in the triumph of the cause of justice and liberty. And that is not all; for never, it seems to us, has a bolder or surer hand unmasked the fate which awaits all political and social organization in this period, quite aside from all questions of nationality or party. His poetic imagination has taken root in the midst of the symbolism, as national as it is evangelical, which he employs to make his work formally available to the most simple intelligence, while the substance of his work puts it on the level of the highest thoughts that have distinguished mankind. To this end he has drawn upon the biblical language that has been stabilized and popularized in Poland, as in Germany and in England, by the translations of Holy Scripture that were made in the middle of the sixteenth century.

Charles-Augustin Sainte-Beuve (1804–1869), the outstanding French literary critic, author of *Portraits littéraires, Port Royal, Causeries du lundi,* and other works, published in the paper *Le National* of July 8, 1833, a review of Mickiewicz's book under the title: *The Books of the Polish Pilgrims.*

This little volume is a work apart. A profoundly national and religious conviction has dictated it to the fervent poet; it is intended as a moral viaticum for the people, wandering or in bondage, in whom the old Catholic faith seems to have allied itself with the most modern feeling for liberty.

Monsieur Mickiewicz has approached the great Polish disaster from that ardent and mystic view which is so favorable to poetry. The style of the Bible is his model. He who formerly breathed his patriotic sorrow in *Crimean Sonnets* or, as in *Konrad Wallenrod,* seemed to borrow from Byron his ethereal images, now writes in the simple biblical verses of the Apostle; he speaks in parables in the style of the Gospel and gives to the exiles in the desert the plain bread of a popular and powerful eloquence.

We have seen, above all, in this a thoroughly noble use of poetic genius in a time of national disaster. We have admired in it, thanks to the precise and bold translation of Monsieur Montalembert, the beauties of a thought that is serious and virile and quite naturally biblical. To tastes that are too often sated, it has been bread of a distinguished and acrid flavor, rather strange, kneaded in a Slavic manner.

To most of our Catholics *The Books of the Polish Pilgrims* should seem excessively democratic and rebellious. Will it seem too Catholic in manner to the Republicans? We do not fear to recommend it to all those who dare study and accept, in its most various aspects, in the most unaccustomed disguises, the idea of future freedom.

GEORGE SAND (1803–1876), the well-known French novelist, showed a lively interest in Poland, Polish literature and art. Her article, "Essai sur le drame fantastique: Goethe, Byron, Mickiewicz" (Essay on the Fantastic Drama: Goethe, Byron, Mickiewicz) in the *Revue des deux Mondes,* December 1, 1839, was at that time one of the longest and most exhaustive about Mickiewicz. Excerpts from it follow.

The right description for these strange and audacious works which were products of a century of philosophical inquiry, and to which nothing in the past can be compared, would be that of metaphysical drama. Among several attempts more or less remarkable, three take their place in the first rank: *Faust,* which Goethe called a tragedy; *Manfred,* which Byron calls a dramatic poem; and Part III of *Forefathers' Eve,* which Mickiewicz describes more slightingly as an act.

The drama of *Faust* marks, in my eyes, a boundary line between the era of the incredible simpleton used in good faith as a dramatic device and an effect, and the era of the incredible savant used philosophically as an expression that is metaphysical and . . . shall I say religious? I will say it, since these great works of which I speak belong to philosophy, that is to say, to the religion of the future—the skepticism of Goethe, as well as the despair of Byron, as well as the sublime rage of Mickiewicz.

It is a question of nothing less than of restoring to two of the greatest poets who ever lived the share of originality which each of them displayed in renewing what it has pleased criticism to call the same work. I see myself fulfilling a religious duty toward Mickiewicz in asking criticism to weigh well its decisions when such names are under consideration.

Thus all literary Europe took Goethe at his word when he announced, with superb kindness, that Byron had appropriated his *Faust* and had used for his own passions, the motives which impelled Doctor Faustus. Byron himself had been alarmed by the resemblance which struck Goethe, when he wrote with an affected frivolity: "Its first scene, meanwhile, finds itself resembling that of *Faust*." Thus the few French critics who have deigned to glance at the magnificent improvisation of Mickiewicz have hastened to say: "This is another imitation of Faust," as Goethe had said that *Faust* was the original of *Manfred*. Well, so be it: *Faust* has served as a model in the art of dramatic design to Byron and Mickiewicz, as Aeschylus did for Sophocles and Euripides, as Cimabue did in the art of painting for Raphael and Correggio; and their dramas resemble that of Goethe much less than an ordinary classic drama in five acts and in verse resembles another ordinary classic drama in five acts and in verse; as *Athalie* resembles *Le Cid,* as *Polyeucte* resembles *Bajazet,* and so on. The metaphysical drama is a form. It has been established; it fell into the public domain on the day it was conceived. It is an invention for which the honor goes to Goethe and for which a sufficiently magnificent apotheosis has been given him. Now it belongs to the future, and the future will develop it, as Byron and Mickiewicz have already begun to demonstrate, according to its capacities.

I have attempted to show that there is neither plagiarism nor servility in modeling one's work upon an established form. It remains for me to show that the substance, range, and execution of the three metaphysical dramas which I am discussing differ essentially. I shall not return again to the defense of the two great poets who are supposed to have imitated the first. I shall try to throw into relief, as regards both content and form, the great philosophic and religious progress that distinguishes these three poems, although they were created in closely related periods.

Since Konrad is the name of the character preferred by Mickiewicz and in particular that of the hero of *Forefathers' Eve,* I call by his name the fragment of Mickiewicz's work of which I am going to give an account, although this fragment has no title at all, either in the translation or the original, and is merely called *Forefathers' Eve,* Part III, Act I. It is therefore a simple fragment that I am going to put beside *Faust* and *Manfred*. But what does it matter if there is a gap between the work published in 1832 and that which the author is no doubt continuing at this moment? What does it matter if there is a break in the development of the characters and in the march of events, if these events and these characters have already been put down and portrayed by a hand so sure that we know at first glance that the poet is the equal of Goethe and Byron? Let us be content, for the present, with the Mickiewicz fragment. We shall see that it is quite enough to put him on an equal footing with his illustrious predecessors.

We have said that the novelty of this form created by Goethe consists in the mingling of the metaphysical world with the exterior world.

But perhaps one has the right to say that Byron has gone too far in his opposition to *Faust,* which remains too much in the real world, while *Manfred* remains too much perhaps in a dream-world. Mickiewicz's treatment seems the best. He does not mix background with idea, as Goethe has done in *Faust*. Neither does he separate the background from the idea, as Byron has done in *Manfred*. Real life is itself a vigorous painting, startling and tremendous, and idea lies at its center. The world of fantasy is not outside or above; it is at the bottom of everything, it moves everything, it is the soul of all reality, it lives in all facts. Each character, each group carries it in itself and shows it its own way. All hell is let loose, but the celestial army is there also; and while the devils triumph in the material order, they are conquered in the intellectual order. They have the temporal power, the autocratic decisions of Tsar Flog, the tortures, the hangmen's agents, exile, shackles, instruments of punishment. The angels have the spiritual power, the heroic soul, the devout loftiness, the holy indignation, the prophetic dreams, the divine ecstasies of the persecuted. But these heavenly rewards are extorted by martyrdom, and it is scenes of martyrdom that the melancholy brush of Mickiewicz makes us witness. Now, these descriptions are of a kind that neither Byron nor Goethe nor Dante could have created. Since the lamentations and denunciations of the prophets of Zion, no voice has been raised with so much force to sing of an event so stupendous as that of the fall of a nation. But if the lyricism and the magnificence of sacred chants have not been surpassed at any period, there is in our day an aspect of the human spirit which was not brought to light in the time of the Hebrew prophets and which throws on modern poetry an immeasurable brilliance; it is the philosophic feeling that extends into the infinite the narrow horizon of God's chosen people. There are no longer Jews and Gentiles; all the inhabitants of the earth are God's chosen people; and the earth is the holy city which, through the mouth of the poet, invokes the justice and the mercy of heaven.

Such is the immense idea of the Polish drama. It shows the development of the feeling for the ideal from *Faust* to *Konrad,* by way of *Manfred. Faust* might be called the Fall, *Manfred* the Atonement, *Konrad* the Redemption; but it is a bloody Redemption, it is Purgatory, where the Angel of Hope walks amid the tortures, representing Heaven and helping the victims; it is a holocaust where half the human race is immolated by the other half, where innocence is on trial in the criminal court, where liberty is sacrificed by despotism, the civilization of our new day by the barbarism of an earlier time. In the midst of this agony, devils laugh and triumph, angels pray and lament; God says nothing! Then the poet gives forth a cry of despair and rage; he summons all the powers of his heart and his genius, to wring from God grace for perishing humanity. Nothing is more sublime than that despairing cry from man to Heaven; it is the voice of all humanity asking divine intercession and protesting against the reign of Satan. . . . But Konrad has fallen, like the rebellious angel, into the sin of pride. Heaven is deaf. God conceals Himself.

It is clear that this energetic and menacing Catholicism is far from the apathetic resignation of Silvio Pellico. Konrad is far removed from that kind of ecstatic submission, worthy perhaps of India, but certainly unworthy of Europe. His burning energy bursts forth in accents which would make God Himself turn pale, if God were this miserable Jehovah who plays with the people of the earth as a chess-player plays with kings and pawns on a chessboard. Also, the silence of this divinity whose merciless laws Konrad does not understand leads him into rage and into error.

The form is Catholic, it is clear; but this Catholicism has a philosophy more audacious and more advanced than the legendary Catholicism of Faust. Konrad, in his thirst to find in Heaven the justice and benevolence that have been denied him on earth, does not recoil from blasphemy. His savage energy, bearing the stamp of the poetry of the North, lays at the door of the Supreme Wisdom the frightful evils from which the human species suffers; the poet shackled in irons is made to resemble a martyr, a Christ. But there is a great distance between his noble and burning rage—and evangelical resignation! Surely, Konrad is no disciple of the patient Essenian philosophy. Konrad is very much a man of his period, and he does not, like Faust, manufacture a pantheistic nature whose organization and cold beauty console him for the absence of God. He no longer consumes himself, like Manfred, in waiting for a mysterious revelation of God and his being that death alone will realize. Konrad is no longer the man of doubt; he is no longer the man of despair; he is the living man. Like Manfred, he still suffers; he suffers a hundred times more; his spirit and his flesh are breathless in the shackles of slavery; but he no longer hesitates, he feels, he knows that God exists. He no longer questions nature or his conscience or his knowledge about the existence of an all-powerful being; but he wishes to know and understand the nature of this Being. He wishes to know if he should hate It, adore It, or fear It. His faith is established; he wishes to arrange his creed; he wishes to penetrate into the essences and attributes of the Divinity. He does not attain his goal, since he is imperfect, proud of his genius and his love of country to the point of frenzy; he represents the human race at the point it has reached at his time, that is to say, he is at the same time a believer and a skeptic, vain about his strength, angered by his sufferings, full of the feeling of justice and brotherhood, eager to break his fetters, but still ignorant, morally primitive, unable to achieve in a single act the labor of his salvation, and still insistent, through habits of the past and impatience with the future, that Heaven perform one of those miracles which Christianity attributed to God apart from humanity. Heaven is deaf, and the poet falls, overwhelmed, while waiting for his spirit to be enlightened, for his pride to be abased, and for his mind to open itself to a true understanding of divine ways.

To recapitulate, we shall say that we see in Faust the need to poeticize the nature that had been deified by Spinoza; in Manfred the desire to make man play, in the bosom of that idolized nature, a role worthy of his faculties and his aspirations; in Konrad an attempt to improve upon the work of creation, in the eyes of man, by improving the fate of man on earth. None of these poems has realized its aim as well as it might have done. But how many valiant and sorrowing works will still issue from the poetic fever before humanity may produce the bard of hope and certitude!

EDGAR QUINET (1803–1875), French historian and philosopher, was professor at the Collège de France. Quinet, Michelet, and Mickiewicz, bound by friendship and common political and moral opinions, formed the "triumvirate" whose plaque adorns one of the halls of the Collège.

We print Quinet's letter to his mother written on December 23, 1837, and published in his *Correspondance,* together with an excerpt from a lecture in the Collège de France of March 20, 1844, published in *Le Siècle,* March 25, 1844.

Last Thursday I met the famous poet Mickiewicz. It would be impossible to have at the same time an attitude more gracious and more untamed. He is quite remarkable, above all, for a moral loftiness, it seemed to me. I think he is rather mystical, but of a mysticism which goes with a great and beautiful nature. He has a youthful and perfectly genuine air, which nowadays is not customary. We must see each other often.

I must record, hailing it as an important event, what is occurring a few feet away, within the walls of the Collège de France. In the name of the Slavs, the foremost poet of the Slavs, our dear, heroic Mickiewicz, fights with consecrated words for a cause that is quite often at one with our own. Who has ever heard words more sincere, more religious, more Christian, more extraordinary than those of this exile among a remnant of his own people, like the prophet under the willows? Ah, if the soul of the martyrs and saints of Poland is not in him, I do not know where it is. Above all, who has ever spoken of our country, of France, with such filial emotion, if it is not this child of Poland? Let thanks be given him! These men, these brothers-in-arms, have constantly been in the advance-guard of our armies; it is right that they should still wish to be, in the activities of France, in the advance-guard of the future.

EMMANUEL-HENRI MARQUIS DE NOAILLES (1830–1909), French writer and diplomat, was the author of two works on Poland: *La Pologne et ses frontières* (1863) and *Henri de Valois et la Pologne* (1872). His article, "La Poésie polonaise" (Polish Poetry), here translated, was published in *Le Correspondant,* March 25, 1866.

Polish poetry has a character which is at the same time general and particular. It also treats the great problems of the human soul and of the inner life, but as a Polish soul conceives and feels them, under the influence of the misfortune with which Poland has been stricken.

Other poets in their works take the point of view of an entirely speculative philosophy; Polish poets write under the impact of an implacable reality; in them the weak side of poetry, if one may dare to say it—that which is invented—does not exist. The evils, the moral anguish which Werther and Hamlet suffer have causes which at bottom concern us very little; but Hamlet and Werther move us when, allowing us to forget their personal fortunes, they make us see in their souls all the passions of the human soul. In the Polish poets, on the other hand, the cause of suffering is as great and as real as the suffering itself; they move us doubly; one feels that their own sadness is still more poignant than that of the imaginary characters whom they put through their paces. Everyone knows the magnificent soliloquy in which Hamlet questions the meaning of life. Never, in the opinion of critics, has the genius of Shakespeare risen higher. But how can one be still not more moved while reading that other soliloquy, in the great drama of Mickiewicz, *Forefathers' Eve,* where Konrad, the new Polish Hamlet, a prey to the same hallucination, to the same poetic delirium as the young Prince of Denmark, allows himself to be carried away by despair, questions God, provokes Him, defies Him, mocks Him, and with an impassioned logic proves to Him that it is not He who governs the world—it is the Tsar.

Another characteristic of contemporary Polish poetry, a characteristic which is peculiar to it and which is not to be found in any other country or in any other period, is the unity of this poetry. Poets of other countries will cull from all peoples and all times the subject matter of their compositions, and follow the compulsions of their genius, which sweeps them along the most varying paths. But with the Polish poets all is national; subjects are always taken from Polish history; it is a single spirit which animates this poetic galaxy, a single feeling which makes their hearts beat, a single idea which guides them along the varying paths which the diversity of their skills makes them follow, a single enthusiasm which inspires them, a single goal which attracts them. They are all in a community of thought and patriotism, and the union of their works forms a perfect poetic cycle.

At their head strides Mickiewicz. His vast genius has run ahead of them in the way which they must follow. He is the unchallenged national poet of Poland. The two great works of his youth, *Wallenrod* and *Grażyna,* are two historical epics. We shall see the patriotic principle embodied in the heroes of these two epics: a warrior and a woman.

In the former work Mickiewicz has admirably described the character of the national bard, repository of patriotic enthusiasm, personification of all the great national traditions, voice of the lost fatherland, which still sings from the depths of his heart, reanimates and fortifies it. Wallenrod is the prototype of the *émigré* poet with a deep sense of mission.

Opposite this figure of the ancient bard, opposite his austere power, Mickiewicz has placed an appealing young woman, Aldona, daughter of Prince Kiejstut, who is loved by Wallenrod and marries him. Mickiewicz has put all the charm and delicacy of his talent into portraying her. She is the bright moment in a dark picture, she is the only ray of youth and joy in the midst of a sad epic. There is nothing more appealing, perhaps, in all modern poetry, than their first meetings and the birth of their love; and there is nothing more touching than their final scenes at the end of the poem.

In the second historical poem by Mickiewicz, *Grażyna,* the entire action turns about a woman. Grażyna is a heroine in the full sense of the word. She is proud, energetic, enterprising; the sight of a sword does not frighten her; she loves, on the contrary, to wield the weapons of warriors. It is by submissiveness and the power of love that Aldona contributes to the work of Wallenrod; Grażyna advances upon the enemy and saves the honor of her husband, which had been for a while in danger. If the role of one woman is more dramatic and more brilliant, the character of the other attracts us more. In these two poetic creations of Mickiewicz we find the whole range of the character of Polish women; full of enthusiasm and energy, of devotion and sacrifice; glorying in patriotic fervor, capable of every self-denial; going to bury in Siberia their gifts of youth and beauty, in order to look after an aged father or to follow a convict-husband; sisters of charity in hospitals and prisons; sometimes risking their lives on the battlefield and not afraid to put up with the sufferings and dangers of war.

At the time when the first works of Mickiewicz appeared, the great struggle between Classicists and Romanticists had not been settled. The young poet was reproached for having allowed himself to be corrupted by the new school; he was accused of violating the eternal rules of art. He replied by publishing *Grażyna,* a national work, modern in its ideas but classicist in purity of form. Here Mickiewicz has confined himself to the most severe conventions; the classic unities are strictly observed; the plot is very cleverly handled; interest is sustained with matchless art. One feels a Homeric breath which animates the entire epic. The young Polish poet made himself in this work a disciple of the creator of the *Iliad;* he has borrowed from him a certain poetic manner, together with those great comparisons which appear from time to time and which embellish the story in such a remarkable fashion.

Victor Hugo (1802–1885), the great romantic poet, novelist and champion of liberty, was one of the most devoted friends of Poland—to quote only one of his statements in a letter to Charles Montalembert: ". . . Je suis presque aussi Polonais que vous, mon bien cher ami, et vous savez combien je vous aime de l'être plus que moi, combien je me blâme de l'être moins que vous. En amour pour cette noble Pologne, je ne le cède qu'à vous" (R. P. Lecanuet, *Montalembert,* Paris, 1895, p. 365).

We print here a letter of Victor Hugo written on May 17, 1867, to Władysław Mickiewicz, son of the poet, upon the occasion of the dedication of a monument to Adam Mickiewicz at the cemetery of Montmorency, near Paris. The letter was published in *Inauguration du monument d'Adam Mickiewicz à Montmorency,* Paris, Librairie du Luxembourg, 1867.

I have been asked to say a word at this illustrious tomb. . . . To speak of Mickiewicz is to speak of the beautiful, the just, the true; it is to speak of the cause of which he was the soldier, of the duty of which he was the hero, of the liberty of which he was the apostle, and of the deliverance of which he was the forerunner.

Mickiewicz was a reminder of all the classic virtues which have in them the power of making us young again; he was a priest of the ideal; his art is in the grand manner; the deep breath of sacred forests is in his poetry; he has understood both humanity and nature; his hymn to the infinite was combined with a holy revolutionary fervor. Exiled, outlawed, conquered, he proudly cried to the four winds the lofty claims of the fatherland. The reveille of the people, it is genius which sounds it; in former times the prophet, today the poet; and Mickiewicz is one of the trumpeters of the future.

There is life in such a sepulchre.

Immortality is in the poet; resurrection is in the citizen. One day the United People of Europe will say to Poland: Arise! and from the tomb will emerge her great soul.

Yes, that sublime shadow, Poland, lies there with the poet. Hail, Mickiewicz! Hail to the noble sleeper who will arise! He hears me, I know, and he understands me. We are, he and I, two exiles. If I do not have, in my isolation and my gloom, any crown to give in the name of glory, I have the right to fraternize with a shadow in the name of misfortune. I am not the voice of France, but I am the voice of exile.

ADOLPHE CRÉMIEUX (1796–1880), French lawyer and politician, was a member of the provisional government of the French Republic in 1848, then Minister of Justice, President of the "Alliance Israélite Universelle," member of the "Défense national" in 1870. We quote his letter of May 20, 1867, to Armand Lévy, written on the same occasion as that of Victor Hugo and printed in the same publication.

Your letter reached me here, and you will understand my sorrow, you who know how much Mickiewicz inspired me with esteem—I almost said with affection. Our young people in the schools, who happily applaud all great men, do not separate the glorious name of Mickiewicz from the glorious names of Quinet and Michelet: three men in whom patriotism fired genius and who understood each other so marvelously. As to him, I can only recall with a feeling of pious gratitude all that his voice and his writings proclaimed in the cause of bringing the Polish Jews into the great Polish family. He stirred the feeling of love of country in that part of the population which had been alienated by religious prejudice, and also the feeling of human brotherhood in the hearts of those who treated the Jews as pariahs and outlaws.

The Revolution saw the Jews unite nobly with Catholics nobly insurgent; and thrown together in the same slaughter, Jews and Christians generously watered with their blood the sacred soil of the common fatherland. In unfortunate Poland there are only friendly hands, joined together and swearing, in a fraternal handclasp, the redemption of beloved Poland: the Israelites have shown themselves and will show themselves devoted, like the Christians, to the same cause.

It was Mickiewicz who with his eloquent pen and his friendly voice preached the brotherhood of religions and the equality of all men born on the same soil. He was understood. When the day of victory comes, bringing the rebirth of this people of martyrs and heroes, the name of Mickiewicz will be sacred to all the children of Poland, whom difference of faith will no longer divide. Since I can say nothing at his tomb, on the day of tribute to his memory, will you kindly at least deliver to all our friends this expression of all my sympathy.

JULES MICHELET (1798–1874), noted French historian and writer, author of the *Histoire de la Révolution,* was a friend and colleague of Mickiewicz in the Collège de France. His article "Le Collège de France," appeared in *Paris-Guide par les principaux écrivains et artistes de la France. Première partie, La Science, l'Art* (Paris, Librairie Internationale, 1867).

The same path was followed at the same time by two outstanding intelligences, Quinet and Mickiewicz, who came from two different parts of the world, had imaginations quite dissimilar, and yet were united with each other and with me by a deep sense of life, by a deep understanding of the mind of the common man.

Quinet exhibited this especially in his recent book on the *Genius of Religions*. Mickiewicz put it into his poems of suffering, *Forefathers' Eve* and *The Books of the Polish Pilgrims,* which were read by many millions of people, from the Vistula to Siberia.

For a long time Quinet and I went together along paths closely related. Without ever arranging a common plan of action, we were always in harmony in our books and our lectures.

Mickiewicz, using different forms, had been at one with us through feeling, through the nature of his thought. In hailing the work done by Saviors and Messiahs, he believed that the origin of their divinity was popular. Everyone could become a savior of his people, of his fatherland. Consequently, this course, Oriental in language and imagery, fitted in intimately with ours, which were the work of two Occidentals. It was a call to heroism, to great and noble desires, to unlimited sacrifice. Thus these three solitary men communicating very little among themselves, found themselves forming more than a group and an organization, but—something decidedly rare—they enjoyed a continuous unity, a powerful harmony of thought and words. External differences only made internal unanimity the stronger. No teaching ever had more power or authority.

And that day of May 11, 1843, was one of the best of my life. Quinet and Mickiewicz, one at the right, the other at the left, were present at my lecture and announced our mutual agreement, and gave to the students in the classroom (who later were to see so much disharmony) the most beautiful spectacle in the world, that of great friendship.

Let us be thankful for unison of hearts, which so fortunately allowed our fathers to join two causes, the brotherhood of man, the brotherhood of countries. Poland and France, together with the many illustrious foreigners whom I saw before me—Italians, Hungarians, Germans—made me feel a single spirit in my breast, that of Europe.

ERNEST RENAN (1823–1892), distinguished French historian and writer, author of *Origines du christianisme, La vie de Jésus,* and other works, delivered an oration in the name of the Collège de France upon the occasion of the removal of the ashes of Adam Mickiewicz from the cemetery of Montmorency, June 28, 1890.[1] The oration was published in *Le Temps,* June 29, 1890, and reprinted in *Feuilles détachées,* Paris, 1892.

GENTLEMEN:

The Collège de France thanks you for having been so kind as to include it in this noble project: the return to his fatherland of the remains of an outstanding man whom Poland lent us and whom she takes back from us today. This is justice. Our Collège, founded for the purpose of studying nature and explaining the spirit of men

1. In 1890 the remains of Mickiewicz were transported to Poland and deposited in the vaults of the royal castle Wawel in Cracow.

through language and literature, is a kind of universal meeting place of minds. Bodies do not belong to us. Therefore take these illustrious remains, which were fired by genius.

Adam Mickiewicz does not entirely take leave of us. We shall have his spirit, his memory. Our ancient halls will retain the faraway echo of his voice. Some survivors of those heroic days can still tell us of the rapture in his words, of their magic, of their fascinating power. United in a glorious trinity with two other names that are dear to us, those of Michelet and Quinet, the name of Mickiewicz has become a symbol to us, an inseparable portion of former glories and former delights.

Your illustrious compatriot, gentlemen, had the sovereign quality by which one dominates one's era, the sincerity, the impersonal enthusiasm, the absence of self-interest which create a state of being in which one does not do, one does not say, one does not write what one's self desires, but one does and says and writes what an external power dictates. This power is almost always derived from one's period, that everlasting invalid that wishes to have its wounds treated and its fever calmed by sonorous words. It is derived still more from one's racial inheritance, from the inner voice of one's ancestors and one's blood. Mickiewicz had these two great sources of inspiration.

When like a true sister Madame George Sand perceived his genius from the first word, she felt keenly that his heart had felt all our wounds and that it had beaten in sympathy with our suffering. The glory of our century lies in having wished to achieve the impossible, to solve the insoluble. Let it be praised for that!

The men of action who will wish to carry out such a stupendous program will be powerless; the men of reason will only end in contradictions. The poet who does not doubt, who after each defeat applies himself again more eagerly and more skillfully to his task, is never beaten. This was the kind of man Mickiewicz was. He had in him the wellsprings of endless rebirth. He suffered the cruelest tortures, but never that of despair; his unshakable faith in the future came from a kind of deep instinct, from something which is in us and which speaks more forcibly to us than painful reality. I mean the spirit of past times, solidarity with that which does not die. Strong men are those who thus embody a portion of universal consciousness, who accomplish their human destiny as the ant labors, as the bee makes honey.

Bound to former centuries by secret lines of communication, Mickiewicz was a Seer of the past. He was at the same time a Seer of the future. He believed in his race; but he believed above all in the divine spirit which animates all those who carry within them the breath of life, and through all clouds he saw a brilliant future where suffering humanity would be consoled for its miseries. This great idealist was a great patriot; but he was above everything else a believer. And as the real reason for believing in immortality was the existence of martyrs, even so his imagination, inspired by his human kindness, persuaded him that humanity has not worked so hard and that unfortunate people have not suffered so much in vain.

This is why enlightened French society received so gladly this great and noble intelligence, made a place for him among that which it held most dear, made him officially and almost without consulting him, a member of a triumvirate which supported freedom and denounced false religion. The day when the Slavic mind had taken its place among national minds, which are studied in a scientific manner, and when the creation of a chair of Slavic language and literature was arranged, a distinguished and generous decision was made by those who were then in charge of intellectual things in France, and Mickiewicz was given this commission. The poet, the man who represented the soul of a people, who was familiar with its legends, who understood intuitively its origins, seemed better, for the profound study of a race, than a library-bred scholar who had worked only with books. It was a correct decision. The flowery meadow is superior to the dry herbarium, which represents only a wan memory of life. The volumes which contain the first lectures of Monsieur Mickiewicz are a treasury of original data of the ancient history of the Slavic people, which the professor expounded with learning and felt with the heart of a man of the common people.

He has been charged with departing from his program. Ah! it is difficult to lock oneself up in a narrow program when one is drunk with the infinite. He was such a man, with his bold insights, his overflowing aspirations, his exalted prophetic visions, that we are proud of him, and although the decree of his official investiture was held up for political reasons, we have inscribed his name on the marble tablets which contain the names of our elders. He had the best of decrees, that which was countersigned by the enthusiasm of the public. From this hospitable earth where he has lain for thirty-five years, you are going to remove him to your Saint-Denis, to the vaults of Wawel, where your former kings lie in state. He will be there beside Kościuszko and Poniatowski,[2] the only ones in that noble assemblage of the dead who were not kings. Next to those who bore the sword you have wished to place the poet who gave a voice to your ardent and powerful spirit, to your exquisite legends, to all which in your land moves and consoles you, makes you weep and smile. You teach thus a great lesson in idealism; you announce that a nation is a spiritual thing, that it has a soul which cannot be crushed by the methods which crush bodies.

Great and illustrious colleague, remember France when you are in the royal tomb which your compatriots have prepared for you. Poor France, she will not forget, you may be sure of it. Those whom she has once loved she will love always. What she applauded in your words she would still applaud. The rostrum that she offered you she would offer again more freely. You would falter if you tried to recall your victories, but you would have words of encouragement to point out the duties of the conquered. Go to the glory that you have deserved; return, amidst the praise of nations, to that fatherland which you loved so dearly. We limit our desire to one thing only, that it may be said at your tomb that you were one of us, that it will be known in the Poland of the future that there was, during the days of trial, a generous France who welcomed you, applauded you, loved you.[3]

2. Tadeusz Kościuszko (1746–1817), Polish and American hero; Prince Joseph Poniatowski (1762–1813), Polish general and Marshall of France, commander of a Polish force in the campaign of 1812. He was called the Polish bayard for his bravery, faithfulness, and sense of honor. [Ed.]

3. The excerpts above, from Mantalembert, George Sand, Quinet, de Noialles Michelet, and Sainte-Beuve, are taken from *Adam Mickiewicz et la pensée Française, 1830–1923,* ed. S. P. Koczorowski, Paris, 1929. [Ed.]

PAUL CAZIN, noted French poet and writer, is the author of a distinguished book on the Polish poet of the eighteenth century, Ignacy Krasicki. We give here Cazin's translation of two ballads by Mickiewicz: "The Three Budrys" and "The Ambush."

## LA BALLADE DES TROIS BUDRYS

Le vieux Litwanien Boudrys
A trois bon lurons de fils:
—"Hé!—leur crie-t-il, de sa cour,—mes gaillards,
Détachez vos palefrois,
Ajustez votre harnois
Et fourbissez vos glaives et vos dards.

"Car on m'a dit, à Wilno,
Qu'on va publier bientôt
Trois incursions contre trois coins du monde:
Olgherd sur les Russes cogne,
Skirghello sur la Pologne,
Keystoutt chez les Teutons fera sa ronde.

"Vous êtes forts et hardis,
Allez servir le pays,
Et que nos dieux litwaniens vous assistent.
Cette année je reste ici,
Mais écoutez mon avis:
Vous êtes trois et vous avez trois pistes.

"Que l'un suive avec ardeur
Olgherd qui marche en vainqueur
Du lac Ilmen aux murs de Novgorod,
Pour conquérir des hermines,
Des brocarts, des perles fines,
Chez les marchands aussi riches qu'Hérode.

"Que de Keystoutt le second
Rejoigne le bataillon

Qui va piller ces chiens de Teutoniques:
Ils ont d'ambre autant que sable
Et des chapes admirables,
Brodées d'orfrois et de gemmes uniques.

"Du Niemen, sous Skirghello,
Le dernier va franchir l'eau:
Les gens, la-bàs, ne sont pas très à l'aise,
Mais qu'il m'apporte un bon choix
De sabres et de courreois,
Et me ramène une bru polonaise.

"Car de toutes nos captives
Il n'en est point de plus vives:
Calines, gaies, folâtres à merveille;
Un teint plus blanc que le lait
Des cils plus noirs que le jais,
Des yeux brillants, aux étoiles pareilles;

"Des seins en fruits de poirier,
Et de si fins petits pieds,
Que, pour chaussure, à la mutine enfant,
Suffirait, je crois, sans peine,
La "sandale de la reine,"
Le plus mignon des muguets de nos champs.

"Voilà plus de cinquante ans,
Quand j'étais jeune et fringant,
C'est de là-bas que j'ai pris une femme.
Bien qu'elle soit déjà morte,
Quand mon regard s'y reporte
Dans mon vieux coeur se rallume la flamme . . ."

Les ayant bien sermonés
Il bénit la randonnée
On saute en selle, on file à fond de train.

L'automne et l'hiver passent,
Des trois garçons plus de traces
Boudrys les croit restés sur le terrain.

Par la neige et la rafale
Accourt un homme à cheval,
Son manteau cache un gros ballot qui pèse:
—"De Novgorod? Quel trésor!
Montre ces beaux roubles d'or!"
—"Non, père, c'est une bru polonaise!"

Après une autre rafale,
Encore un homme à cheval,
Sa housse tombe et le fardeau lui pèse:
—"Est-ce l'ambre allemand garçon,
Qui charge ainsi ton arçon?
—"Non, père, c'est une bru polonaise!"

Enfin sort de la rafale
Un dernier homme à cheval,
Sous son manteau gonfle un riche butin . . .
Mais, avant qu'il n'ait rien vu,
Le vieux Boudrys a couru
Prier son monde au troisième festin.

L'EMBUSCADE

De son beau jardin d'Ukraine
Le palatin, hors d'haleine,
Court au château, plein de rage et d'effroi,
Par le rideau de cretonne
Il glisse un oeil et frisonne:
Que fait sa femme, hors du lit vide et froid?

Son oeil se fixe immobile,
Tandis que sa main fébrile

Tortille sa moustache grisonnante;
  Pirouettant brusquement,
  Ses long manches au vent,
Il fait trembler l'air de sa voix tonnante:

  —"Cosaque! Holà, mon escorte!
  Maraud, qui garde la porte?
La nuit ni chien, ni valets? Damné drôle!
  Hardi! prends ta carnassière
  Ton mousquet de janissaire,
Et dépends-moi du clou mon espingole."

  En armes il s'élancèrent
  Et prudemment se glissèrent
Vers la tonnelle où s'accrochait la treille.
  Sur un tertre de gazon,
  Dans l'ombre qu'aperçoit-on?
La palatine en très simple appareil.

  De cette blanche bacchante
  L'une des mains tatonnante,
De son sein nu protège la pudeur;
  Et l'autre main pouce à pouce,
  Assez mollement repousse
Les bras d'un homme, à ses genoux, en pleurs.

  Tendre et amer tour à tour,
  Il lui dit: "Mon cher amour,
Ai-je donc tout perdu sans espérance?
  Tes soupirs et tes émois,
  Les frôlement de tes doigts,
Ce roquentin a tout payé d'avance.

  "Pareil aux âmes damnées,
  Brulant depuis tant d'années,
Suis-je de toi réprouvé sans recours?

L'autre avait plus de ressources,
Il a fait tinter sa bourse
Et tu lui as tout vendu pour toujours.

"Chaque soir, ce vieil indigne,
Au creux d'un duvet de cygne,
Sur ton giron bercera sa folie,
Et de ta lèvre enfiévrée
Et de ta joue empourprée
Butinera les douceurs que j'envie.

"Moi, sur mon roussin fidèle,
Avec Phébé pour chandelle,
J'accours ici, bravant des temps de chien,
Pour pleurer, en arrivant,
Et te dire, en m'en allant:
Bonne nuit, belle, et amusez vous bien!"

Elle demeure insensible,
Et lui, sans répit la crible
De ses soupirs et de ses remontrances.
Tant qu'enfin, la pauvre amante,
Epuisée et pantelante,
S'abandonne entre ses bras, tout en transes.

Le cosaque et le barbon
A l'affût sous un buisson,
Tirent des bandoulières les cartouches,
De leurs dents les déchiquettent,
Puis, à renfort de baguettes,
Chargent balles et poudre en double couche.

—"Monseigneur," dit le cosaque,
"Quelque diablotin m'attaque.
Permettez-moi d'attendre un tantinet.
Voilà qu'armant mon fusil,

Un tremblement m'a saisi,
Une larme a mouillé le bassinet."

—"Plus bas! race de kroumir,
Je vais t'apprendre à gémir,
Attrappe-moi ce sac de poudre fine.
Vite, garnis la lumière,
Grattes de l'ongle la pierre,
Et puis, choisi: toi ou la gourgandine.

"Plus haut. . . A droite. . . Tout doux!
Laissez-moi le premier coup,
Je veux d'abord toucher ce galantin."
Le cosaque arma, visa,
Et sans attendre, cassa,
A bout portant . . . la tête . . . au palatin!

# SWITZERLAND

## *At Lausanne*

University of Lausanne authorities and officials of the Cantonal College of Lausanne reported on Mickiewicz's services as professor of Latin literature there, 1839–1840. From these reports the following excerpts are taken.

The Faculty of Letters, University of Lausanne, to the Swiss Council of Public Instruction

*February 15, 1840*

The University . . . would consider itself deficient in its duty if it did not submit in this report the expression of its gratitude toward the higher authorities on the occasion of the appointment of Mr. Mickiewicz. The appearance of one of the foremost poetic geniuses in a chair of the University of Lausanne and the splendor which his European fame casts over our institutions constitutes an event too important, too honorable, not to be welcomed with joy. Since Mr. Mickiewicz's first lectures his students have recognized in him a great talent for literary criticism, rarely found in a gifted poet; however he sustains it, imbues it with inspiration, and broadens its horizons. The knowledge of the intimate life of the Roman people with regard to the arts and letters, of the spirit of the Latin language and that of the poets and orators whom this language served as their tool, an astonishing perspicacity in penetrating their individual characters in connection with the investigation of their writings, felicitous comparisons between the ancient literature of Rome and various modern literatures, the ability to express himself in a foreign tongue, finally the interest of freshness lent to a subject which seemed exhausted and the inspiration of a poet's soul enlivening these gifts of nature and these fruits of labor—these are in the eyes of Mr. Mickiewicz's audience, the reasons for the growing success of a course which captivates the young people, attracts each day more listeners, and most charms those who are best suited to judge it.

If the long-standing desire to revive in our cantonal teaching institutions strong classical studies inspired the two laws of December 21, 1837, we have indeed cause to congratulate ourselves and to be astonished at the singular good fortune of our canton in having found, to crown the studies so well begun at the College, a man combining vast literary knowledge and poetic genius.

Report of the Director of the Cantonal College at Lausanne to the Rector of the University

*Lausanne, February 26, 1840*

. . . The forty-five classes given each day at the College, to all of which I must devote my attention, have not permitted me to listen to many of Mr. Mickiewicz's classes; but I must state that all the classes of that professor which I was able to attend have profoundly interested me. Though for many years he seems not to have made Roman literature his principal work, nothing in his exposition shows notions acquired or resuscitated overnight. The thought is always precise and complete; the judgments solid; the views broad and just. Listening to him one feels that his is a mind that has absorbed an immense amount and compared much, and that, as a result, sees all things from above. He is thoroughly familiar with the works of the most learned philologists, but he does not use them slavishly; he evaluates them according to their worth, and his erudition is always utilized with judicious comprehension and superior reason. Those who, in particular, hear him talk either of some little-known author, such as Lucretius, or of one well-known, such as Cicero, may observe that his opinions, equally sound in both cases, are his own. And when his subject leads him to compare authors of different nations, as he has done, for instance in the case of Catullus, it may be seen to what extent the eye of this experienced writer grasps ingenious connections without abandoning the truth and to the enhancement of beauty. . . .

And as far as the translation of an author is concerned, Mr. Mickiewicz shows a precision which demonstrates a rare grasp of the French language, one which is not always found in other professors who have a more natural knowledge of our language. In translating, for instance, Horace's *Poetic Art,* he demands not only a clear and faithful rendering, but he wants to have it concise, colorful, poetic, like the work of the author. If some excerpt from a comedy writer such as Plautus or Terence is involved, he seizes upon the familiar expressions in our language that render the Latin phrases with such finesse that on the basis of this proof alone he could be regarded as a writer of the highest merit.

Report of the Rector of the University of Lausanne

*Lausanne, February 27, 1840*

We speak of genius. The genius of the poet Adam Mickiewicz, celebrated in all countries where letters are held in esteem, is not contested by anyone. Instead of joining this concert of eulogies, we seek and we find in such a lofty poetic mind the guarantee of literary sentiment, enthusiasm for the beautiful and the good, which uncover and reveal the most beautiful secrets of the soul and talent of great writers, elevate the thought of the students, and impart to them a sacred fire.

It would, however, be a mistake to believe that Mr. Mickiewicz's teaching merely scintillates with imagination and captivates by its verve. If he penetrates to the core of literary beauty and makes the student love it, if the warmth of life may be felt in his words, the dominant feature of his lectures is the solidity of teaching, wisdom, common sense, a firm and at the same time delicate taste, new but always judicious observations, ingenious but not far-fetched ideas: in his originality he displays the good faith of a mind which aspires to the truth and forgets itself.

Apart from his talent and his intellectual qualities we must take into consideration his knowledge and erudition. Mr. Mickiewicz has constantly given proof of his profound knowledge of Roman history and literature in relation to the character and development of the Roman spirit; his general views open a wide horizon; the details, chosen with sagacity, are instructive; the flow is steady, and each author occupies precisely the place which belongs to him in the literary and national movement of ancient Rome. The professor recognizes with astonishing perspicacity the individuality of each of the great writers of Rome, brings to the fore the characteristic features of his life and of his talent, and chooses the principal moments and the works which signify the phases of his development. One feels and one may be sure that Mr. Mickiewicz does not derive all his knowledge at second hand, that he has dipped not only in books written on Latin literature but in the study of the Roman writers themselves, assisted by the intuition of genius which sees at one glance what others gather or deduct slowly.

Mr. Mickiewicz's knowledge of the Latin language is no less solid. His slightly foreign pronunciation does not offer any difficulty to students used to the French or German pronunciation of Latin; his reading is prosodic and has no defects with which the Polish people are reproached in this respect. He quotes from memory fragments, often rather long ones, from Latin authors, compares them with others and analyzes them, points to their peculiarities of vocabulary, construction, syntax, explains the learned structure of the periods and the other literary beauties of the language. In order to demonstrate the qualities of the language and of the poems, he improvises in Latin prose a translation of the lines of a poet and shows the devices and resources of the poetic idiom.

Finally, Mr. Mickiewicz knows the works of the old and more modern philologists, the works of the Dutchmen, Germans, and Englishmen; he makes use of them, but as a superior man whose good sense forms a striking and instructive contrast with erudition more enchanted by itself than by the works of genius.

If he does not yet improvise with fluency, he at least speaks French without difficulty, even with ease, and generally correctly; when he translates a Latin passage or judges a printed translation he evaluates correctly and with precision even the niceties of our language.

# ITALY

## *Mickiewicz's Position in Italy* [1]

by ENRICO DAMIANI

THE POSITION of a poet outside his own country rests inevitably upon the knowledge of his language among other nations.

The Polish language, while one of the richest and most expressive and most compelling in the world, is unfortunately not one of the most widespread. Therefore the ability to make a direct acquaintance with the treasures of its literary output, and in particular its poetry, is limited in other countries to small circles of specially privileged people.

For this reason the "position" of such a truly important poet as Adam Mickiewicz, both in Poland and internationally, must be more restricted, and always will be more restricted, than the position of a great Polish scientist or a great Polish musician—for example, Copernicus or Chopin—or even of a great storyteller, as for instance, to limit ourselves to one example that is universally known, Sienkiewicz.

The works of Mickiewicz, therefore—and they are works of the highest order—remain for this reason a shrine that is closed, or only imperfectly accessible, to the uninitiated. This is why his popularity in Italy is all the more strange and significant.

His position among us has no doubt been aided by the frequent translations that have been made of many of his works, although these translations are always inadequate, to greater or lesser degree, as happens to every first-rate poet. His position among us has also been aided by the literature of varying kinds and varying importance that has been appearing in Italy for a century, on the subject of the

1. From G. Maver, E. Damiani, M. Bersano Begey, *Mickiewicz e l'Italia* . . . Naples, Raffaele Pironti e Figli, 1949 (publication of the "Seminario di Slavistica dell' Instituto Universitario Orientale di Napoli").

great Pole. No less a factor—perhaps a greater one—has been the repercussions of the fraternal part played by the poet in the struggles of the Italian nation, during our national Calvary and our fight to liberate ourselves from foreign oppression. But the greatest single factor was the personal charm of the man who, by his works, his activities, his words, his example, felt in his heart the union of Italy and Poland in a common cause, through identification of their destinies, their sufferings, their struggles, their sacrifices, their heroism in the service of a supreme common ideal.

Mazzini, who was the first and the greatest of the Italians to become intimate with Mickiewicz, was also—together with Tommaseo—the first to understand intuitively the greatness of his spirit and his intellect, when in 1838 in an anonymous article published in the periodical *The Polish Monthly Magazine,* he did not hesitate to call him "more than a poet: a prophet. A prophet of the same kind as were the great poets of Israel." He stressed this latter comparison.

What above all had impressed Mazzini and what brought him close to Mickiewicz was the deep humanitarian sentiment which was part of both of them and which, extending without barriers their sympathy to all oppressed peoples everywhere, made them regard each other as fellow victims, because each came from a country that was persecuted. Thus Mazzini writes: "All this world-wide work of rejuvenation, all this struggle to reinvigorate Europe, this purpose which characterizes our era and is certain to be accomplished—all this must be expressed in a general social organization which will have the cause of humanity as its final objective and fatherland as its point of departure."

These are Mazzini's words [2] and Mickiewicz's ideas. "Now is my soul incarnate in my country," said Mickiewicz-Konrad, merged in the hero of his poem *Forefathers' Eve,* Part III. "And in my body dwells her soul; my fatherland and I are one great whole! My name is million, for I love millions: their pain and suffering I feel." [3]

Mazzini called Mickiewicz *the greatest of living European poets,*

2. G. Mazzini, *Scritti politici editi ed inediti,* Vol. V, Imola, 1910. (This is the national edition of the writings of G. Mazzini.)
3. *Forefathers' Eve,* Part III. (Soliloquy, or Improvisation, of Konrad.)

and translated him himself, evidently relying on a French or English translation, since he did not know Polish. He translated "To a Polish Mother," "Farys," and part of *Forefathers' Eve*. He did not translate *The Books of the Polish Pilgrims,* but he was deeply moved by it and showed now and then its occasional influence.

When therefore these two great men met each other in Milan a century ago, in 1848, they felt that they had been brothers for a long time and talked to each other as if they were brothers.

Mazzini wrote Mickiewicz: "Brother, let me call you so. I am not united to you in the brotherhood of genius, but I feel like a brother to you in purpose, hope, and faith."

Mazzini's admiration and profound respect for Mickiewicz were also shared completely by Cavour, who called Mickiewicz "the greatest poet of the century," and he based on Mickiewicz his faith in the future of Poland.

"History shows," such were Cavour's words at the meeting of the Chamber of Deputies on October 20, 1848, "that when Providence inspires geniuses such as Homer, Dante, Shakespeare, or Mickiewicz, the nations to which they are born are summoned to great destinies."

The opinions of the two greatest Italians of the nineteenth century were very beneficial to the reputation of Mickiewicz in Italy. And this was also the opinion, more or less, of many of the famous representatives of Italian culture, from Carlo Cattaneo to Niccolo Tommaseo, from Terenzio Mamiani to Tancredi Canonico, from Tommaso Gallarati Scotti to Attilio Begey, to mention only the best known.

Mamiani, in Rome in 1877, upon the occasion of the unveiling of the commemorative plaque of Mickiewicz in the Via del Pozzetto, said: "I had the good fortune to be his contemporary and to have intimate talks with him, to be at times his table-mate, to be present, with great pleasure, at his lectures at the Collège de France. Every time I heard him speak, and the cheering welcome that he received, I went back to my own small room, reinforced in purpose and spirit."

And as early as 1835 Niccolo Tommaseo wrote to Gino Capponi:

This piece [he referred to the *Paroles d'un croyant* of Lamennais] is childish, compared with *The Book of the Polish Pilgrims* by Mickiewicz. I reread it last night. . . . The last prayer in "The Pilgrims' Litany" made me weep. Towards midnight I read them aloud, and understood the simplicity of affection and faith. In Lamennais's book there is not one line that comes from the depths of the soul, not even one. And he is imitative in his chapter: "We cry unto you, O Lord!" But Mickiewicz, in his *Kyrie Eleison,* is so much greater! Do read him! . . . Read Mickiewicz, you will enjoy him: less universal but no less daring, he is a truer poet than Lammenais. You would also find Mickiewicz agreeable personally. He is simple, sincere. His speech is colorful and his friendliness spontaneous. He has an understanding of Italy, for religion, for beauty. He does not pretend to have good qualities, as some people do, or to have bad qualities, as others of small stature do. To meet Mickiewicz in Paris is like picking a violet in Siberia.[4]

The tributes might be continued. But it is not without significance that, considering the extraordinary difficulties of the undertaking, there have been many Italian translations of the chief works of Mickiewicz, beginning with the ones mentioned in connection with Mazzini, as well as the first clandestine Italian edition of *The Books of the Polish Pilgrims,* issued by the Swiss Press at Capolago. Also, a great many writers and speakers and journalists in Italy have discussed Mickiewicz at different times during the past century. At present there are no fewer than fifty Italian translations of different works by him. There have been five or six or more versions of certain poems, such as *Konrad Wallenrod,* "Farys," *The Book of the Polish Pilgrims,* and so forth. And the case of the late Aglauro Ungherini is eloquent, since he chose to study the very difficult Polish language for the sole purpose of reading Mickiewicz in the original, and then to make him accessible, through Italian translations, to his fellow countrymen.[5]

4. Niccolo Tommaseo and Gino Capponi, *Carteggio inedito,* 1833–1874, I (1911), 272–273.

5. The careful and faithful translation by A. Ungherini was actually published in 1898 at Turin by the firm of Roux Frassati & Co., under the title *Gli Dziady, il Corrado Wallenrod e poesie varie. Traduzione dal polacco di Aglauro Ungherini, preceduta da una lettera del sig. Ladislao Mickiewicz.*

There is no space here for a list of the translations into Italian of Mickiewicz's works, or of the writing that has been done in Italy about him.[6] I shall limit myself to mentioning, as contributory factors in the establishment of Mickiewicz's position in Italy, the publication in Milan, during the fateful days of the revolution, of an anonymous version of "The Pilgrim's Litany," which was circulated secretly on the eve of the Five Days, under the title of *The Lombard Pilgrim's Litany*.[7] There was also a felicitous adaptation of *Konrad Wallenrod* as a melodrama, which was done by Antonio Ghislanzoni in 1874, as the libretto for an opera composed by Ponchielli which was performed with notable success in Milan on March 7 of the same year, under the name of *The Lithuanians*.[8]

In discussing Mickiewicz's position in Italy, it is impossible not to make some mention, however brief, of the courses that have been given at the University of Rome in the last twenty years on the subject of his work, first by Professor Pollak and later by Professor Maver. Mention must also be made of the very recent course, from 1947 to 1948, given on the same subject at the Institute of Oriental Studies in Naples, where a competition for prizes was announced, the subject being the *Crimean Sonnets* of Mickiewicz. . . .

Today's solemn ceremonies in the Capitol at Rome, part of a series of tributes to the great Pole which were arranged and will continue to be arranged by the chief Italian cities, mark an important date in the secular relations of Italy and Poland, a furtherance of an Italo-Polish *rapprochement* which has been in existence since the beginning of the Polish nation.[9]

This is the second time that Rome honors Adam Mickiewicz in her Capitol. Seventy years ago similar honors were paid, with a similar spontaneity, on the day of the Legion's anniversary, by the Mayor

6. See the full listing in the very careful bibliography of M. and M. Bersano Begey, pp. 33 ff.

7. After the liberation of Milan, *The Lombard Pilgrim's Litany* was published in the "Gazzetta di Venezia" of March 30, 1848.

8. Published by Ricordi (Milan) without date, under the title of *I Lituani: Dramma lirico di A. Ghislanzoni, Musica di A. Ponchielli.*

9. This refers to a convocation on March 4, 1948, to honor the centennial of the founding of the Polish Legion. [Ed.]

of Rome Venturi, Terenzio Mamiani, Tancredi Canonico, the Marquis Guerrieri-Gonzaga, Armand Levy (intimate friend of Mickiewicz, who was present at his deathbed in 1855, at Constantinople). That was also an historic occasion, when Rome and Italy's love for the Polish bard was solemnly proclaimed; a plaque was dedicated and attached to the wall of the house where Mickiewicz lived in the Via del Pozzetto; while a bust, done by the sculptor Brodski, was placed the following year in the Capitol among memorials of the great Italians.

And there was another historical occasion, a little more than a year later, in 1879, at the University of Bologna, when the University created a department of Polish and Slavic history and literature, named after Mickiewicz. Finally, in 1880, twenty-five years after the poet's death, the Archiginnasio of Bologna also honored him with a tablet, at the unveiling of which his son, Ladislav Mickiewicz, was present.

Thus Rome and Bologna took the lead in honoring the prince of Polish poets, both expressing the sentiments of the entire nation. But today's ceremonies are not restricted to Rome and Bologna; they are also being observed in Milan, Turin, Genoa, Naples, Florence, Sicily, and throughout Italy, on this occasion of the one hundredth anniversary of the Legion, as part of the greatest and most spontaneous demonstration of affection ever given on Italian soil for a great foreign poet.

But Mickiewicz is not a foreign poet to us. He himself did not feel a stranger in Italy. When he addressed the students of Florence in the Via Larga (the Via Cavour today) on April 21, 1848, Mickiewicz called this land "your and *our* Italy." In Italy and among Italians he could not believe himself a foreigner, and he never was, is not now, and never shall be a foreigner to Italy, to any Italian, from the Alps to the three seas.

## *Adam Mickiewicz in Rome in 1848* [1]

by GIOVANNI MAVER

Coming from Marseilles, Adam Mickiewicz landed at Civitavecchia on February 5, 1848. By the next day he was in Rome and had settled himself in the Hotel Minerva. Eighteen years earlier he had visited Rome, as an exceptionally serious student and as an impassioned Romantic poet; now, however, mature in years and in experience, he returned to seize, at the right time and in the right place, the opportunity that had been offered him by destiny to bend this moment to his strong will. In the words of a contemporary journalist, those were days when Rome lived in a continual ecstasy, with "hearts serene, lips smiling, souls hopeful." In those weeks, however, in spite of his sympathy with the Romans, nobody was able to discover a smile on the lips of Mickiewicz, and there were not many moments when his face appeared serene. His attitude, his words, his actions were marked by a resolute firmness of purpose, even before his purpose had taken clear and concrete form in his mind. His countrymen knew that his nature was generous and impulsive, that he was not given to easygoing conformity, that there was going on within him a difficult struggle toward a radical rebirth of moral and religious values. His strange self-confidence in the field of political action seemed enigmatic to the Polish colony in Rome of 1848; also, only a few of them were irresistibly attracted to him; many more, disturbed and frightened, distrusted all his plans. And yet, if one studies it today without prejudice, the personality of Mickiewicz in 1848 appears neither contradictory nor enigmatic. The yearning for power which had been in evidence since his youth was now both more conscious and more justifiable, in view of the self-discipline to which he had been subjecting himself for many years; and a tenacious study of his own mind had resulted

1. From G. Maver, E. Damiani, M. Bersano Begey, *Mickiewicz e l'Italia,* Naples, 1944.

in a deeper understanding of the highest values of humanity, besides sharpening his prophetic insight, which manifested itself spontaneously in poetry.

The conviction that the time had come to act, and that action must begin in Rome, slowly matured in his mind and assumed the form of an unshakable purpose which, even if he had wished to withdraw from it, could not have been abandoned.

An interesting, though not always clear revelation of these various stages are the speeches that he delivered in Paris at the meetings of the Circle of God's Work when, during the absence of its leader, Andrew Towiański, he served as its spiritual chief. On February 27, 1847, he had said to his companions in faith: "Let us resist the world, so that the sacred spark may not be extinguished." A few days later Mickiewicz was speaking of the need "to descend from the spirit to the earth," and he observed that in these new conditions, "resignation, humility, self-contemplation" might become so many sins. On March 9 he is more explicit, and sketches a concrete program: the unquestionable right of the peasant to the land where he makes his home; the unavoidability of great political changes; the insufficiency of purely spiritual activity. At the end of the month he is asking his fellows to answer him squarely: if, in their opinion, "they were approaching the moment to put an end to their exile, would this not require more than only spiritual measures?" "The world is in ferment and presses upon us." "Many are the roads that lead to the fatherland; the question is, which one to choose and when." In his own heart Mickiewicz had already decided; and when his decision was announced, on October 5, in finely chiseled prose, he left a reminder of the language employed by the Circle of God's Work: "The manifestation of the Christian spirit, the construction of the state for Christ, must originate in Rome, which is both church and state. Summoned to conquer for the spirit a state on the earth, we must proceed on the earth, starting from Rome, which is our support." [2]

2. Comparison can now be made between these statements and what Mickiewicz wrote during the same months to Margaret Fuller Ossoli, who was at that time in Italy (see E. Detti, *Margaret Fuller Ossoli e i suoi corrispondenti*, Florence, 1942). "My trip to Italy is very doubtful. However, since I am not

In Rome, therefore, begins this unique undertaking, national and universal, religious and social, political and military, through the labor of one man entirely without means—he arrived in Rome with only nine *paoli*. In the beginning he had nothing but the moral support of a few faithful comrades, waiting in Paris for his summons; but he was sustained by the mighty power of his faith, which had been matured by spiritual torments, as well as by his political intuition, which he trusted religiously. He was also entirely optimistic about getting help from the man who at that time was the hope of so many who yearned for justice and liberty, Pope Pius IX.

And yet at the beginning of this wonderful spring Mickiewicz felt terribly alone. The majority of the Poles living in Rome were not favorably inclined toward him, and quite a few opposed him openly: the clergy, for his adherence to Towiański, whose doctrines approached heresy; the aristocracy, for his bold social ideas, as well as because, led by Prince Czartoryski, the uncrowned King of the Poles in exile, they did not wish to lose the initiative—they were rich, powerful, and unquestionably patriotic—in a political struggle which they desired to limit in aim to the regaining of political independence for Poland. On behalf of Mickiewicz, Zygmunt Krasiński, who was his friend in art but his adversary in politics, describes his intentions in a letter written in Rome on February 14: "His main idea, his stubborn purpose is to create a power which by its holiness will be able to destroy the edifice of evil in one blow. . . . He wants saints with military training, saints led by sergeants, officers, colonels."

The opinion of the poet Krasinski, if it is tinged with sarcasm and wavers between respect and fear, is also on the whole correct. The fact was that Mickiewicz did want saints who would fulfill the mis-

making any plans and am obliged to await developments, my plans may well change" (Letter of April 26, 1847, p. 310). "Write to me at Milan, general delivery" (Letter of August 3, 1847, p. 311). "I do not know now if it will be possible for me to go to Italy" (Letter without date, p. 312). "I do not make any plans for the future. It is therefore not impossible that we shall meet, whether in Italy or between Italy and France" (Letter of September 16, p. 314). "I hope, my darling, to see you in Rome. It is possible that I shall be there before the end of the year. Don't send any more letters to me at Paris" (Letter of November 17, p. 314).

sion with which destiny had entrusted him. One is touched by his need to remain in the skies, even as he has to descend to earth for a practical prosecution of his plan. With deep humility he takes part in the pious pilgrimage of the Holy Stairs and accepts as confessor a man whom he knows to be one of his most embittered foes.

A small group of compatriots had already rallied round the poet when on March 25 a delegation that included him was received by Pius IX. We have various accounts of this audience, but none is completely trustworthy; in any case, there is no doubt that Mickiewicz pleaded passionately not only the cause of the Poles but of all oppressed peoples, and that the Pope, while showing great interest in his appeal, tried to restrain his fiery eloquence, neither rejecting nor at the same time wholly approving his plans.

Independently of this attempt to win the moral support of the pontiff, Mickiewicz proceeded four days later to formulate the constitutional program of the Polish Company, which had the purpose of returning to the fatherland from Italy and "forming a union, if God wills it, with Slavic brothers." The initial step—the struggle against Austria on Italian soil, with the help of Slavic deserters from the Austrian Army—all this is merely sketched in this constitutional program; and the final aim is stated in a very general way. On the same day was also issued the text of the famous "Political Symbol for Poland," which in fifteen short articles included an organic plan for a radically reformed constitution for the Poland of the future, or better, a suggestive vision of the future ideal state. In this ideal state would be found, with perfect freedom, the Christian spirit of the Holy Roman Catholic faith; God's word, announced by the Gospel, would become civil and social law; the fatherland would become the field of action for God's word on earth; Poland, resurrected in the flesh which had suffered and been buried a hundred years earlier, would arise as a free and independent nation and would stretch out her hand to the other Slavs; every citizen would be equal in rights and before the law; every family would have its own land, under the trusteeship of the community; every community would have its communal land under the trusteeship of the nation; and every extant private property, respected and intact, would be under the trusteeship of the national government.

Meanwhile the provisional government in Milan issued a proclamation that harmonized remarkably with Mickiewicz's plans, including as it did a warm invitation to the Poles, "generous brothers in adversity and hope," to speed the fight against the common foe, since time is growing short and "the day is arriving when oppressed people will revolt and gain new strength in the fresh air of freedom."

The signers of the constitutional program of the Polish Company numbered fourteen, including Mickiewicz, who was the last to add his name. The smallness of the number did not at all discourage Mickiewicz, who had complete faith in the magnetic force of this tiny nucleus and the idea it embodied, in the achievement of both immediate and distant aims.

Before leaving Rome, as he was about to begin his march through Civitavecchia and Leghorn to Milan, Mickiewicz assembled his Company in the Church of Sant'Andrea della Valle and addressed his comrades as follows:

In the name of God, under our Eagle, which was blessed by the highest Magistrate of the Church on the same day that witnessed the celebration of the miraculous discovery of the relics of Saint Andrew, patron saint of the Slavs, we begin our march toward our fatherland. We are only a handful of men, but God protects us and sees our spirit. God and His protection will be with us as long as we are faithful to the spirit that unites us. Let this spirit show itself throughout our pilgrimage, during our encampments, in the midst of our struggle. Through our actions we shall deserve the name of the Polish Company, a name which we took in a baptism of faith; through our actions we shall be worthy of our Polish brothers and our Slavic comrades and we shall see them join us. Lord, in the name of Christ and through the intercession of our Queen, His Mother, bless this beginning of the Polish Regiment!

On April 11 this handful of men left Rome and began its march through Italy—an action which even today, after one hundred years, still seems to us one of the most beautiful acts of brotherhood between two nations, especially in view of the spontaneity which everywhere marked it. The Poles had a friendly reception in Leghorn, a most tender one in Empoli, and a frankly triumphal one in Florence, where they stayed a week. During one of many demonstrations of the Florentine people, Mickiewicz addressed the crowd in Italian and said among other things: "The will of God is that Christianity should become in Poland and through Poland everywhere not a dead letter of the law but the living law of governments and civic associations. . . . While you have been fêting unarmed foreign pilgrims on their way to challenge the greatest powers on earth, you have only been honoring in us that which is spiritual and deathless—our faith and our patriotism."

Popular enthusiasm overflowed when the Poles passed through Bologna, Modena, and finally Milan, where Mickiewicz, showing extraordinary ability as an organizer, was able to attract a great number of Poles who had been scattered throughout Italy, Switzerland, France. He managed to overcome many difficulties and to make an agreement with the government of Lombardy, according to which the Polish Legion would be dependent on this government, agreeing to serve the Italian cause until the moment when the Austrians had been driven from Italian territory; and then the Polish Legion would be free to go at once where the interests of their fatherland called them. The Polish Legionnaires observed this vow, taking part, among other things, in the Battle of Lonato.

But it was the decision of destiny that Mickiewicz's Legion, which had been born in Rome, should end its brief life in Rome. During the defense of Rome, inspired by Mickiewicz, who at that time was once more in Paris, the Legion wrote its most beautiful pages, fighting heroically near the Porta di San Pancrazio, near the Porta Cavalleggeri, and especially around the Ponte Milvio. It was certainly not the Legion's fault that it could not contribute more to the struggle for the freedom of Italy, Poland, and mankind.

But the legacy of the Polish Legion is not limited to its military deeds on Italian soil. Several years later, Mazzini, who had met Mickiewicz in Milan, remarked to his son: "If the Polish Legion of '48 had been nothing more than a political symbol, that alone would have assured its renown." To this significant judgment of Mazzini, who often demonstrated his profound understanding of the entire work of Mickiewicz, we should like to add a simple statement: that only in Rome could have been created this moment in history, which unites the noblest religious, political, and social aspirations of Poland and of Italy.

## *Commemorative Orations*

MARQUIS ANSELMO GUERRIERI-GONZAGA (1819–1879), member of the provisional Government of Lombardy in 1848 and of the Italian Parliament, and translator of Horace, Goethe and Schiller, delivered on March 29, 1877, in the Capitol at Rome the following oration, upon the occasion of the unveiling of a marble plaque in commemoration of Adam Mickiewicz. The oration was published in *Honoration de la mémoire d'Adam Mickiewicz en Italie* (Paris, Librairie de Luxembourg, 1881).

When those in charge of this reunion designed to honor the memory of Adam Mickiewicz were kind enough to ask me to take part, they certainly only thought of me as one of the survivors of the provisional government of Lombardy, which welcomed with so much joy the help of the Polish Legion, which had arrived from Rome under the leadership of the great poet. They have perfectly understood the desire of my soul to repeat here, before his son, the expression of our profound gratitude for the eminently patriotic aid given us by his illustrious father. Despite the many emotions that we have experienced since 1848, the memory of the first of May of that memorable year is still as much with me as if it were yesterday. There appeared before me for the first time the austere figure of the Polish bard, respectfully surrounded by a crowd of people; and I heard the tones of that vivid eloquence which poured out of his profoundly religious and patriotic soul and found so quickly a response in the soul of our people, despite the difference of race and culture.

It was a time when history seemed to become legend, and poetry seemed to become action; one would have said that a general transformation, religious and political, was going to take place throughout

Europe. Those who experienced the fascination of that truly extraordinary period keep so deeply its memory within them that they might repeat with the poet:

"I know the ardor of the ancient flame."

Nowadays, every time some solemn occasion returns us to those days of enthusiasm and faith, we old fellows feel young again and we beg the young to keep alive within them the divine torch of the ideal. Also, we are grateful to Mickiewicz, who was the untiring and generous bearer of that torch. He showed by his example that it is useless to try to divide a man who was at once a great poet and a great citizen; he demonstrated how certain doctrines, which seek to establish a vain formula of liberty without religious and social action, are stillborn doctrines, useful only to the transitory interests of certain privileged personages, but unable to satisfy the best and the continuing needs of the masses; he taught us that nations will not rise at all, or if they do rise, will fall again, unless they are conscious of the function they are called upon to fulfill in the intercourse of sister nations.

The spirit of Mickiewicz was profoundly religious, but of a religion which would not submit to the constraints of the Roman Curia. His Christianity, or better, his Catholicism, was to Vaticanism what the Gospel is to the Syllabus [a decree of Pius IX issued in 1864] or what the Sermon on the Mount was to the words of its official interpreters.

His great intelligence had understood the deep importance of the religious and social question, and had proclaimed the necessity of harmonizing patriotic feeling with religious feeling. If he had lived to see these latest phases of the ecclesiastical question, the proclamation of the Syllabus, the reunion of the Council, the fall of the temporal power, I am certain that his writings would have been declared once more anathema by the Roman Curia. He would have declared himself against the separation of Church and State which is going forward today; he would also have repudiated the medieval claims which menace not only Italy but the independence and liberty of all civil governments.

I allow myself to recall to the Poles, so eminently Catholic, these opinions and feelings of their great national poet, because I am persuaded they understand that their beliefs are worthily represented by that glorious figure whom I should like to see brought back today among us. From him we should be able to draw inspiration, with boldness and certitude, for the new tasks that destiny spreads out before us.

I believe, indeed, that we shall not be able to pay a better tribute to the memory of dead great men than by seeking to carry out a portion of that ideal which they have given us in their immortal visions.

ARMAND LÉVY (1827–1891) was a writer and politician, associated with the leaders of the national liberation movements, whether Poles, Rumanians, Yugoslavs, Italians, or others. Lévy, during his studies in Paris, became acquainted with Mickiewicz, whose friend and disciple he remained. He assisted the poet in Italy in 1848 and went with him to Constantinople in 1855. The following speech was delivered on the same occasion as that of Guerrieri-Gonzaga and printed in the same publication.

When Count Cavour,[1] in one of his famous speeches, spoke of Adam Mickiewicz as a spiritual brother of Homer, Dante, and Shakespeare, he expressed a genuine political and literary intuition. Mickiewicz was indeed one of those men who give a direction to their time and whose stamp is preserved for many centuries. In him the word was not merely the clothing of his thought; it was its very flesh. And love of country inspired all his creations. . . .

The works of Mickiewicz make one think now and again of Schiller and Goethe, of Shakespeare and Byron, of Petrarch and Dante, even of Homer and Isaiah. It is not at all that he has imitated them, any more than it can be said that Napoleon imitated Hannibal, Alexander, Caesar, and Charlemagne, although often he shows characteristics of one or another of these heroes. But the great poet, like the great general, has an inner light in common with his most illustrious predecessors.

After *Konrad Wallenrod,* Adam Mickiewicz was called "the Polish Byron," because like Byron he was admired for the ardor and strength of his thought, for a clean-cut style, for a poetic *brevitas*

1. Camille Cavour (1810–1861), Italian statesman, one of the promoters of Italian unity. [Ed.]

*imperatoria,* for the consistency of word and story; in the same way after *Forefathers' Eve* he was hailed as the Polish Dante, because like Dante he suffered exile through great love of his country, and like Dante he celebrated in immortal verse the martyrdom of his country; and the estimates he made of living and dead people have become, in turn, a school of patriotism.

Adam Mickiewicz has been no less well appreciated in other Slavic countries than in Poland. And he has also been understood by the Latin and Germanic races. He is one of the spiritual leaders of the new Europe.

When after the French Revolution of July 29, 1830, the Polish uprising of November 29 broke out, Adam Mickiewicz was at Rome. But his spirit had fought at Warsaw; the people had chanted at the city hall of that city the final stanzas of his *Ode to Youth.*

Adam Mickiewicz wished to return to Warsaw. But the same thing happened to him as had happened to Petrarch when he learned at Avignon of the insurrection of Cola da Rienzi and desired to join him at Rome, but delayed and finally was stopped at Genoa by the news that there was no longer anything for him to do in Rome. Mickiewicz, unable to get further than the Grand Duchy of Posen, suffered keen disappointment.

He had had a foreboding of this. At the first news of the glorious days in Paris he had foreseen the Warsaw uprising and the Polish disasters; and from Genova, where he was at the time, he wrote in his "To a Polish Mother" the prophetic message that her son would grow accustomed to suffering, because the days of great suffering approached. After the fall of Warsaw, while in Dresden where he had sought refuge, he praised the heroism of a lost cause, notably in "The Redoubt of Ordon," which is the glorification of a hero who preferred death to surrender.

The soul of Mickiewicz had never been charged with a stronger current of electricity. The moral force which, in spite of his own desires, Providence had not allowed him to spend in active service, overflowed in works of the first order. One after another he produced his two principal compositions: *Forefathers' Eve,* Part III, and *The Books of the Polish People and the Polish Pilgrims.*

In exile Mickiewicz was a comfort to his compatriots, and the admiration that he won abroad redounded to the credit of his fatherland.

When he was given a position teaching Latin literature at the University of Lausanne he made a deep impression by the breadth of his scholarship, by the choice of his ideas, by the originality and soundness of his observations. He believed that the study of ancient literature is the indispensable basis for all serious education, and he believed that Latin has many secrets still to teach new generations. He liked to say that reliving intellectually the centuries that have gone before is an essential condition for being a rounded man, a necessary preparation for satisfactory fulfillment of our social duties.

When he was called to Paris to teach Slavic literature at the Collège de France he did his work with a superhuman impartiality, and although Polish he was able to speak of Russia not only without bitterness but with a fraternal justice. He explained the characteristics that Slavic peoples have in common, as well as their distinctive national traits—both the kinship and the individuality of Poland, Russia, Bohemia, and Serbia. After tracing both the history and literature of these nations, he demonstrated how the literary vigor of a nation is in direct proportion to the intensity of its national life. Going against the prejudices of the Occident, he declared that literary activity could not be separated from political activity, and that political activity could not be separated from religious activity. After having announced the awakening of the Slavs, outlined their mission and weighed their potential strength, he showed how it depended on France and the Occident whether this Slavic current would be turned to the profit or loss of civilization, and he described what the Occident and France must do to raise their thinking to the level required by the new historical situation.

The only response of the Government to these admonitions, was to suspend the course he was giving. But the memory of this course made a deep impression on those who had the good fortune to hear it. Several years later Michelet told us at the Collège de France: "I still see on these walls the flaming words of Mickiewicz."

Adam Mickiewicz meditated for a while on the planning of the religious jolt needed to startle and win the international heart and to initiate the politics of a new era; then he turned his eyes towards the Eternal City. It was the period when a breath of liberty, starting in Rome, was blowing through all Italy. Mickiewicz, with one of those intuitions that were not at all rare in him, announced that when he returned soon to France he would not find the government of Louis-Philippe, which was already, he said, no more substantial than a dream. And, as a matter of fact, February 24 arrived, with its many repercussions throughout Europe. At the first word of the heroic days in Milan, which followed so closely upon those at Vienna, together with the immediate march from Ticino of the army of Charles-Albert, Mickiewicz immediately formed at Rome a nucleus of the Polish Legion, and by way of Florence and Bologna hurried to Milan, where he had a meeting with his compatriots. This Legion, open to all Slavic patriots, was planned as a powerful means of disorganizing the Austrian army, which was largely composed of Slavs, and as the beginning of a practical plan to unite the Slavic peoples under the same flag of liberty. The first detachments of Legionnaires fought bravely at Desenzano for Italian independence. The following year, after Italy's disasters in the north, they fell back on Florence, whence, increased by new detachments arrived from France, they came to defend in Rome itself the principle of Italian unity. Thus the Poles gave to Italy, as previously they had given to France, the proof of their feeling of solidarity.

It was this greatness of heart that makes Mickiewicz no less dear to Italy than to France.

# THE UNITED STATES

## *Mickiewicz on America and the American Potato*

by MANFRED KRIDL

AMONG MICKIEWICZ'S *juvenilia* there is a poem entitled "Kartofla" (The Potato) which may be of special interest for American readers. Written in 1819 it was originally planned as a poem consisting of two parts, but was never finished, and only its first "song" and some fragments (written in 1821) are known today. The subject of this first "song" is the discovery of America by Christopher Columbus and the discovery of the American potato, which was afterward to play such an important role in the nutrition of mankind.

"Kartofla" belongs to the genre of didactic-descriptive poems numerous and popular in eighteenth century neo-classic poetry. The genre goes back to the *Georgics* of Vergil, which was a model for Delille (*Les Jardins, L'Homme des champs,* and so on) and for a number of other poets, as Saint-Lambert (*Les Saisons*), Roucher (*Les Mois*), Voltaire (*Sept Discours sur l'Homme*), and others. There also existed parodies of such poems, for instance Joseph Berchoux's *La Gastronomie,* devoted to—recipes for preparing food.[1]

The little poem of Mickiewicz (508 lines) is a mixture of serious and humorous elements, sometimes approaching parody, sometimes —historiosophy. The very beginning is a travesty of the classic "argument" (a summary in verse); as the poet is starting to praise various plants, a potato cries out from the stove and suggests to him the subject of the poem: the glorification of the potato and of all that led to its discovery. The poet, ashamed and repenting, changes his subject and recites a parody of an apostrophe, not to the Muse, but to the potato, asking it to inspire him and promising to immortalize its beauty and its "inner" qualities.

There follows a description of the creation of the "New World"

1. See Wacław Borowy, "Studia Mickiewiczowskie," Pamiętnik Literacki 1948, pp. 16–17.

and of the expedition to it. The picture of Columbus's boat and of its crew belongs to the most vivid in the poem. They are sailing bravely and hopefully, when suddenly a calm stops them far away from the "Old World." Neptune takes advantage of this and anchors the vessel to the sea bottom by a chain. Then he appears at a meeting of the gods of ancient Olympus—after the victory of Christianity in Europe they had moved to the other side of the Atlantic—and presents the danger arising from the invaders. But thunder disperses the old gods and the scene shifts to heaven where the saints are to decide the fate of Columbus. St. Dominic whose "watchword is crosses, tortures and war" favors him because of all the material gains the world can expect from his discovery. Other saints are opposed because of "the tears and innocent blood of the savage tribes" which will be shed in connection with it. The scale held by St. Michael tips:

> The gold weighs less than human blood and tears.

St. Raphael presents a new argument in favor of Columbus:

> We, heavenly denizens, a verdict are to pass
> Which is to bear on future destinies.
> The earth five hundred orbs around the sun describes.[2]
> Look at the night under which Europe lies.
> Laments and weeping, groans heard everywhere,
> Pyres in flames; and clattering chains resound.
> Driven together by the despots' whip
> The throng of slaves contends in their defense.
>
> . . . .
>
> Then freedom's star o'er the New World rises
> Virtue and learning seek shelter in its rays.
> Broken are monkish fetters and threats of autocrats.
> The golden Capitol's dome towards the heavens soars.
> Mortals, astonished, fall upon their knees,
> The Sovereign People is holding equal sway,
> Tyrants of old before it bow in awe,
> In Europe freedom's spark new fires kindles.[3]

2. That is, five hundred years will pass.
3. This applies to the role of America in promoting universal freedom.

Both sides of the scale are now in balance; on the one are the tears and blood, on the other the treasures and liberties. Presently St. Dominic exhibits an object which causes general astonishment. It is a potato:

> Inside, the fruit was pliable and soft,
> Pale spots were scattered on its greyish hull,
> It was enveloped in a tender skin.
> This fruit, as you have guessed, was the potato.
> All Saints transfix it with astonished gaze.
> Shaking it trice, St. Dominic lifts it high. . . .[4]

In a long speech St. Dominic expounds the qualities of the potato. While the growth of other plants depends upon climate and soil, the potato "feels well" and prospers in every country, in the Ukraine, in Arabia, in snow-covered Russia, and in Asia. Everywhere other vegetables may perish because of frost or drought and thereby cause starvation; only the potato, hidden deeply in the earth, survives under any circumstances and saves people from hunger.

This argument proves to be a decisive factor. The potato thrown on the scale by St. Dominic tips the balance. Columbus is saved, the New World will be discovered.

Columbus and his men know nothing about this decision and are exposed to suffering on the motionless vessel. Finally a revolt breaks out. Columbus's life is in danger. All of a sudden the crew discovers a potato on the water driven toward the boat by a light wind. This is a sign that land is near, and the calm is over. And indeed, the wind increases, the boat slips anchor and sails on. The crew forget their troubles and Columbus, as an act of gratitude, puts the potato in a gold frame and hangs it on his breast.

In this way America and the potato were honored by young Mickiewicz.

The poem is written in a classic style full of long comparisons, inversions, periphrases, artificially constructed sentences, replete with pomp, rhetoric, and mythology. Within this general character of

4. The lines of the poem quoted here were translated by Ludwik Krzyżanowski.

poetic language the poet frequently achieves vivid descriptions, humorous images, and rhetorical force. He does not shrink, however, from using colloquial expressions and even dialect, which provides his language with a special flavor. In general, he is here a faithful disciple of Polish and foreign classicists, but a disciple who already shows originality and invention.

## *Cooper and Mickiewicz: a Literary Friendship*

by LUDWIK KRZYŻANOWSKI

On April 25, 1830, *Kurier Litewski* reprinted the following news item from *Gazeta Warszawska:*

"Mickiewicz continues his stay in Rome. He may be often seen roaming through the city with the famous American novelist Cooper and the Russian authoress M-lle Klustine." [1]

The names of the two writers had been linked in print at least once before. Their affinity was noted by no lesser man than Mickiewicz's fellow poet and rival, Juliusz Słowacki. Defending himself against the suggestion that his *Mindowe* may have been influenced by Mickiewicz's *Grażyna,* Słowacki wrote, as follows, in the introduction to his tragedy:

"Modern poets, like poets of the past, must meet one another in thought, and even more often, for they faithfully depict man's nature and heart; there is only this difference: the poets of the past consciously strove to imitate, while the others imitate accidentally whenever they cannot avoid it. And if we wished to analyze each work of genius, would it then be difficult to say that *Wallenrod* itself is Cooper's *Spy?"*

What opinion Mickiewicz himself held about the American writer may be gathered from an account by the former's traveling compan-

1. Władysław Mickiewicz, *Żywot Adama Mickiewicza* (Poznań, 1931), II, 81.

ion and amanuensis, Antoni Edward Odyniec. Basking in the splendor of his illustrious compatriot this minor poet recorded the events of their travels through Europe following Mickiewicz's departure from Russia in 1829. In Weimar, memorable for Mickiewicz because of his visit with Goethe, the French sculptor David [2] and the German poet Holtei had gathered in the hotel room shared by Mickiewicz and Odyniec in the morning of August 28, 1829, and engaged in a literary discussion. Odyniec hastened to apprise his friend Julian Korsak of his impressions:

But do you know what image this whole conversation of this morning reflected in my imagination? I see as if an azure sky spread over the entire earth. The West, still burning with the vivid flame and splendor of an already extinguished sun—that is Byron. The East, radiant with the morning star—that is Adam. The moon in its fullness and in the zenith of its way—that is Goethe. The triad of stars-suns of first magnitude—Chateaubriand and Walter Scott over Europe, and Cooper over America. The pleiad of sunny planets—Manzoni, Moore, Béranger, Lamartine, Tieck, Tegner and our Ursyn.[3] The misty flaming planet—that is Hugo; the Northern star—Pushkin.[4]

Arriving in Rome on November 18, 1829, Mickiewicz was at once introduced to the busy social life of the cosmopolitan colony in the Eternal City which, to use Cooper's words, "at this moment contains a congress of all people of Christendom . . . a society uniformly elegant and high-toned." [5] Very helpful to the Polish poet in establishing social contacts was his old friend from Russia, Princess Zinaida Volkonskaya, through whom he acquired a wide circle of acquaintances. It is undoubtedly this lady to whom Cooper refers as "the Princess V—, a Russian, now in Rome for her health," [6] who

2. Pierre-Jean David, usually called David d'Angers, who a few years later was to execute in Paris busts of both Cooper and Mickiewicz.

3. Julian Ursyn Niemcewicz (1758–1841), Polish poet, novelist, playwright, satirist, statesman, author, *i.a.*, of a life of George Washington. He lived in America about eight years and was married to an American, Mrs. Levingston-Kean.

4. Antoni Edward Odyniec, *Listy z podróży*, quoted by Mieczysław Haiman, *Z przeszłości polskiej w Ameryce* (Buffalo, 1927), p. 152.

5. James Fenimore Cooper, *Excursions in Italy* (London, 1838), II, 169.

6. *Ibid.*, p. 196.

gave a picnic on Monte Mario which "included Russians, Poles, French, Swiss, Germans, Italians, etc." [7] Most certainly Mickiewicz attended this party.

Notable among Mickiewicz's new friends were a distinguished Russian lady, Mme Vera Klustine, née Countess Tolstoy, the wife of a high ranking Russian army officer, and her daughter Anastasie, a person of literary tastes and refinement, "whose delicate health could not bear the Russian climate." Soon to become the wife of the French Count Adolphe de Circourt whom she had met in Paris during the winter of 1826–1827, she had in 1829 published in the *Bibliothèque Universelle* an article on "The Present State of Russian Literature" which was reprinted by several French publications. Under the name of Corinne Borysthénide she was awarded the diploma of the Rome Academy of Arcades. Remarkable for intelligence, education, nobility of mind and a soul full of goodness, "she attracted the attention of distinguished men wherever she appeared." [8]

It was at the house of these ladies that the authors of *Wallenrod* and of *The Spy* met for the first time. Let us again turn to Odyniec for a description of this event. On March 9, 1830, he wrote to Ignacy Chodźko:

> In turn I must tell you about a new acquaintance which you will envy me, I'm sure. I met Fenimore Cooper! He had come here from Paris, and since he had from there letters to Mlle Anastasie Klustine, her mother arranged for him a splendid soirée at which all local and artistic celebri-

7. *Ibid.*, p. 207. Princess Volkonskaya's house in Rome was described by F. Buslayev, "Rimskaya villa kniagini Z. A. Volkonskoy," *Vestnik Evropy*, 1896, I, 5–32.

8. Cf. *Count Cavour and Madame de Circourt.* Some Unpublished Correspondence, edited by Count Nigra, translated by Arthur John Butler, London, 1894, Introduction, p. 7; and Huber-Saladin, *Le Comte de Circourt, son temps, ses écrits. Madame de Circourt, son salon, ses correspondances*, Paris, 1881, pp. 23, 25. De Circourt, writer and diplomat, was honorary member of the Massachusetts Historical Society and translator of George Bancroft's *Histoire de l'action commune de la France et de l'Amérique pour l'indépendance des Etats Unis*, Paris, 1876. The Circourts' Paris "salon was frequented by the most celebrated people of Europe" (*La Grande Encyclopédie*, XI, 439). Mme Vera Klustine became on July 22, 1838, in Paris, the godmother of Mickiewicz's son, Władysław. See Władysław Mickiewicz, *op. cit.*, II, 438.

ties could see, welcome and honor this star of the other hemisphere, who out of simple curiosity had come to glance at ours and sweeps across it like a comet with the whole constellation of his family, that is, his wife and four daughters. Therefore, when, after hearing that he was supposed to go to Dresden, I asked him whether he did not also intend and desire to visit Poland, which knows and appreciates him with the rest of Europe, he answered very politely that he would indeed sincerely wish to see and know the country of Kościuszko. "Mais, Monsieur," he added with a good-humored smile, "qui voyage avec cinq jupons, n'est pas maître de sa volonté." This answer alone, not to mention the tone of voice, if you had heard it, would at once given you an idea about the singularly good-natured simplicity and unpretentiousness which is manifested in his manner of speaking and in his whole behavior. Mr. Krivtsov, an official of the Russian Embassy, a great dandy and a man of the world, was introduced to him by the hostess and greeted him with choice words, saying among others: "Je m'estime heureux, Monsieur, de faire la connaissance d'un homme dont la gloire remplit les deux mondes." Cooper, who was then engaged in lively conversation with those surrounding him, got embarrassed at this compliment. Obviously confused, he bowed very politely in return, apparently not finding on the spur of the moment another reply than the indeed strange "Oui, Monsieur." Those present bit their lips in order not to smile, especially when seeing the mutual embarrassment of Mr. Krivtsov who at this unexpected answer forgot the tongue in his mouth, as the saying goes. "C'est un rustre," he later told his friends; but as far as I am concerned, this very simplicity and bashfulness in such a man seems to me the summit of greatness, for it is evident from them that he is superior to vanity and pride. In this respect he reminded me of our Karol Lipiński,[9] probably the most modest of all famous artists whose heads are often turned by continuous praise and applause.

To judge from his physiognomy and figure, Cooper seems to look more like a goodly country farmer than the great author he is. But they say the same thing about Walter Scott. He must be already over 50 years old.[10] Tall stature, grave movements; the expression of his face quiet and mild, a slow voice, blue eyes. In conversation he listens more than he talks. He talked with Adam for quite some time and enquired particularly about the spirit and the character of the Slavs and about the nomad tribes in the

9. Polish composer and violinist (1790–1861); he set to music Mickiewicz's sonnet "Niemen."

10. This is inexact, since Cooper was then only 40 years old.

steppes. Mlle Anastasie had probably not neglected to tell him in advance who Adam was.[11] Indeed, he treated him with distinct respect but did not pay him any compliments. In general he did not seem to feel that he was the hero of the reception, or if he felt it inwardly, he apparently deliberately tried not to leave this impression. As long as he stood in the group of men in the middle of the drawing room I tried to be as near him as possible in order to hear what he was saying. But these were common, routine conversations: about travels, Italy, Rome, etc. I would be particularly interested in what he said to the ladies and how he said it, but I could not get near because the ladies quickly surrounded him. I only saw from a distance how he bowed in all directions, probably acknowledging compliments. His wife and daughters were not present at this soirée though they had been also invited. He excused them with ill health and fatigue from the journey. . . . During the general conversation Adam spoke a few minutes aside with the painter Vernet Sr. . . . Cooper listened from a distance but did not himself mix in the conversation. When this was protracted too long, Mlle Anastasie, wishing to put an end to it . . . sat down at the piano and played a few tender Ukrainian melodies. All came closer and surrounded the instrument. Cooper stood next to her chair and extolled the tenderness of the melodies.[12]

Mickiewicz's biographers either do not mention the acquaintance with Cooper at all or devote to it a sentence or two, managing to be inaccurate even in such brief references. Thus Chmielowski speaks of Cooper's visit in Rome with his "only daughter, later also famous in literature." [13]

The poet's son Władysław supplements the picture with this interesting, though partly inexact, information:

"In March Mickiewicz met the outstanding novelist Fenimore Cooper who was staying in Rome with his only daughter and soon

11. The nature of her remarks may be guessed from a letter Anastasie de Circourt wrote on October 28, 1838, to Augustin P. Candolle, ex-rector of the University of Geneva, in support of Mickiewicz's candidacy for a professorship of comparative literature in that institution: "Je puis vous garantir, en ma qualité de *Slave,* que, dans toute *la famille* de nos langues, Mickiewicz est reconnu d'un accord universel, pour le premier poète vivant" (Władysław Mickiewicz, *op. cit.,* II, 556).

12. Odyniec, *op. cit.,* quoted by Haiman, *op. cit.,* pp. 152–154.

13. Piotr Chmielowski, *Adam Mickiewicz, zarys biograficzno-literacki* (Warsaw, 1901), II, 57.

became friendly with him. Cooper, seven years Mickiewicz's senior, had already won European fame. He praised the American landscape and so ardently encouraged Mickiewicz to visit the United States that in the Rome salons some already envied the poet the great dowry of Miss Cooper." [14]

A reflection of this statement may be found in a history of American literature written in Polish: Cooper's "close association with Mickiewicz who was then staying abroad as an émigré almost developed into a father-in-law–son-in-law relationship." [15]

Cooper's biographers have almost all a word to say about the acquaintance of the two writers:

"He [Cooper] made friends with the Polish poet Mickiewicz who roused him to an interest in Poland's woes, which endured after his return to Paris." [16]

"Even more a haunt of artists and poets than of pleasure seekers, the city on the Tiber offered the American many congenial acquaintances among her émigré group. . . . The Polish patriot-poet, Adam Mickiewicz, released at the age of thirty-one from his Russian prison, was spending the winter in Rome, and it was presumably he who accompanied the novelist on those rides on the white horse Chingi, which form the topic of several letters of his *Italy*." [17]

"Cooper was . . . linked with Poland by his friendship with Adam Mickiewicz, the Polish patriot and poet, whom he had met . . . in Rome." [18]

"The feelings of Cooper were profoundly stirred in behalf of [the Polish] people. With this his personal friendship with the Polish poet, Mickiewicz, had probably a great deal to do; for at Rome a close intimacy had sprung up between him and that author." [19]

14. Władysław Mickiewicz, *op. cit.*, II, 100.

15. Władysław Tarnawski, *Literatura angielska,* Tadeusz Grzebieniowski, *Literatura półn.-amerykańska* (Warsaw, n.d.), p. 270.

16. Henry Walcott Boynton, *James Fenimore Cooper* (New York, 1931), p. 203.

17. Robert E. Spiller, *Fenimore Cooper, Critic of His Times* (New York, 1931), p. 160.

18. James Grossman, *James Fenimore Cooper* (The American Men of Letters Series, William Sloane Associates, New York, 1949), p. 75.

19. Thomas R. Lounsbury, *James Fenimore Cooper,* Boston, 1895, p. 107. Cf. also Van Wyck Brooks, *The World of Washington Irving* (New York, 1946),

However, the most striking and eloquent description of the American-Polish Rome episode comes from the pen of the novelist's daughter and the poet's would-be bride, as she had been labeled by Polish monographers:

It was the especial delight of the American author to ride for hours over the Campagna, lingering here about some ruin, now pausing a moment to enjoy an impressive view, or dismounting, perchance, to examine more closely a statue or fragment of ancient days. He seldom rode alone; ever social in feeling and tastes, he generally found some agreeable companion for the morning ride among the European friends who, at Rome, as at Florence, took pleasure in the cheerful American fireside. Among those who rode with him, there was none, perhaps, whose society gave the author more pleasure than that of the distinguished Polish poet, Mickiewicz, a man whose appearance, manner and conversation were full of originality and genius, while the sad fate of his country enlisted Mr. Cooper's warmest sympathies in his behalf. The two writers were constantly roaming together over the Campagna, or amid the ruins of Rome.[20]

Susan Fenimore Cooper repeats essentially the same description in a magazine article sixteen years later. The two writers no longer appear as constant companions, but "were frequently seen roaming together."[21]

The passage quoted above must have been the source on which Mary E. Phillips based her reference to the Polish poet whose portrait appears in her book: "Perhaps none who rode with him [Cooper] gave him more pleasure than the famous Polish poet Adam Mickieowicz [*sic*] a man full of originality, genius and sadness for the fate of his lost country. All of this won Cooper's sympathy and help in zealous writing and speaking for the suffering Poles."[22]

Rather unexpectedly an additional reference to Cooper and Mickiewicz is supplied by Samuel F. B. Morse, the inventor of the telegraph.

p. 261: "Cooper had been intimate with Mickiewicz in Rome and had ridden with him every day on his white horse Chingi, and his house in Paris . . . was the hospice of St. Bernard of the Polish refugees."

20. Susan Fenimore Cooper, *Pages and Pictures from the Writings of James Fenimore Cooper* (New York, 1861), pp. 229–230.

21. "A Second Glance Backward," *Atlantic Monthly*, October, 1887, p. 481.

22. Mary E. Phillips, *James Fenimore Cooper* (New York, 1913), pp. 218–219.

In a letter to his brothers from Rome, dated April 15, 1831, he relates the following incident:

We have recently heard of the disasters of the Poles. What noble people; how deserving of their freedom. I must tell you of an interesting circumstance that occurred to me in relation to Poland. It was in the later part of June of last year. . . . As I approached the Coliseum . . . a party of gentlemen also approached to the entrance. One of them addressed me. Perceiving that he was a foreigner, I asked him if he spoke English. He replied with a slight accent, "Yes, a little; you are an Englishman, sir?" "No," I replied, "I am an American, from the United States." "Indeed!" said he, "that is much better," and extending his hand, he shook me cordially by the hand, adding: "I have a great respect for your country, and I know many of your countrymen." He then mentioned Dr. Jarvis, and Mr. Cooper, the novelist, the latter of whom he said was held in the greatest estimation in Europe and nowhere more so than in his country, Poland, where his works were more sought after than those of Scott, and his mind was esteemed of an equal, if not superior, cast. . . . I asked him about the literature of Poland, and particularly if there were now any living poets of eminence. He observed "Yes, sir, I am happily travelling in company with the most celebrated of our poets, Meinenvitch [*sic*], and, who, as I understood him, was one of the party walking in another part of the ruins.[23]

There seems to be no doubt that Morse's Polish interlocutor was Odyniec, while "Meinenvitch" can only be a misspelling of the name Mickiewicz.

Unfortunately no record of the conversations of the American novelist and the Polish poet exists. It may only be surmised that Mickiewicz, who had a thorough classical training acquired at the University of Wilno and who several years later was to become professor of Latin literature at the University of Lausanne, could offer his American friend many an enlightening observation and penetrating remark on the Roman antiquities they were visiting together. Thus it may perhaps not be extravagant to conjecture that Cooper's *Excursions in Italy,* contains matters which had been the subject of the two writers' discussions.

23. Cf. Samuel Irenaeus Prime, *The Life of Samuel F. B. Morse, LL.D.* (New York, 1875), pp. 209–210.

Since both were authors they certainly spoke about literature. In this respect not everything must be left to conjecture. Władysław Mickiewicz relates that his father possessed an album with entries handwritten by Ryleyev, Bestuzhev, and other victims of Tsar Nicholas I. In this album he also preserved a description of the American wilderness offered him by Cooper in Rome. This cherished possession was spirited away in Paris by some misguided autograph collector when in 1836 Mickiewicz brought the album to the poet Bohdan Zaleski who wanted to compare his own poems of the Ukrainian steppes with Cooper's autograph text.[24]

"The sad fate of his country," so vividly described and poetically transformed by Mickiewicz two years later in *Forefathers' Eve,* Part III, could not be left unheeded in the intimate talks of the two sightseers. Visits to the scenes of the persecution of the early Christians brought to mind comparisons with the sufferings of the Poles. "Poland," the poet was to write in the Preface to *Forefathers' Eve,* "for the last half century has presented a picture of such continual, unwearied, and inexorable cruelty on the part of tyrants, and of such boundless devotion and such obstinate endurance on the part of the people, as are unexampled since the times of the persecution of Christianity." [25] Mickiewicz probably interpreted Polish history for Cooper, corrected various misconceptions, spoke of the Polish conception of freedom which before long he was to formulate in *The Books of the Polish Nation:* "And God gave unto the Polish kings and knights freedom, that all might be called brothers, both the richest and the poorest. And such freedom never was before. . . . And finally Poland said: 'Whosoever will come to me shall be free and equal, for I am Freedom.' " [26]

Cooper's association with Mickiewicz bore rich fruit. When on November 29, 1830, a rising against Russia broke out in Warsaw, Cooper, who was then in Paris, wholeheartedly rallied to the aid of

24. Władysław Mickiewicz, *op. cit.,* 1929, I, 182.
25. *Poems by Adam Mickiewicz,* ed. George Rapall Noyes (New York, 1944), p. 247.
26. *Konrad Wallenrod and Other Writings of Mickiewicz,* tr. George Rapall Noyes (Berkeley, Calif., 1925), p. 141.

the oppressed nation for whom Mickiewicz had aroused his sympathy. He became the chairman of an American Committee to aid the cause, first of the Polish insurgents, and then, after the failure of the rising, of Polish exiles. In this capacity he wrote an eloquent appeal to the American people, in which he said:

When Poland was overcome, the fifth power in Christendom was trodden upon. There are circumstances of unmitigated wrong, of peculiar aggravation, that must be added to the picture. The crime of Poland was too much liberty; her independent existence, in the vicinity of those who had reared their thrones on arbitrary will, was not to be endured. Fellow-citizens, neither the ancient institutions, nor the ancient practices of Poland have been understood. . . . There was wanting but a single aggravating circumstance to render the partition of the fine country more odious, and, unhappily, this too is to be enumerated among its sufferings. When Poland was subdued, by far the larger portion of her territory became subject to a people less advanced in civilization than her own citizens. . . . Against the injustice of their lot, and the further accumulation of their manifold wrongs, the Poles have risen before God and man. . . . We have put the case of Poland simply before you. Her cause is so obviously just as to require no aid from the embellishments of language, or to need any laboured appeal to your charities. . . . We should be false to our origin, our principles, and that mild religion in which we are nurtured, could we hesitate between Poland and her enemies. . . . Come then, people of America, to the relief of this much injured and gallant people. Your aid will be offered to those who are willing to work out their own redemption; who have already shown themselves worthy of their ancient fame in twenty fields and who will never yield until resistance shall have been carried to extremity.[27]

Cooper's activity in behalf of Poland is a separate subject and transcends the scope of the present note.

Further documentation of the friendship so auspiciously begun at Rome is extremely sparse, though it is not impossible that a search of the Cooper papers now preserved at Yale may yield some results.

27. Reprinted in full by Mieczysław Haiman, *Polacy wśród pionierów Ameryki*, Chicago, 1930, pp. 309–312, from *Buffalo Journal and General Advertiser* of September 7, 1831.

The two writers never again saw each other personally, but they intermittently kept informed about each other through friends or direct correspondence.

On April 29, 1832, the Polish *émigrés* in Paris founded a Literary Society. Mickiewicz attended its meeting for the first time on September 20, 1832, soon after his arrival from Dresden. He inaugurated his participation in that Society by moving that Cooper should be elected a member. Mickiewicz's motion was unanimously adopted.[28]

About the same time, on September 4, 1832, an English correspondent, Elizabeth Marlay, supplied Cooper, who was then in Geneva, with a bit of news about Mickiewicz which seems to be a proof of the American writer's continued interest in the Polish poet:

Poor Michiewitz [*sic*] is come, agreeable as ever, but out of health, and out of spirits, and I see little of him. He seems to have taken an aversion to Paris, and to see all things in a gloomy point of view, as well he may, tho' latterly the Government appears to treat the Poles better. He and Chodzko are printing another edition of his poems, with what object at this inauspicious moment I cannot divine, but I suppose, half patriotic, half pecuniary. The first—alas. The second, must, I trust, offer some certainty or they would not have engaged in the undertaking.[29]

Not until seventeen years later can a trace be detected indicating that Cooper must have occasionally received news about Mickiewicz which he considered interesting enough to communicate to his wife. On December 9, 1849 he wrote her from New York:

"A Count Gurowski, a Pole who came to see us in Paris, a one-eyed man, is in the house, and spoke to me this morning. Bearnatzki [*sic*] is still living, but Louis Plater is dead. Michiewitz invented a religion but submitted to Pius IX. He is still flourishing. Janski is connected with the press, etc., etc." [30]

Perhaps the two writers still occasionally exchanged letters. The following is a proof that at least one letter of Mickiewicz to Cooper

28. Władysław Mickiewicz, *op. cit.*, II, 192.

29. *Correspondence of James Fenimore Cooper,* ed. by his grandson James Fenimore Cooper (New Haven, 1922), I, 287–288.

30. *Ibid.*, II, 640. The names mentioned are those of Polish *émigrés* in Paris after the November Insurrection.

was in existence. On September 22, 1850, he informed his wife: "My French letter was from Michiewitz. He tells me that Mad. Marlay is just dead—that he often heard of us through her—*how,* I cannot say. His object was to get my interest in favour of a German artist, as he says of uncommon merit." [31]

On September 30, 1850 he apparently refers to the same letter: "Michiewitz speaks of Mad. Marlay's death." [32]

Thanks to the efforts of a Polish scholar, Leopold Wellisz, the original document in question was recently found and reproduced in facsimile and in Polish translation in a weekly published in London. The letter, dated Paris, June 3, 1850, reads:

MONSIEUR

C'est pour moi une heureuse occasion de me rappeler à votre souvenir que de vous adresser le porteur de la présente, Monsieur Müller. Je connais votre goût pour l'art européen. L'art, si je me rapelle bien, est la seule chose que vous admirez dans notre vieille Europe. Monsieur Müller est un artiste sculpteur des plus distingués. Il se rend en Amerique et il y transporte son oeuvre qu'il vient dernièrement d'executer, très estimé des connaisseurs d'ici et que je trouve moi au dessus de leur estimation. Il a l'idée de l'exposer au public americain. J'ignore quel [*sic*] sont en ce moment les dispositions artistiques de ce public. Quant à notre hemisphère, l' expatriation de Monsieur Müller vous prouvera suffisamment l'état de nos arts et la position de nos artistes. Pour vous en donner une idée complète je vous dirai que l'on parle parmi nous, chez les artistes, du régime de Louis Philippe comme d'un age d'or de l'art, comme d'une époque de Periclès et de Médicis! Les artistes se trouvent actuellement réduits à la position des réfugiés polonais; c'est une des causes de plus de ma profonde sympathie pour Monsieur Müller et c'est ce qui me fait espérer que vous ne lui refuserez pas votre bienveillante protection.

Vous avez mon cher Monsieur probablement reçu le triste avis du décès de notre amie Marie Marly. Tant qu'elle vivait, je recevai quelquefois par elle de vos nouvelles. Maintenent je suis réduit à en demander aux voyageurs de vos compatriotes; ils me parlent bien de vos ouvrages mais ils ne savent pas rien de précis sur vous et votre famille. Je vous prie de m'en dire quelques mots par Monsieur Müller, ce sera une preuve que

31. *Ibid.*, p. 689.
32. *Ibid.*, p. 690.

vous conserver quelque souvenir de votre ancien très affectueux et très dévoué serviteur

ADAM MICKIEWICZ

*Paris*
*Batignolles*
*42 rue de la Santé*
*3 Juin 1850*
P.S. Vous faisiez autrefois des projects d'un voyage artistique en Europe. Persistez vous dans ce projet? Visiterez vous encore Paris? [33]

In characterizing the two writers' association one is tempted to repeat the words which Mickiewicz used in connection with himself and Pushkin in "The Monument of Peter the Great":

> Although their friendship had not flourished long,
> They were united by a great regard.[34]

33. Leopold Wellisz, "Mickiewicz i James Fenimore Cooper," *Wiadomości,* No. 114, June 8, 1948. The English translation of the letter is as follows: "It is a happy occasion for me to recall myself to your memory by recommending to you the bearer of this letter, Mr. Müller. I know your taste for European art. Art, if I remember well, is the only thing which you admire in our old Europe. Mr. Müller is one of the most distinguished sculptors. He is on his way to America and is taking with him works which he has recently completed, highly valued by experts here and considered by me to be even above their estimation. He plans to exhibit them to the American public. I do not know what its artistic disposition is at present. As far as our hemisphere is concerned, the expatriation of Mr. Müller will be for you sufficient proof of the condition of our art and of the situation of our artists. To give you a full idea of it I will say that among our artists the reign of Louis Philippe is referred to as a golden age of art, as an epoch of Pericles and of the Medicis! The artists are now reduced to the status of Polish refugees; this is one more reason for my profound interest in Mr. Müller, and a circumstance which makes me hope that you will not refuse him your kind protection.

"You have probably received, dear Sir, the sad news of the death of our friend Marie Marly. While she was alive I sometimes received news about you through her. At present I can only ask your travelling compatriots for it; to be sure, they tell me about your works, but they do not know anything definite about you and your family. Please let me know a few details about this through Mr. Müller. This will be proof that you have retained some recollection of your old, very affectionate and devoted servant.
"P.S. You had planned some time ago an artistic trip to Europe. Do you still hold to this plan? Will you still visit Paris?"
34. *Poems by Adam Mickiewicz,* p. 349.

Mickiewicz admired America as "the land of freedom, a holy land." [35] Cooper esteemed the "constancy . . . martial promptitude . . . frankness and dignity" of the "heroic [Polish] nation." Believing in the "sacred justice" of the Polish cause, he bowed "to the majesty of truth" when choosing "between Poland and her enemies." [36]

The story of their relationship is incomplete and full of gaps. However, there exist a few incontestable facts which may form the basis for a fuller reconstruction of this noble and fruitful friendship and throw light on the relationship of *Konrad Wallenrod* and *The Spy,* those two works which, though widely apart in time and space, express a kindred idea of the heroes' service to their nations.

## *Adam Mickiewicz and Margaret Fuller*

Margaret Fuller was the second American whom Mickiewicz met and with whom he was united by a closer friendship than that with James Fenimore Cooper. They met for the first time in February, 1847, in Paris. It seems that this American writer and fighter for women's rights, beautiful, sensitive, very intelligent, and somewhat extravagant, made a deep impression on Mickiewicz. She was at that time the author of several books (*Summer on the Lakes, Papers on Literature and Art*) and of articles in the *Dial,* the organ of the "Circle of Transcendentalists" (headed by R. W. Emerson) and in the *New York Daily Tribune.* She was interested in philosophical, social, literary, and moral problems and distinguished herself by a kind of enthusiasm and faith akin to Mickiewicz's. Their first meeting must have had a very unusual character: what Mickiewicz said to her must have been extremely touching and exciting, since—according to some

35. "The Books of the Polish Nation," *Konrad Wallenrod and Other Writings,* p. 127.
36. Words in quotation marks are from Cooper's appeal to the American people; see *supra,* note 27.

sources—she "fainted away on the sofa." Equally extraordinary is Mickiewicz's letter written to her in French after this first meeting. It begins with very lofty general statements and continues by defining her spirit as "linked with the history of Poland, of France and America" and her "mission" to contribute "to the deliverance of Polish, French and American womanhood." [1]

The uninitiated reader should realize that Mickiewicz was at that time deeply absorbed in mysticism and in activity among "brothers" of a mystic Circle. The character and tone of Mickiewicz's letter to Margaret Fuller reflects precisely the method of those mystics in approaching people and "converting" them to their faith; they tried to convince them that they had a special and important "mission" to fulfill, in this way awakening their faith in themselves and in the sacred "cause."

Margaret Fuller's account of this meeting is much simpler in expression (see below), but her later letters approached—according to Wellisz—to some extent the tone of Mickiewicz. They probably met more than one time in Paris, but Margaret Fuller left shortly for Italy (in February, 1847) and further relations were confined to correspondence. What is interesting is that Mickiewicz's letters of that time are different in mood, limited rather to personal affairs, full of tenderness and worry about her health, although from time to time the "mystic" tone manifests itself. One is tempted to speculate whether Mickiewicz had not a more "earthly" interest in the attractive American than to convert her to his faith and to help her in carrying out her "mission"; the more so since at the time Emerson was preparing Margaret Fuller's *Memoirs* "a story was being told of how the poet Mickiewicz had wanted a divorce to marry Margaret and how Mazzini had offered to marry her." [2]

Be that as it may, the friendship and correspondence between them continued, and Margaret Fuller did not lose interest in the "Cause" and her possible role in it. When Mickiewicz arrived in Rome in

1. See Leopold Wellisz, *The Friendship of Margaret Fuller d'Ossoli and Adam Mickiewicz* (Polish Book Imp. Comp., New York, 1947), whence all these details are taken.

2. Ralph L. Rusk, *The Life of Ralph Waldo Emerson* (New York, Charles Scribner's Sons, 1949), p. 378.

February, 1848, to organize the Polish Legion, "they met often" (Wellisz, p. 28). Margaret Fuller's letters from Rome (see below, Nos. 3, 4, 5) pertain to this period of their relationship. She was also further informed by him about his trip to Milan and followed with interest reports in newspapers on his expedition and the attitude of the Italian people (see No. 5). Then she herself took part in the Italian revolutionary movement and directed an army hospital throughout the siege of Rome by the French (Wellisz, p. 36). She received one more letter from Mickiewicz in 1849, proposing that she write articles for the *Tribune des Peuples* published by him in Paris. Almost a year later, in July, 1850, Margaret Fuller d'Ossoli met her death in the Atlantic together with her husband and child.

The following excerpts from her letters illustrate her sentiments toward Mickiewicz and Poland.

1

To Ralph Waldo Emerson

*Naples, March 15, 1847*

Mickiewicz, the Polish poet, first introduced the *Essays* [3] to acquaintance in Paris. I did not meet him anywhere, and, as I heard a great deal of him which charmed me, I sent him your poems, and asked him to come and see me. He came, and I found in him the man I had long wished to see, with the intellect and passions in due proportion for a full and healthy human being, with a soul constantly inspiring. Unhappily, it was a very short time before I came away. How much time had I wasted on others which I might have given to this real and important relation.[4]

2

To E.H. [Elizabeth Hoar]

*Paris, January 18, 1847, and Naples, March 17, 1847*

. . . Afterwards I saw Chopin, not with her [George Sand], although he lives with her, and has for the last twelve years. I went to see him in his room with one of his friends. He is always ill, and as frail as a

3. *Essays* of R. W. Emerson (1841). The latest biographer of Emerson, Professor Ralph L. Rusk, seems to confirm this statement in writing: "Mickiewicz, presumably the first to make Emerson known in France . . ." (p. 350).

4. *Memoirs of Margaret Fuller Ossoli,* by R. W. Emerson, W. H. Channing, and J. F. Clarke (Boston, Roberts Brothers, 1874), II, 207.

snow-drop, but an exquisite genius. He played to me, and I liked his talking scarcely less. Madame S[and] loved Liszt before him; she has thus been intimate with the two opposite sides of the musical world. Mickiewicz says: "Chopin talks with spirit and gives us the Ariel view of the universe. Liszt is the eloquent *tribune* to the world of men, a little vulgar and showy certainly, but I like the tribune best." [5]

### 3

To Ralph Waldo Emerson

*Rome, March 14, 1848*

Mickiewicz is with me here, and will remain some time; it was he I wanted to see, more than any other person, in going back to Paris, and I have him much better here. France itself I should like to see, but remain undecided, on account of my health which has suffered so much, this winter, that I must make it the first object in moving for the summer. One physician thinks it will of itself revive, when once the rains have passed, which have now lasted from 16th December to this day. At present, I am not able to leave the fire, or exert myself at all.[6]

### 4

Letter XXIII to the *New York Daily Tribune*

*Rome, March 29, 1848*

I have seen the Austrian arms dragged through the streets of Rome and burned in the Piazza del Popolo. The Italians embraced one another and cried, *Miracolo! Providenza!* The modern Tribune Ciceronacchio fed the flame with fagots; Adam Mickiewicz, the great poet of Poland, long exiled from his country or the hopes of a country, looked on, while Polish women, exiled too, or who perhaps, like one nun who is here, had been daily scourged by the orders of a tyrant, brought little pieces that had been scattered in the street and threw them into the flames—an offering received by the Italians with loud plaudits. It was a transport of the people, who found no way to vent their joy, but the symbol, the poesy, natural to the Italian mind. The ever-too-wise "upper classes" regret it, and the Germans choose to resent it as an insult to Germany; but it was nothing of the kind; the insult was to the prisons of Spielberg, to those who commanded the massacres of Milan—a base tyranny little congenial to the native German

5. *Ibid.*, p. 198.
6. *Ibid.*, p. 234.

heart, as the true Germans of Germany are at this moment showing by their resolves, by their struggles.[7]

5

Letter XXIV to the *New York Daily Tribune*

*Rome, April 19, 1848*

The Poles have also made noble manifestations. Their great poet, Adam Mickiewicz, has been here to enroll the Italian Poles, publish the declaration of faith in which they hope to re-enter and re-establish their country, and receive the Pope's benediction on their banner. In their declaration of faith are found these three articles:

"Every one of the nation a citizen—every citizen equal in rights and before authorities.

"To the Jew, our elder brother, respect, brotherhood, aid on the way to his eternal and terrestrial good, entire equality in political and civil rights.

"To the companion of life, woman, citizenship, entire equality of rights."

This last expression of just thought the Poles ought to initiate, for what other nations has had such truly heroic women? Women indeed—not children, servants, or playthings.

Mickiewicz, with the squadron that accompanied him from Rome, was received with the greatest enthusiasm at Florence. Deputations from the clubs and journals went to his hotel and escorted him to the Piazza del Gran Duca, where amid an immense concourse of people some good speeches were made. A Florentine, with a generous forgetfulness of national vanity, addressed him as the Dante of Poland who, more fortunate than the great bard and seer of Italy, was likely to return to his country to reap the harvest of the seed he had sown.

"O Dante of Poland, who like our Alighieri has received from Heaven sovereign genius, divine song, but from earth sufferings and exile—more happy than our Alighieri, thou hast reacquired a country; already thou art meditating on the sacred harp the patriotic hymn of restoration and of victory. The pilgrims of Poland have become the warriors of their nation. Long live Poland, and the brotherhood of nations!"

When this address was finished, the great poet appeared on the balcony to answer. The people received him with a tumult of applause, fol-

7. *The Writings of Margaret Fuller,* selected and edited by Mason Wade (New York, The Viking Press, 1941), pp. 452–453.

lowed by a profound silence as they anxiously awaited his voice. Those who are acquainted with the powerful eloquence, the magnetism of Mickiewicz as an orator, will not be surprised at the effect produced by this speech, though delivered in a foreign language. It is the force of truth, the great vitality of his presence, that loads his words with such electric power. He spoke as follows:

"People of Tuscany! Friends! Brothers! We receive your shouts of sympathy in the name of Poland; not for us, but for our country. Our country, though distant, claims from you this sympathy by its long martyrdom. The glory of Poland, its only glory truly Christian, is to have suffered more than all the nations. In other countries the goodness, the generosity of heart of some sovereigns protected the people; as yours has enjoyed the dawn of the era now coming, under the protection of your excellent prince. (Viva Leopold II!) But conquered Poland, slave and victim of sovereigns who were her sworn enemies and executioners—Poland, abandoned by the governments and the nations, lay in agony on her solitary Golgotha. She was believed slain, dead, buried. 'We have slain her,' shouted the despots; 'she is dead!' (No, no! Long live Poland!) 'The dead cannot rise again,' replied the diplomatists; 'we may now be tranquil.' (A universal shudder of feeling in the crowd.) There came a moment in which the world doubted of the mercy and justice of the Omnipotent. There was a moment in which the nations thought that the earth might be forever abandoned by God, and condemned to the rule of the demon, its ancient lord. The nations forgot that Jesus Christ came down from heaven to give liberty and peace to the earth. The nations had forgotten all this. But God is just. The voice of Pius IX roused Italy. (Long live Pius IX!) The people of Paris have driven out the great traitor against the cause of the nations. (Bravo! Viva the people of Paris!) Very soon will be heard the voice of Poland. Poland will rise again! (Yes, yes! Poland will rise again!) Poland will call to life all the Slavonic races—the Croats, the Dalmatians, the Bohemians, the Moravians, the Illyrians. These will form the bulwark against the tyrant of the North. (Great applause.) They will close forever the way against the barbarians of the North—destroyers of liberty and of civilization. Poland is called to do more yet: Poland, as crucified nation, is risen again, and called to serve her sister nations. The will of God is that Christianity should become in Poland, and through Poland elsewhere, no more a dead letter of the law, but the living law of states and civil associations (Great applause); that Christianity should be manifested by acts, the sacrifices of generosity and liberality. This

Christianity is not new to you, Florentines: your ancient republic knew and has acted upon it; it is time that the same spirit should make to itself a larger sphere. The will of God is that the nations should act towards one another as neighbors, as brothers. (A tumult of applause.) And you, Tuscans, have today done an act of Christian brotherhood. Receiving thus foreign unknown pilgrims, who go to defy the greatest powers of the earth, you have in us saluted only what is in us of spiritual and immortal —our faith and our patriotism. (Applause.) We thank you; and we will now go into the church to thank God."

All the people then followed the Poles to the church of Santa Croce, where was sung the Benedictus Dominus, and amid the memorials of the greatness of Italy collected in that temple was forged more strongly the chain of sympathy and of union between two nations, sisters in misfortune and in glory.

This speech and its reception, literally translated from the journal of the day [*Patria,* April 17, 1848, No. 233], show how pleasant it is on great occasions to be brought in contact with this people so full of natural eloquence and of lively sensibility to what is great and beautiful.

It is a glorious time too for the exiles who return and reap even a momentary fruit of their long sorrows. Mazzini has been able to return from his seventeen years' exile, during which there was no hour night or day that the thought of Italy was banished from his heart—no possible effort that he did not make to achieve the emancipation of his people, and with it the progress of mankind.[8]

## *Mickiewicz and Emerson*

In his lectures on Slavic literature at the Collège de France, Mickiewicz sought to stress the characteristics of the Slavic mind. Deeply interested in the problems of national spirit, he was always on the alert to find its mark upon the writings of poets and philosophers. He

8. *Ibid.,* pp. 461–464.

discovered, for example, a sharp difference between the philosophic thought of all Slavic nations and the German philosophic thought which then dominated Europe. And it was while he was trying to define more exactly the Slavic mind that he discovered Emerson. In the Yankee thinker he found a kindred spirit, he believed, because like himself, like all Polish writers, Emerson put his emphasis not upon intellectual speculation but upon intuition and moral force.

In this connection it may be interesting to recall that Emerson's intellectual background was Unitarian, and sixteenth century Poland had been the birthplace of the first organized Unitarian movement, as is made clear in *A History of Unitarianism* by Earl Morse Wilbur, which deals at length with the Poland of that period.[1] In a sense, therefore, when Mickiewicz armed himself with Emerson's thought he was merely taking back some of what his country had indirectly given Emerson. It is one of those historical paradoxes which delight the impersonal student of man and civilization.

Mickiewicz mentioned Emerson for the first time in his lecture of January 31, 1843, while he was discussing *The Undivine Comedy* of the Polish poet Zygmunt Krasiński.[2] In passing, it might be noted that this work, written in 1833, is an extraordinary drama which has not paled with age even today, more than a century after its publication. Its subject is a great imaginary social revolution in Europe, and it presents the last stage of the revolution: the people's troops, led by a ruthless and intelligent upstart named Pankrace, surround the fortress of the Holy Trinity, which is defended by all that remains of the aristocracy, under the leadership of Count Henry. A genuine tragic feeling is created; the reader feels keenly the inevitability of the catastrophe; and the characters who are caught in their own doom are no less aware of it. This use by Krasiński of a method peculiar to ancient tragedy, together with its application to a social theme, afforded Mickiewicz an opportunity to analyze the character of one of the heroes, the revolutionary leader Pankrace.

1. Harvard University Press, 1947.
2. Adam Mickiewicz, *Les Slaves,* cours professé au Collège de France, 1842–1844 (Paris, Musée Adam Mickiewicz, 1914), pp. 78–79.

The character of Pankrace [he said] recapitulates all these characters; he is a compendium of Cromwell, Danton, and Robespierre. He is, however, exaggerated, and he does not ring true, because the poet has only given him intelligence. Now, that gift alone—intelligence—never succeeds in leading men. It cannot stir the masses. Still, it is noteworthy to see that the Polish poet gives the strongest intelligence to a creature who is degraded and destructive. You recall that according to the scale of psychological values of the Polish philosophers, intelligence is classed among the lesser qualities of the soul.

An American philosopher, whose work has just been reissued in London—work which I have scarcely had time to look through—accepts this set of values, and is certainly the first among other thinkers to do so. He has grasped this principle by intuition. He also assigns the intelligence to a lower place. This American thinker, Emerson, whom I shall often quote to you later on, because you will see in his works several chapters which seem made to order to explain the Polish poets and philosophers, this thinker believes also that the embryo, the center of all action is the soul. This soul acts either through thought or feeling; it creates a philosophy, a poetry. But in its lesser activities it appears first as prudence; it scarcely raises itself above the level of the brute; later it becomes philosophy; slowly it raises itself toward poetry, which Emerson places above philosophy; and finally it becomes wisdom. Thus on the ladder of humanity prudent men occupy the lower rungs; then come the intellectuals; then the poets; and finally the true sages. Emerson believed that, as in nature, the fluids and forces we call imponderable, such as magnetism, light, and electricity, are only material forces rarefied and released; thus the intelligence of man is nothing but a material force of this type, raised to a third or fourth power. The soul of man can take hold of the earth, steam, electricity, intelligence, to employ them for its purposes; but it must raise itself toward what he calls the Over-Soul, that is, toward God.

Since he goes on with his analysis of *The Undivine Comedy* in several lectures, Mickiewicz refers again to Emerson on February 21, 1843:

We shall not take up for the moment the question of the marvelous in poetry, because we shall have much to say on this subject, of which we shall speak soon and for the last time. The poet [Krasiński] says farewell to this supernatural world, while introducing it into the fourth part of his poem. On this occasion I shall read to you some lines from a philosopher whose name I have already given you, Emerson. The ideas which his philosophy expresses coincide in an extraordinary way with the Polish national idea, and convey incomparably well the needs of our epoch.

We have said, in our preceding lecture, that the fundamental dogma upon which rested Slavic nationality in general and Polish nationality in particular was the belief in the uninterrupted influence of the invisible world upon the visible world; and we use "nationality" here in the broadest sense of this word; we consider it as being the source of all national truth, of all national strength, of all national power. We have been careful to test our opinion against historical evidence, and to show the progress of this idea as it demonstrated itself also in Slavic poetry and in Slavic philosophy.

Listen now to the words of the American philosopher. Emerson certainly does not belong to the philosophic schools of Western Europe; he fights against them, he even heaps ridicule upon them. He seems to me to belong to one of the nonconformist sects of the established church; he is a practical philosopher, a kind of American Socrates.

The following lines are taken from a lecture delivered in Boston before a society of reformist workers, and published in 1841 in an American magazine very little known, *The Dial.* [The lecture is *Man the Reformer,* and it was delivered before the Mechanics' Apprentices' Library Association in the Masonic Temple in Boston on January 25, 1841, and appeared in *The Dial* for April, 1841.] It fell into our hands by chance. He speaks to his fellow-countrymen, who are reputed to be the most practical and the most materialistic people on earth.

The passage from Emerson follows:

Let it be granted that our life, as we lead it, is common and mean; that some of those offices and functions for which we were mainly created are grown so rare in society that the memory of them is only kept alive in old books and in dim traditions; that prophets and poets, that beautiful and perfect men we are not now, no, nor have even seen such; that some sources of human instruction are almost unnamed and unknown among us; that the community in which we live will hardly bear to be told that every man should be open to ecstasy or a divine illumination, and his daily walk elevated by intercourse with the spiritual world. Grant all this, as we must, yet I suppose none of my auditors,—no honest or intelligent soul will deny that we ought to seek to establish ourselves in such disciplines and courses as will deserve that guidance and clearer communication with the spiritual nature.

Mickiewicz goes on, in the same lecture: "If that is the manner in which the American people are addressed, people whom Emerson himself accuses of lacking the two necessary virtues, hope and charity, what should be the language of politicians and philosophers who address themselves to the Slavic people, to whom no one will dare deny these virtues, charity and hope? What frightful responsibility would weigh upon men who desired to rouse this people, while making use of the formulas of a dead society, which lacks precisely these virtues and which has only created these formulas as a result of the awareness of that lack of an internal strength! What responsibility would it not be to speak to this people which has preserved intact its faith, its great national traditions, and a feeling of humanity so pure and so exquisite, while avoiding mention of God, religion, and charity!" [3]

It is not, of course, the purpose of these present notes to attempt to evaluate the ideas of Mickiewicz, strange as they may sometimes seem. Here the purpose is simply to present them, from the historical point of view—which makes us recall, when we turn to his lecture of March 14, 1843, that anti-industrial views were not rare among moralists of that period. We find the following:

A very interesting aspect of the Slavic problem reveals itself just now. We arrive once again at the question of the future of this people. Everyone feels that this people is called to action. Not only the Slavs themselves, foreigners also say it. In general I only mention, in connection with these problems, the names of foreigners, so as to avoid all suspicion of partisanship. If this people is called to action, what will it have to do in the present-day world? In a world which is so opposed to it, in the world of science, art, and industry, what role can be played by an agricultural people who know no other life than that of villages, who have no other instrument of art than the axe, who are artistic, artisan, philosophic, who until now have not even known the rudiments of the division of labor? And this people is called upon to act in a period when intelligence has taken possession of the globe, when we are continually being astounded by new industrial

3. *Ibid.*, pp. 95–97.

inventions! All those who have written about the reform of the Slavic peoples express the wish to Europeanize them. They wish first of all to civilize them, that is, to make them merchants, shopkeepers, industrialists, to make them English, German, or French, to strip them of their Slavic characteristics.

To show you what is false about this, and I dare to apply the word sacrilege to such attempts, I shall quote to you some further lines from the American philosopher Emerson. In his land, teeming with industry, with railroads, with banknotes, with division of labor, the practical philosopher sighs for the agricultural life. He shows that the manner in which European nations have lived, whereby they have exploited Christianity for private profit, has put them into a condition so wretched that they can no longer feel what is true. If Christianity gives strength to man by showing him the inferiority of nature, it is not for the purpose of inspiring within him a single desire, the desire to lay hold of nature; if Christianity proclaims the equality of men, it is not only for the purpose of stirring up jealousy and competition.

Let us see what Emerson says, in a harmonious, thriving society, at Boston. [The following passage from Emerson is taken, like the previous one, from *Man the Reformer*.]

". . . we must begin to consider if it were not the nobler part to renounce it [the advantage offered by a civilized society] and to put ourselves into primary relations with the soil and nature, and abstaining from whatever is dishonest or unclean, to take each of us his part, with his own hands, in the manual labor of the world.

"But it is said 'What, will you give up the enormous advantages reaped from the division of labor, and set every man to make his own shoes, bureau, knife, wagon, sails, and needle? This would be to put men back into barbarism by their own act.'

". . . I confess I should not be pained at a change which threatened a loss of some of the luxuries or conveniences of society, if it proceeded from a preference of the agricultural life out of the belief that our primary duties as men could be better discharged in that calling. Who could regret to see a high conscience and a purer taste exercising a sensible effect on young men in the choice of their occupation?" [4]

Again on May 16, 1843 Mickiewicz returns to this theme, the relationship of man to nature, when he says: "Everyone begins to have

4. *Ibid.*, pp. 121–122.

a presentiment that there is a tie more intimate than we had believed until now between man and what we call nature. An American philosopher, Emerson, whom I like to quote often, addresses himself also to this question: what is the animal? what is the tree?"[5]

A month later, in his lecture of June 13, 1843, Mickiewicz takes up the question of the criterion of certainty, as the question absorbing the chief attention of the French philosophers De Maistre, Lamennais, Leroux, as well as some Polish philosophers. He draws a parallel between Leroux and Emerson:

Emerson, in his religious opinions, is very much like Leroux. He believes also in the existence of a universal soul (the Over-Soul) which absorbs individual souls. More profound than Leroux, he seeks above all to teach us the importance of maintaining ourselves in a state of being where it is possible to communicate with the universal soul; he seeks to detach us from prejudices, from received opinions, and even from all affections; he advises us to concentrate our attention on ourselves, to have a lively faith in God, and to lend an attentive ear to His inspirations. Meanwhile he leaves us too isolated, while paying no attention to time, to nation, to earth. Humanity, in Emerson, is a humanity left dangling I don't know where. As to Leroux, he leaves us at least the support of nationality.[6]

In 1844 Mickiewicz's lectures became increasingly imbued with faith in the power exerted over nature by exceptional men who had received illumination from above. On March 19, 1844, he touches upon the hiatus that exists between the life that we know historically and the life that is beyond the reach of our knowledge. Before quoting again from Emerson, he discusses the unknown life of animals:

It is curious that philosophers, who have meditated on the causes of the silence of sub-human species, have never suspected that there might be a formidable mystery hidden in the very center of the life of every kind of animal and vegetable. Already some scientists begin to realize that it is not enough to apply the scalpel to the brain of an animal, nor to cut it up still living in order to understand what goes on in its spirit. But what am I saying? "In its spirit!" The spirit that is not spoken of! Gassendi spoke of

5. *Ibid.*, p. 169.
6. *Ibid.*, p. 202.

it, however; Descartes sought to understand the vital principle in animals. In the midst of all the trash produced by modern philosophy, we find only vague formulas on this subject. Meanwhile ordinary human beings continue to hold for the silent companions of their work and their danger an invariable sympathy which deserves to be explained philosophically, since it assumes in the beings to which it is directed the existence of a sympathetic principle. Scientists even declare that more than once they have seen an animal, under torture, manifest, with a final effort, an expression of suffering that is almost human, an inexpressible internal cry which makes the anatomist turn away. One of your great writers has said that suffering gives the right to immortality. A fellow creature which dies while suffering thus, has it nothing to hope for?

There are scientists, and I might even cite their names, who concern themselves actively with this question. It is one of the unsettled questions of the present time. To demonstrate it, I shall quote to you some words from the American philosopher Emerson, from one who represents best the needs of the present time, who, it is true, does not succeed in settling any question but who has stated important questions with an admirable precision and clarity. This is what he says [In "History," *Essays, First Series*]:

". . . what is the use of pretending to know what we know not? But it is the fault of our rhetoric that we cannot strongly state one fact without seeming to belie some other. I hold our actual knowledge very cheap. Hear the rats in the wall, see the lizard on the fence, the fungus under foot, the lichen on the log. What do I know sympathetically, morally of either of these worlds of life? As old as the Caucasian man—perhaps older—these creatures have kept their counsel beside him, and there is no record of any word or sign that has passed from one to the other. What connection do the books show between the fifty or sixty chemical elements and the historical eras? Nay, what does history yet record of the metaphysical annals of man? What light does it shed on those mysteries which we hide under the names of Death and Immortality? Yet every history should be written in a wisdom which divined the range of our affinities and looked at facts as symbols. I am ashamed to see what a shallow village tale our so-called History is. How many times we must say Rome, and Paris, and Constantinople! What does Rome know of rat and lizard? What are Olympiads and Consulates to these neighboring systems of being? Nay, what food or experience or succor have they for the Esquimaux seal-hunter, for the Kanàka in his canoe, for the fisherman, the stevedore, the porter?" [7]

Mickiewicz's lecture of April 30, 1844, has for its subject "The Eternal Man." The following passage is interesting because of the reference made to Emerson. It occurs during a discussion of the relation of the knowledge gained through books and the knowledge gained through a direct experience of life. Mickiewicz says:

Does the European literature of civilized nations find itself already in a state like that of the Greeks and Romans of the fifth century? There are Western European writers who think so. What is sure is that the books which delight most the leisure hours of readers have very little influence on their actions, and represent very rarely the true feelings of their authors.

Poland learned first by a great national experience that the European word had no political value. This nation, attacked by a formidable enemy, had on its side all the books, all the newspapers, all the eloquent tongues of Europe; and from this entire army of words came not a single action. The word which should have been the source and principle of national life was only an echo, a deceitful echo.

The experience was decisive. Polish thinkers and poets had a presentiment of what would happen, and they understood its full significance. They turned away with disgust from all that was merely literary, from all that was merely well thought out. One of these poets, a philosopher and a soldier, took leave thus of books: "Let us allow the worms to take up lodging in these musty volumes; let them feed and grow fat on them in tranquillity. As to me, I have discovered nothing in my long journey through so many pages and so many volumes. I have got nothing from physics or chemistry. Who has ever read so much, has ever kept such a patient vigil with books and laboratory instruments? Today, O philosophers, you know me for one of you, for your equal. I understand the secret of your profession, and if I were to ask you what you know, shame would redden your forehead and your brains—if you are still capable of feeling shame, O philosophers!"

This latest cry from Polish literature finds an echo on the other side of the globe, in America. There Emerson preaches the same holy war against bookmen and their systems, against the world that is artificial, spoiled, and rotten. We have nothing more to learn there about our future; even the

7. *Ibid.*, pp. 310–312.

past is no longer there. It is not outside ourselves, says Emerson, that we must seek our history; we must learn to read it within ourselves. History must cease to be an old volume; we must absolutely break with old books. History must be incarnated in every honorable and wise man.[8]

And Mickiewicz goes on in the same lecture:

The doctors of the Church have said that each Christian should, during his lifetime, pass through all periods of the history of the Church; that he should relive in himself that history. Emerson, who agrees on this point with the Christian doctors, bids us relive in ourselves the history of our nations, to complete it within ourselves and to begin a new chapter.

Fifty years before Emerson, a Polish poet—[Ignacy] Krasicki—seized upon the same idea of the unity of the individual soul passing through the multiplicity of forms, and developed it in an historical novel.[9] This novel contains the story of an imaginary being, of a deathless man, a kind of Wandering Jew, but more interesting than the Jew. For he, pursued unceasingly by the same curse and the same remorse, remains always the same, while the man of Krasicki, possessing the secret of rejuvenation, is reborn from age to age, changes at will his family and his nationality, and becomes in turn Chinese, Carthaginian, Roman, and finally Polish. He has lived in this way the life of several nations, of several peoples, and of a great number of centuries. He has been happy and he has suffered with them.[10]

It would be difficult to present all the ideas developed by Mickiewicz in his lectures in the Collège de France. We have therefore limited ourselves to those places where he directly mentions Emerson. It is clear which aspects of Emerson's thought appealed to him.

So far as we know, these portions of Mickiewicz's lectures in Paris have never been translated from the original French into English. They may contribute to a better understanding of the little-known tie between Transcendentalist New England of the mid-nineteenth century and Europe and particularly Poland.[11]

8. *Ibid.*, p. 332.
9. Mickiewicz refers here to Krasicki's work, *History Divided into Two Parts* (1778).
10. *Les Slaves,* pp. 335–336.
11. Mickiewicz also published in the *Tribunes des Peuples,* in 1849, two translations from Emerson: "L'Homme religieux réformateur" and "Essai sur l'histoire."

# INDIA

## *The* Crimean Sonnets *in India*

The penetration of Mickiewicz's sonnets into India is an item which we have considered worthy of inclusion in this book. We are indebted for this "discovery" to Mr. Alexander Janta, Polish poet and writer, who, during his stay in India before the Second World War, met the distinguished Hindu poet Uma Shanker Joshi, awoke his interest in Polish literature, and suggested to him a translation of the *Crimean Sonnets*. Mr. Janta provided the Hindu poet with an English version of the sonnets, and in 1939 Uma Shanker Joshi's Gujrati translation appeared in Ahmedabad, Bombay Province, with an introduction by Mr. Janta. In English, the title reads: "The Flower of Poland, a Translation of the *Crimean Sonnets* by the Polish Poet Mickiewicz, with an Introductory Essay on the Sonnet Form and Its History."

Gujrati, spoken by twenty-five million people of Gujrat and Kathiyawar in Bombay Province, is the native tongue of Gandhi and the language in which he wrote his autobiography.

Uma Shanker Joshi was born in 1910. He early joined the "Gujrati Vidhja Pith," the National Institute founded by Mahatma Gandhi at Ahmedabad, continued his university studies, receiving his M.A. in Gujrati literature, and worked in the Gujrat Research Society. His works include *Gangotri* (1934), a collection of poems on the social, political, and economic problems of India; eleven one-act plays; a collection of short stories (1937); and a book of poems, *Nishit* (God of Night), 1939. His place in Gujrati literature is considered high and compares to that of Nanalal, the outstanding poet of the language. Joshi is credited with having created new forms of the sonnet in his native poetry, which may account for his interest in Mickiewicz.

His translation of the *Crimean Sonnets* is preceded by an essay devoted chiefly to the art of the sonnet. To Mickiewicz, the Hindu poet

# ગુલે પોલાંડ

પોલિશ કવિ મિત્સ્કિયેવિચના 'ક્રીમિયન સૉનેટ્સ'નો અનુવાદ

સૉનેટના બંધારણ તથા તેના ઇતિહાસ વિષે વિસ્તૃત
અભ્યાસપૂર્ણ અને આધારભૂત નિબંધ સાથે


તૈયાર કરનાર

ઉમાશંકર જોષી

પ્રકાશક

કુમાર કાર્યાલય ૧૪૫૪ રાયપુર અમદાવાદ


TITLE PAGE OF UMA SHANKER JOSHI'S TRANSLATION
OF THE *CRIMEAN SONNETS*

pays tribute as a master of this form, while stressing the patriotic element which appealed especially to him as a fighter for India's independence. Each sonnet in the Gujrati translation is provided with a summary (not always exact) in which its characteristics are explained.

# INDEX

# CONTRIBUTORS

WACŁAW BOROWY

*Late Professor of Polish literature, University of Warsaw*

PAUL CAZIN

*French writer and critic*

ENRICO DAMIANI

*Professor of Slavic language and literature, University of Rome*

ABRAHAM G. DUKER

*Student of Jewish culture*

MARIAN JAKÓBIEC

*Professor of Slavic literature, University of Wrocław*

KAREL KREJČI

*Professor of Polish literature, Charles University, Prague*

MANFRED KRIDL

*Adam Mickiewicz Professor of Polish Studies, Columbia University*

LUDWIK KRZYŻANOWSKI

*Lecturer on Polish language, Columbia University*

GIOVANNI MAVER

*Professor of Polish literature, University of Rome*

CZESŁAW MIŁOSZ

*Polish poet and writer*

GEORGE R. NOYES

*Professor Emeritus of Slavic languages and literature, University of California*

Ernest S. Simmons

*Professor of Russian literature, Columbia University*

John N. Washburn

*Instructor in Russian, Dartmouth College*

Józef Wittlin

*Polish poet and writer*

Czesław Zgorzelski

*Professor of Polish literature, University of Lublin*